THE RAILWAY CONQUEST OF THE WORLD

Frederick A. Talbot

Foreword by Christian Wolmar

AMBERLEY

Front cover: Photograph courtesy of Gordon Edgar.

First published 1911

This edition by Amberley Publishing 2015

Amberley Publishing
The Hill, Stroud
Gloucestershire, GL5 4EP

www.amberley-books.com

British Library Cataloguing in Publication Data.
A catalogue record for this book is available from the British Library.

ISBN: 978 1 4456 5221 4 (print)
ISBN: 978 1 4456 5222 1 (ebook)

Typesetting and Origination by Amberley Publishing.
Printed in the UK.

Contents

Foreword

The construction of the rail network in the nineteenth and early twentieth centuries was the most extensive civil engineering project the world had ever seen. By far. It is impossible to exaggerate the significance of the building of this network in terms of the economic, social and political history of the world. Nothing that preceded it was on a comparable scale. Building the pyramids was akin to making a sandcastle in comparison with the creation of the railway network given the scale, extent and importance of the endeavour.

The world's first railway, the Liverpool & Manchester, opened in 1830 and would be the example that almost every nation in the world would follow in the next hundred years. While the Liverpool & Manchester had various primitive predecessors, such as the Stockton & Darlington and numerous waggonways built as far back as the seventeenth century, it was the first to operate passenger and freight services on a double-track line between two major towns hauled entirely by locomotives rather than horses. The line was, too, a conspicuous commercial success which is partly why it triggered off the railway revolution that changed the world.

The simple figures of the iron road's subsequent takeover of the globe are impressive. In the eighty or so years following the opening of the Liverpool & Manchester, a staggering 500,000 miles of railway were built across the world. That is 16 miles opened every day of that period, and the influence of this development cannot be exaggerated. People were able to travel faster than a horse could gallop for the first time in history and goods could be transported far greater distances and much more cheaply. Whole industries sprang up as a result of the creation of the railways and peoples' lives were changed, mostly for the better. Commuting to work became a possibility which, in turn, allowed the expansion of towns into vast cities. The very roots of today's civilisation lie in the spread of the railways which allowed the pace of economic development to accelerate beyond anything ever experienced before.

Nor is it possible to exaggerate the achievement of building the iron road in many inhospitable parts of the world, opening up swathes of territory that formerly was barely connected with the outside world. Frederick A. Talbot's book on the development of the railway, originally published in episodes, captures so well the difficulties faced by these railway pioneers. He focussed on the most ambitious civil engineering projects, whether in Europe, Asia, America or Africa. Heroic is an overused word to describe the construction of the network, but how else does one depict the battles against the elements and the topography? Snow, heat, swamps, cliffs, mountains and even the sea proved to be no barrier to the railways' advance. It is impossible to choose which of the railways Talbot describes was the most difficult to build. There is the sheer scale of the Trans-Siberian, a railway that stretches 5,700 miles from Moscow to the Pacific Coast in territory where temperatures can range from 30° Celsius to -30° Celsius. The construction of a narrow gauge railway across South-West Africa (now Namibia) is one of the craziest enterprises described by Talbot, but there is no shortage in that category, notably the Florida Overseas Railroad that reached from across more than 100 miles of sea and small islands to reach Key West, which was nearer Havana than Miami. There is, too, the story of the first tunnels through the Alps and the first railway passes over them, but my particular favourite is the efforts of Henry Meiggs, who managed to build the highest lines in the world in the Andes through territory that seems completely unpassable. All the lines, except the Florida Railroad, which is now Highway 1, the main road to Key West, survive, a testimony to the fact that this fantastic endeavour was worthwhile.

Talbot never forgets the cost in human terms of these efforts. Many lives were lost due to the crude construction techniques or, more often, by disease or even attacks by wild animals. The pay was often minimal, the work extremely onerous, the food lousy, and the housing primitive. It was not just the navvies and labourers who suffered. The surveyors, as he describes, were probably the bravest of these men, many of whom perished as a result of the elements or hostility from local people, but many engineers and managers, too, succumbed to disease or overwork. Yet, it was thanks to the efforts of this amazing workforce that the world became connected for the first time, enabling travellers to go round it in eighty days as famously described by Jules Verne.

Talbot's accounts, written before history had settled, do not always fit in with subsequent research on railway history. On the building of first transcontinental railway across the United States, he gives far too much emphasis to the battles with the Native Americans and far too little to the amazing achievements of the workforce brought in from China to carry out much of the work in the most difficult terrain through the Sierra Nevada. In his account of the building of the Trans-Siberian railway, he fails to point out the militaristic ambitions behind the scheme and the various political manipulations that resulted in a route through Manchuria being chosen. Understandably, too, Talbot writing in 1911 was overoptimistic about the chances of the completion of the Cape to Cairo railway, the most ambitious scheme ever attempted and which failed because of the way that Africa had been parcelled up between colonial powers and the sheer scale of the enterprise.

But he gets far more right than wrong. Talbot's descriptions of early railway construction, written at a time when many contemporaneous sources were still alive, are invaluable. His style is still very much Victorian, with long evocative descriptions enhanced by lots of anecdotes and descriptions of the wonderful characters who were responsible for this fantastic enterprise. They have an earthiness and a breathless energy that entertains and enchants. His work is a major contribution to what we know about the construction of the iron road and it is great that it is being revived.

Christian Wolmar
September 2015

Editor's Note

This is a new edition of Frederick A. Talbot's classic work, *Railway Conquest of the World*, first published in 1911. Talbot explores some of the most innovative railways of the golden age of railway building; he considers the many obstacles that the enterprising engineers faced, such as boring the Gotthard tunnel and the sheer scale of the Trans-Siberian. Throughout, Talbot praises the vision of the engineers who designed them and the men who built them.

The original language has been retained as it appeared in the original edition of the book, which truly captures the excitement and pioneering spirit of the time. Although sometimes surprising, the volume nevertheless offers the reader an important historical and cultural insight in to the development of the world's most ground-breaking railways.

Preface

There is the unfathomable fascination of romance connected with the construction of great railways, though little is known of the beginning and the growth of the great trunk roads of the world; of the heavy tax which their construction imposed upon the ingenuity, skill and resource of their builders. Speeding along swiftly in a luxurious Pullman car over a roadbed as smooth as an asphalt pavement conveys no impression of the perils and dangers faced or of the infinite labour expended in the making of that steel highway. Today, the earth is girdled with some 700,000 miles of railways, and there are few countries in which the locomotive has not made its appearance.

This volume has been written with the express purpose of telling in a popular manner this story of romance. It is obviously impossible to deal with every great railway undertaking in the compass of a single volume, but those described may safely be considered representative, and they are the largest and most interesting enterprises between the two poles.

In the writing of this volume I have been assisted by innumerable friends who have been identified closely with the introduction of Stephenson's invention into fresh fields of conquest. I am indebted especially to the following gentlemen: Messrs Norman B. Dickson, M.INST.C.E.; A. M. Cleland, the Northern Pacific Railway Company; the late J. C. Meredith, chief engineer, the Florida East Coast Railway; A. L. Lawley; R. R. Gales, M.INST.C.E.; H. E. Gwyther, chief engineer, the Leopoldina Railway Company Ltd; Francis B. Clarke, president of the Spokane, Portland & Seattle Railway; William Hood, chief engineer, the Southern Pacific Company; F. A. Miller, the Chicago, Milwaukee & Puget Sound Railway; the I. R. Austrian Railway Ministry; W. Weston, the Denver, North-Western & Pacific Railway Company; the Pennsylvania Steel Company; W. T. Robson, the Canadian Pacific Railway Company; the Cleveland Bridge & Engineering Company, and Frederic Coleman of Darlington; the Swiss Federal Railways; H. R. Charlton, the Grand Trunk Railway Company of Canada; the chief engineer, the New Zealand Government Railways; the Peruvian Corporation; the chief engineers of the New South Wales, South Australia and West Australia Government Railways; the Minister of Ways of Communication of the Russian Empire; the Transandine Railway Company; the chief engineer, the Imperial Japanese Government Railways; J. J. Gywn, chief engineer, and S. K. Hooper, the Denver & Rio Grande Railway; G. J. Ray, chief engineer, the Delaware, Lackawanna & Western Railroad; Virgil G. Bogue, vice-president and chief engineer, the Western Pacific Railway Company; and S. J. Ellison of the Great Northern Railway, USA.

Frederick A. Talbot
Hove,
29 September 1911

CHAPTER 1

The Railway Surveyor's Adventurous Life

One's experience is varied from camping out in tents at fifty degrees below zero, to spending a large amount of time in the wilderness, when provisions are very short and one has to depend upon fish for food.

This was the description of the task of discovering a path for the iron road through a new country, as related to me by the late John E. Schwitzer, one of the most brilliant railway engineers that Canada has produced, and one who had climbed the ladder of success from the humble capacity of rodman at a few shillings per week, to the position of chief engineer of the Canadian Pacific railway, within the short space of twenty-two years. From his unique experience he was fitted to speak with authority, and his statement sums up the life of a surveyor in a nutshell.

So far as the loneliness and the need to fish for food are concerned I can speak from experience. This article of diet is plentiful, but its monotony palls very quickly, while at times one longs for the excitement of the city. But once this feeling has been lived down, one would not exchange the virgin country, with its invigorating air and life of exciting adventure, for a smoke-begrimed stifling centre of activity for any consideration.

In Great Britain, owing to its completely settled condition, the difficulties incidental to this class of work do not exist. The wrestles with heat, sun-baked desert, ice-bound forest and extreme cold have never been experienced in connection with the driving forward of the ribbon of steel in these islands. There is an utter lack of that thrilling romantic interest and adventure associated with similar work in an unknown country, where the surveyor is not merely a surveyor, but an explorer as well. In any of the four continents beyond Europe he fulfils an important mission. He is the advance-guard of civilisation. He spies out the country for the greatest settling force that has yet been devised, and although the work more often than not is extremely perilous, he revels in the dangers. One must be prepared to face any emergency: be ready to fulfil any duty. One may be buried for months amid the strongholds of ice-capped mountains, isolated upon the sweltering desolate expanses of broiling deserts, imprisoned in the hearts of yawning ravines, or immersed amid reeking dismal swamps, cut off by hundreds of miles from the nearest town or settlement. Then Nature is the surveyor's sole companion, and in her silent company, herculean and heroic tasks often have to be fulfilled, of which the world at large never gleans an inkling.

The surveyor is the personification of happy-go-luckiness. He pursues his path doggedly, laughs at obstacles, no matter how forbidding they may be, and accomplishes glorious deeds unsung. Often his sudden death through accident, disease or misadventure goes unmourned beyond the limits of his own camp. Yet an everlasting and omnipotent monument to his memory is raised – the thin thread of steel that annihilates time and space.

These men show a devotion to their calling which it is impossible to fathom. They brave perils beyond conception and face death in a hundred different forms. It may be a slip on a treacherous foothold at the brink of a yawning gulch, the upset of a frail bark in a swiftly rushing rapid, a land or rock slide, an avalanche, or a tree snapping under the fury of the storm which hurries them to their doom. In silence they suffer the torments of thirst, the pangs of hunger, physical exhaustion, frostbite, snow-blindness, disease, the hostility of mankind and a thousand other dangers. When they have emerged from the ordeal, they laugh at their experiences and consider them no more fearsome than those confronting the ordinary city dweller as he walks along a crowded thoroughfare.

As one travels over the railway through Mexico, interest is aroused by four primitive little wooden crosses beside the track. It is a small God's acre in an undulating expanse. The probability is that it would miss the eye unless one were bent on its discovery. Yet those four monuments tell a silent story of grim adventure. The Mexican Central was being driven through a hostile country, and the Indians were being forced back relentlessly by its influence. They were sullen but not subdued.

A little squad of four surveyors were busily engaged in pegging out the path for the line. They were deep in the intricacies of their task. Suddenly there was a savage blood-curdling whoop. A horde of Indians, in the full panoply of war paint and feathers, were bearing down upon them on mischief bent. The engineers discarded their instruments hurriedly and grabbed their rifles. They were outnumbered hopelessly, but undaunted, they kept blazing away, picking off their foes with that stubbornness born of despair. There were no thoughts of surrender to the implacable enemy. Nor could they hope for aid; they were too far distant from their base. One by one they fell, and when at last their comrades came up, their mutilated corpses were the sole evidences of that forlorn struggle. Today, those four wooden crosses serve to recall that grim episode. Such dramatic incidents unfortunately were only too frequent in the early days of railway building upon the American continent, though they were far from being peculiar to the New World. They have been, and still are, repeated occasionally in connection with such enterprises in other parts of the globe.

It was only a year or two ago that one of the most ferocious acts of savage barbarity, such as is difficult to parallel in the annals of railway engineering, was perpetrated in South America. Only the fringe of that vast territory has been opened up by the iron horse. The greater part is more unknown today than the land around the North Pole.

A small party of engineers set off up country to map out a projected extension. They plunged boldly into the depths of the primeval forest. But they never returned. What happened when they disappeared within the tangled labyrinth of trees no one knows. The time slipped by, and their comrades outside, fretting at their prolonged absence, grew so alarmed that a relief party was organised. The worst was dreaded, for the hostility of the natives to the locomotive was known only too well. The relief party advanced warily, weapons in hand, ready for the slightest sign of fight. However, they were safe from molestation, but had not ventured far into the tangled jungle before they solved the mystery, and were able to reconstruct a tragic adventure only too realistically.

The steps of the surveying engineers had been dogged silently and relentlessly by the remorseless savages. When the former had gained a point sufficiently remote from the belt of civilisation, they were laid low by poisoned arrows. The relief party accounted for every engineer, but one and all were beyond human succour. They were found in a gruesome row, poised upside down, with stakes driven lengthwise through their bodies and heads into the ground. They had been pinned down with no more compunction than the schoolboy secures his etymological prize to a piece of cardboard.

A few years ago British North Borneo was the scene of a similar disaster. It had been decided to drive a railway from coast to coast, and a party set out on the reconnaissance, as the first step in a new railway undertaking is called. The path lay through the dense forest which had never been penetrated by the white man, and where the dreaded Head Hunters held undisputed sway. The prospect was forbidding in the extreme, but it did not dismay the engineers who plunged fearlessly into the bush. As the crow flies, their journey was only one of some 150 miles, but the thick vegetation concealed difficulties innumerable.

That survey was doomed to failure. The party was overwhelmed by the Dyaks and massacred, with the exception of three native porters who succeeded in making good their escape. After experiencing terrible privations, this trio regained civilisation and communicated the sad tidings of the calamity. For years that stretch of forest defied conquest. Finally another attempt was made to traverse the jungle, and on this occasion no interference to progress was offered. The surveyors gained the opposite coast in about six months, being called upon to fight only one enemy – disease. It was a desperate plunge, for the party had to hack and hew its way foot by foot through the matted scrub and trees.

These afford instances of the hostility of mankind which fortunately today are encountered but seldom. It is the hostility of Nature which is feared more greatly now. Yet the work possesses a fascinating glamour. The existence of difficulty only spurs the determined to further effort.

Railway surveying in the effort to roll back the map in a new country offers the young man all the adventure in life that can be desired. As one surveyor who had spent more years than he could remember in the wilds between China and Peru remarked to me, 'If it is not the natural difficulties or the hostility of the natives which lend variety to the work, the chances are a hundred to one that a revolution will fill the gap, especially in China or the South Americas.'

At times the work is exasperating. Perhaps the surveyor who has been imprisoned for months on end in an inhospitable country has been driven to his wits' end to find a practicable location that is immune from the many disturbances of Nature. By dint of supreme effort finally he discovers a route which he congratulates himself to be absolutely safe, only to receive a rude awakening. In the survey of a new line through the Rockies, the mountains barring the engineer's path had achieved an unenviable reputation, owing to the frequency and severity of the avalanches that tore down their steep slopes every spring. The surveyor reconnoitred that mountain chain from end to end, observed every path that the slides had been known to take, searched local records and questioned aged inhabitants to make himself acquainted thoroughly with the conditions.

At last he concluded that he had elaborated a path for the railway which was beyond the destructive efforts of the periodical visitations and work was commenced. Yet in the first spring, while the construction train was crawling along with a load of excavated spoil from the mountainside, the slipping snow departed from its accustomed path, and in its descent caught the unlucky train, threw it into the gulch some distance below, ripped up the metals, buried the grade beneath thousands of tons of debris, and obliterated every vestige of the work.

The surveyor must be a man not to be daunted very easily in his enterprise, not to be cast down by heart-breaking failures, and who has the capacity to gather tangible assistance from apparently insignificant trifles. The search for a rift through a frowning mountain wall often is galling in its hopelessness. When the first Canadian transcontinental line was being forced towards the Pacific coast, the crossing of the Rocky, Selkirk and Gold ranges puzzled the surveyors acutely. Walter Moberly, a surveyor to the manner born, was deputed to complete the conquest of the Gold or Columbia Range. The obvious path to follow was along the bank of the mighty Columbia River, and this was taken by Moberly. Yet the Gold Range had to be threaded somewhere and somehow, though it appeared to defy penetration. He spent months wandering up and down the river, enduring hardships indescribable, seeking for the slightest breach through that terrible wall, wide enough to carry a pair of metals, but no gateway could he find.

Weary and sick at heart at the fruitlessness of his endeavours, he was one day returning despondently to camp. He was compelled well-nigh to admit failure. Suddenly, he espied an eagle wheeling over his head. He followed its movements somewhat nonchalantly, until he saw it make directly for the Columbia Mountains. Then his heart gave a thump! Would the bird rise and clear their lofty summits or would it sweep through a rift? Following its flight through the air, he saw the bird give a majestic dip downwards towards the chain. He turned the head of his jaded horse, and digging his spurs into its flanks, sped in the wake of the bird. Onward it flew as straight as an arrow towards a projecting crest, where it made a sharp turn and was lost to sight.

Moberly galloped madly forward with his eyes glued to that crag. He never turned his head, fearing his sight might play him false, and was oblivious to stumbles and lurches as his steed fell over logs and slipped among boulders in its mad career. He swung round the crest, and there before his eyes the peaks were rolled back on either side, leaving a broad canyon, and of such a character that Nature appeared to have fashioned it expressly for the advance of the steel highway. The Columbia Range was conquered. It was by pure accident that it had been found, but it was an accident that culminated a prolonged industrious quest. Indebted for his success to the monarch of the air,

Moberly christened the break in the rocky wall 'Eagle Pass', and it is through that gulch today that the Canadian Pacific makes its way to the western sea. As one sweeps between the massive ice-crowned teeth of the mountains, one may see the site of the oldest cabin in the mountains, where the indefatigable Moberly passed the winter of 1871/2 completing the preliminary surveys for the line among the fastnesses of the Columbia Mountains.

The task of planning the location through such broken country is attended with the gravest dangers, relieved with exciting adventures. At places among the peaks, a foothold on *terra firma* for the manipulation of the survey instruments is impossible. Then massive tree logs are lowered into the gulch a few feet above the raging foam of a wicked mountain torrent, and along this slender staging the surveyor has to crawl to carry out his task.

Life often hangs upon the veritable thread. It may be that logs cannot be thrown over the cliff face. Then the surveyor has to don a leathern waist-belt fitted with a heavy swivel to which a rope is attached. In this way he is swung over the edge of a cliff to operate his level and transit along the face of a precipice where no foothold exists. Sometimes it becomes imperative to have recourse to dynamite to blast out a ledge along which to advance. Many a promising young engineer has gone to his last account in work of such a desperate character. In the survey of what is now the Denver and Rio Grande through one of Colorado's yawning canyons, a young assistant had to be lowered in this manner. Half a dozen labourers grasped the end of the rope and steadied the surveyor in his descent over the perilous edge. From the brink to the bottom of the canyon was a matter of 200 feet or so straight down. In a few seconds the young fellow was dangling betwixt earth and sky, steadying his descent as best he could down the face of the cliff.

Suddenly, there was a cry of alarm! The rope-man nearest the cliff edge noticed that the rope was bearing upon a piece of rock, the edge of which was as keen as that of a razor. The rope had been sawn almost in two. Lowering stopped. The two men rushed forward to grasp the rope below the point of pending rupture to ease the strain. But they were too late. There was a slight tremor, the last strand snapped, and before the rope-men realised the situation as the end hung limply in their hands, the cry of the lost engineer as he tumbled through the air was echoed from the depths of the canyon.

Life in the field is indisputably hard and exacting, and the task is often aggravated by the scarcity, or monotony, of the food. This condition of affairs, however, is incomparably better today than it was thirty years ago. The surveyors are tended more thoughtfully than they were then, and the perfection of food-preserving science has enabled a camp now to be provisioned with tasty comestibles which formerly were unknown. Pork, beans and bannock – a substitute for bread made from flour and bacon fat with a little baking powder – constituted the staple articles of diet, varied with fish from the streams, game from the forests and wild fruits. The bread was often musty, for immersion time after time in a torrent and storage upon damp ground did not improve the flavour of the flour by any means. The pork or bacon often was rancid, while the cook was invariably an execrable exponent of the culinary art, and his bannock played sad havoc with the digestive organs of the human body. Little wonder that the men, under such conditions, sought to secure additions to the menu from the rivers by methods decidedly unsportsmanlike, but the 'end justified the means'; or delighted in bear steaks and venison. Extreme altitudes such as have to be attained in order to cross the Andes undermine the strongest constitutions and render the surveyor's work increasingly difficult. Struggling, crawling and slipping among crags and loose rocks inflicting cuts and bruises is arduous work indeed, but when the human frame is racked by the tortures of *sorochté*, or mountain sickness, the surveyor's plight is to be pitied in very truth. In such climes the cold and winds are pitiless, the movements of the thermometer between midnight and noon are enormous, the fluctuation in some cases being as much as a hundred degrees in the course of twelve hours. In the middle of the day the heat is well-nigh unbearable, and the surveyor gladly discards his outer clothing. At night he finds it no simple matter to keep warm, for the mercury descends to a very low level and frost prevails. The winds too are so cutting and penetrating that it requires elaborate and special clothing after dark to keep warm.

Now and again a situation develops which relieves the monotony of the daily round of struggle against the forces of Nature. South America is pre-eminently the home of these humorous incidents. The concession for the construction of a railway through one of the tropical republics had been granted, and no time was lost in pushing forward with the preliminary surveys. But when the men with the transit and level reached a certain city they were surprised to meet with unveiled opposition. The municipal authorities point-blankly refused to permit the surveyors to carry out their work in the precincts of the city. Seeing that the latter was to benefit mostly from the steel link, the attitude was somewhat inexplicable at first sight. A little reflection, however, upon the South American methods of transacting business convinced the surveyor that bribery was the root of the trouble. He reported the interruption to his superiors, whose representatives hurried to the city to fathom the reason for the unexpected opposition. It was as the surveyor had surmised. The civic authorities would permit the iron horse to enter the city if the concessionaries would make a handsome contribution to the municipal improvement fund – explained the mayor. 'Well, how much do you want?' remarked the concessionaries, who inwardly had not overlooked this contingency. The mayor could not say offhand, and accordingly several delays occurred until this vital consideration was arranged. As a result of the prolonged parleys, the concessionaries undertook to deliver a certain sum of money to the city.

The bullion was dispatched forthwith and reached the city the night before payment was due, so as to prevent the authorities to withdraw from the bargain on the plea that the concessionaries were dilatory. But law and order were not enforced very strongly, and the surveyor, with his companions, entertained certain qualms. Accordingly they decided to mount guard over the building in which they were passing the night in case of eventualities, at the same time securing a goodly supply of arms and ammunition.

As the first streaks of dawn lighted the scene, the guard thought he descried the forms of men creeping along the ground in the gloom. Silently he roused his companions, and with firearms cocked they waited developments. Not a sign of movement was displayed among the inmates, and the robbers silently forced an entrance through the windows and door. Once inside the building they were greeted with a warm fusillade of lead, and in accordance with the characteristics of their ilk, they did not stop to reply, but beat as hurried retreat as they could under the assistance of bullets, leaving some of their number *hors de combat*. When day broke the besieged party examined the fruits of their marksmanship, and to their intense surprise discovered that the dead included the mayor of the city, and one or two of his companions who had carried out the negotiations for the contribution to the improvement fund, and who had been so remarkably solicitous concerning the city's welfare!

It will be realised that the surveyor who undertakes the plotting of the line through a new country must be a man of illimitable resource and capacity, and at the same time ready to meet any development. It must be confessed, however, that the work, from its adventurous aspect, appeals strongly to the young engineer anxious to get away from monotonous routine.

CHAPTER 2

The Romance of Construction

Though the task of deciding the path for the railway teems with excitement, adventure and privation, the battle with Nature commences in grim earnest when the constructional engineer arrives on the scene. On paper, it seems a simple task to follow the location as indicated by an unbroken row of wooden stakes, but to carry the surveyors' work to completion, and to comply with requirements as to grades and curves, often proves a heartrending undertaking. No matter how formidable any obstruction may appear, it is the work of the builder to beat it down; to overcome it by some means or other with the minimum of expense. He must be baulked by nothing.

Such a task demands a man of illimitable resource and infinite ingenuity, conversant with every phase of civil engineering. At the same time he must possess the happy faculty of being able to organise great armies of men of all nationalities, and in such a manner that he can get the utmost out of them. This is a searching difficulty. The camp of today upon a large railway undertaking is a heterogeneous mass of humanity; the confusion of tongues at the Tower of Babel could not have been more embarrassing. I have lived among the camps of Canada and the United States, and among a hundred men it has been no uncommon circumstance to find representatives of a dozen different tongues. The control of such men is rendered all the more complex for the reason that in the majority of cases they have little or no knowledge of any language but their own. It is not until they have been in one another's company for several weeks that inter-conversation becomes possible. In addition to this drawback there are always the peculiar troubles incidental to racial and religious prejudices confronting the commander-in-chief, and at times he is hard pressed to preserve order and authority.

This trouble is not experienced to any great degree in connection with railway building operations in Great Britain, but abroad the initial difficulties of this character are exasperating to a superlative degree, more especially where reliance has to be made upon native labour. The workmen have to be educated into the use of labour- and time-saving implements. This is no easy matter. The native entertains strong opinions concerning his own ability, and the conversion from the primitive to the up-to-date scientific has to be effected gradually and unconsciously, a task which demands considerable tact and patience. A great amount of time must be expended necessarily in the early days to drill such raw material, but perseverance and an equable temper are the only virtues. In Mexico, the railway pioneers found it almost hopeless to impress upon the paeons, as the navvies are called, that to carry ballast in a basket slung upon the back was not to be compared in speed and efficiency with conveyance by small trucks pushed along a tram road. It was only by carrying out the work themselves in this more modern manner that the engineers could teach them the superior advantage of this method, with its sparing of effort and fatigue. In fact, the only way one can convert the raw native to ideas entirely foreign to his own custom is to show him how he can save himself trouble. Then he will adopt the idea with alacrity.

Now and again, however, the white man, despite his ingenuity in the devising of time- and labour-saving appliances, has to bow to the inevitable. For instance, in India the Hindoos toil at such a low daily wage that in many phases of work the wonders of mechanical invention cannot compare with their crude efforts in cheapness. It comes as a heavy blow to the engineer's pride to realise that he must abandon his elaborate plant and that the native holds the balance between failure and success.

Again, in the South Americas the laissez-faire attitude of the inhabitants galls him to the quick. In the southern part of the New World, the policy is 'Never do today what can be done tomorrow', and the native acts up to the very letter of the aphorism. Religious festivals, each of which is regarded as a holiday, occur with the most tantalising frequency. It is no uncommon circumstance for two or three such orgies – they scarcely can be described as anything else – to occur in a week, and the labourer is a commendable zealot in the observance of the religious feasts. The engineer may fret and fume at the delay, but unless he is in a position to recruit outside labour, he must tolerate the frequent interruptions in the work with the best grace he can muster. In the mountainous regions of South America, the native knows only too well that he holds an unassailable advantage, for he is accustomed to the rarefied atmosphere encountered in the extreme altitudes, whereas it plays sad havoc with the strongest constitutions of Europeans.

Strange to say, one of the most conscientious workmen in railway building, as in other fields of industrial endeavour, is the Chinaman. From a cursory point of view this appears inexplicable, but it must be borne in mind that a Celestial's word is his bond. Johnny will haggle and argue for hours over a bargain, but when he finally accepts the terms he will fulfil the contract to the letter, even should he ascertain before he has completed the task that it involves him in a personal loss. I have seen these men pick up their tools as the clock struck the hour for commencing the daily task, plod along quietly and continually until the hour of cessation, and give an indisputably good return for their daily wage. Can the same be said of the workmen of any other nationality? I am afraid not. In fact, the steadiness of the Chinaman has become so famous and has proved so reliable that it is safe to say that many of the biggest railways of the day never would have been completed but for his aid. It enabled the first transcontinental line to be carried across the United States to link New York with San Francisco; through Oriental labour the Canadian Pacific was consummated, and many another great undertaking of a like nature could tell a similar story.

The same spirit prevails when the scene of activity is removed to China itself. The Celestial may entertain quaint ideas concerning the iron road and its scope of utility. He may slave hard today laying the track, merely to pull it up again on the morrow on the plea that it is disturbing the spirits of his ancestors. But nevertheless, he completes his part of the bargain in the first instance. Strikes are unknown, and disputes never arise unless the employer declines to stand by his side of the contract. China is permeated through and through with secret societies or Guilds – Trade Unions, if you like – to one or other of which every Celestial belongs. The white engineer when he first arrives in the country finds it very difficult to make headway, but in reality he is on probation in the eyes of the Orientals. They are watching closely his methods, fathoming his code of honour, his capacity for handling men – in fact, are investigating him just as closely as if he were under a microscope. Once he has established his reputation and has inspired confidence, he need entertain no further apprehensions concerning trouble.

Yet the Celestials have their own peculiar and effective way of settling disputes among themselves. The engineer in need of a few thousand men negotiates for brawn and muscle through a middle-man or labour contractor. The engineer concludes his bargain with this worthy, and the latter makes his own terms with the men. He recruits the navvies at a certain wage, which he takes care to leave him a wide margin of profit. Occasionally he will be too grasping and will resort to sweating tactics. When the labourers find this out, trouble looms ahead. The men report the matter to their Guilds, who take the avaricious middle-man in hand and make him disgorge some of his ill-gotten gains. If he refuses, well, one day the contractor is missing, and never is seen again by the engineer. No questions are asked and no explanations for his disappearance are offered. He has settled his account with the Guilds to his own personal disadvantage. The engineer, however, knows nothing about the dissatisfaction until he observes the absence of the contractor, for the work meantime continues its daily round undisturbed.

Although labour is a vital consideration, it is but one cog in the complex machine by means of which the iron road is driven forward through a new country. Without tools the efforts of the navvy would count for naught, and as time has rolled by inventive effort and engineering skill have contrived more and more wonderful devices to enable the epoch-making work to be fulfilled in the shortest space of time. There is the steam shovel, which will remove 2½ cubic yards of miscellaneous rubble with every swing of its ponderous arm; the grader, whereby the soil is ploughed up and displaced by an endless chain of buckets into capacious wagons for removal; the drag shovel, a huge scoop attached to the end of a chain which is pulled along the ground from a stationary point by steam power, becoming charged with material in its progress, and thus fashioning the cutting; the monitor, whereby tons of gravel are washed down the mountainside under the disintegrating force of a powerful jet of water similar to a fireman's hose; and a host of other wonderful implements, all devised for the express purpose of expediting the work in hand. Gunpowder and dynamite are invaluable handmaids, and today are used with an astonishing prodigality. Indeed, when the advance is through rock, their services are indispensable. Crags, cliffs and even whole hills are blown away bodily by their agency, and the cost often runs into thousands of pounds, miniature volcanoes being produced by the upheavals.

Those who have travelled over many remarkable railway systems in various parts of the world where striking evidences of the engineer's skill are apparent upon a liberal scale, have pointed to the absence of any such evidences of activity in these islands – 'The Home of the Railway.' But this to a certain degree is inevitable. The engineer was not faced with such physical conditions when he essayed to gridiron this country as confronted him in the Americas or Asia. There are no towering ranges of eternally snow-wreathed mountains to overcome, no wildly boiling wide rivers to span, no yawning canyons to thread or stretches of sterile desert to traverse. Yet when Stephenson and his contemporaries sought to achieve the railway conquest of Great Britain, they encountered many obstacles which to them, with their crude appliances, were every whit as stupendous as those which rear up before the engineer today, although he is equipped with an extensive assortment of heavy artillery to assist him in his contest against the forces of Nature. Moreover, some of the expedients which Stephenson evolved to overcome a difficult situation are practised today merely because the intervening eighty years have not provided any better solution of a problem of a similar character.

Everyone has read how Stephenson was for a time nonplussed by the treacherous bog Chat Moss, across which now speed the expresses of the London and North-Western railway. It is the largest stretch of swamp in the country, and many wiseacres prophesied that there Stephenson would meet his Waterloo when he essayed to carry the Liverpool & Manchester railway over its unstable surface. Yet Stephenson plodded along unconcerned and achieved success in a novel manner. He laid branches of trees and hedge cuttings upon the surface of the bog, and upon the softest patches pressed hurdles intertwined with heather into service. Upon this network he laid a layer of rock and gravel, which caused the foundation to sink somewhat into the morass. This formed the permanent way, and its peculiar character provoked more than one scornful criticism. But its stability confounded the critics.

Today, in foreign countries where huge stretches of swamp bar the progress of the iron road, the self-same principle is adopted, and it is known as 'corduroying' or 'cross-waying'. In the northern states, Canada and Siberia – the latter country and Canada especially – the 'muskeg', or 'tundra', as this treacherous land is called, often stretches for miles. One can sound it sedulously to a great depth, and then will fail to touch the bottom. The soddened decayed vegetable matter merely fills a large depression which cannot be drained. The builders waste no time attempting to build up a solid earthen embankment resting on the submerged solid floor of the bog. They fashion a huge mattress of trees. Large trunks are laid horizontally and longitudinally to the track. Upon these are laid transversely two or three layers of shorter logs, the whole being secured together firmly. A topmost layer of branches forming a kind of thatching completes the structure.

At times, these mattresses assume respectable proportions. I have stood beside some almost as thick as a man is tall, and they constituted quite formidable pieces of work. When the corduroy is completed a layer of rock is applied, and upon this is dumped the gravel and other material forming the embankment. Under the weight thus superimposed, the mattress sinks deeply into the morass and rests firmly. The earthen ridge is continued to the requisite height; the whole of the embankment for the track rests upon the fabrication of tree trunks. Yet the whole is just as solid as if resting upon granite. One might remark that it appears an indifferent foundation upon which to pile up a mass of earth weighing several hundred tons, and that in a short time the wood, under decomposition and collapse, would precipitate a subsidence. But as a matter of fact, the corduroy grows stronger with every passing day. The wood immersed in the viscous liquid and preserved from all contact with the atmosphere becomes waterlogged, until at last it assumes the character of bog oak and is practically indestructible.

Stephenson was called upon to cope with another critical situation upon the same railway. The great tunnel at Kilsby was in course of construction, but work had not proceeded very far when the contractors struck a large pocket of water and quicksand. They combated this adversary for several months, and then, unable to make any appreciable headway, threw up the contract. Efforts were made to induce other firms to accept the task, but in vain. At last Stephenson was called upon to rescue the undertaking from failure. The outlook was far from promising, for the shaft was being sunk through material which the engineer always regards askance – a shale – while the fault in which reposed a large volume of water and sand was of large proportions. Stephenson concluded that the best way to cope with the problem was to pump out the water first, and accordingly he rigged up an elaborate plant capable of handling 1,800 gallons per minute, and this was kept going day and night. Even then, however, it was only by superhuman effort that the water was kept down. One day after Stephenson had been on the scene about six months, the water got the upper hand and flooded the tunnel to such a depth that the men and materials had to be floated in on rafts.

This undertaking, however, served to demonstrate to those anxious to participate in railway-building speculations how estimated expenses for definite work might be sent astray seriously, and how formidable and ubiquitous was the unexpected factor in such work. The original contractor offered to complete the burrow, 7,169 feet in length, under the Kilsby Ridge for some £90,000. By the time the last brick of the lining had been laid and the tunnel was ready for use, over £300,000 had been expended.

The attempt to pierce this tunnel at that time, however, was a far more difficult enterprise than it would be today. The engineers had not the powerful marvellous appliances such as serve the contractor's purposes now. Electric energy was unknown, the hydraulic shield for driving tunnels had yet to be invented, the steam shovel had not been thought of – in short, the contractor was handicapped on every side by the crude character of his tools. Some of these appliances which the modern railway builder uses are little short of wonderful, both in time- and labour-saving qualities, and the majority have been born of necessity.

For instance, in the early railway days on the American continent, too much time would have been occupied in building lofty earthen embankments among the mountains. Accordingly, the rifts and gullies were spanned by timber trestles. But the woodwork was perishable, and there was always the risk of fire demolishing the structure and precipitating disaster to a passing train. The obvious remedy was to replace the wood by metal, but the expense was a deterrent factor.

One day, a workman on one of the mountain sections suggested that the woodwork should be left intact, but buried beneath a mass of earth. The suggestion was received with ridicule because, as the divisional engineer pointed out, several thousand men and several hundred trucks and dozens of locomotives would be required to handle the material, while the time the task would occupy was incalculable. The workman listened to the criticisms, and then interposed with the quiet comment that he did not suggest using any trains and trucks, and that a few dozen men would be ample to complete the work. The divisional engineer was somewhat astonished, and at first thought the man had taken leave of his senses. Then the workman revealed his intentions. He would not resort to steam shovels or any other device of that character. He had observed minutely and tested the power of a jet of water, and consequently had conceived an idea to wash down masses of gravel by means of very powerful jets of water. There was no need even to rig up a steam engine and pump to supply the requisite force to the water flying from the nozzle. High up on the mountainside was a creek. A dam could be thrown across this torrent at little cost, the pent-up water could be led down to the working site below through piping, and the pressure thus secured by gravitation would be more than ample for the purpose. The gravel as washed out of the hillside would be directed into wooden conduits and led to points around the trestles, where it would be discharged to build up the embankment.

It was a simple means of overcoming a perplexing difficulty. The divisional engineer was so impressed with its feasibility that he secured the requisite permission for the workman to put his suggestion into practical form. The creek was dammed by throwing trees from bank to bank, and from the little pond thus formed the water was led several hundred feet down the mountainside through pipes to the large nozzles. A small network of timber conduits was fashioned to convey the displaced gravel to the feet of the timber trestle.

In a short time work was commenced, and as the jets of water struck against the solid face of the mountain, the soft earth and gravel were washed out at a tremendous speed. Heavy streams of mud poured down the conduits. The hill disappeared like magic under the scouring action of the harnessed water, to reappear in a symmetrically shaped ridge around the woodwork, which grew rapidly in height until the level of the railway was gained. The embankment thus formed was found to be as solid and stable as if built by dumping, and the whole task was accomplished in a few weeks. While the work was in progress, the chief engineer and his lieutenant visited the spot and watched the building of the embankment by hydraulic sluicing with intense interest. Its complete success in this initial experiment secured its adoption, and in a short space of time, where the conditions permitted, all the trestles among the mountains were buried beneath a ridge of earth built up by a jet of water.

While I was being shown some of the most impressive pieces of railway engineering among the Cascades, my cicerone, an English engineer and railway builder, after describing the features whereby the Great Northern railway is taken down to the coast, remarked, 'I wonder what Brunel would have done among these mountains? I guess he would have revelled in the difficulties they offered.'

There is no doubt that the great engineer would have found the ascent of the steep slopes and the crossing of the great gulches an extensive field for the exercise of his genius. His work among the vales of Cornwall and along the rugged seashore of Wicklow, Ireland, indicates this fact only too plainly. In these two districts are to be found the nearest approaches to spectacular work that these islands can afford. True there are no wonderful loops and great terraces winding up and down mountainsides, but there is the daring and lofty spanning of yawning valleys, and the driving of a narrow pathway along steep rocky slopes.

For something like half a century Brunel's spidery timber viaducts of Cornwall constituted one of the sights of that county. The location, with its grades and curves, as carried through Cornwall, has been assailed by many critics, but it must be remembered that when Brunel penetrated the English Riviera, railway operation was very different from what it is today. Engines and train loads were light, while money was by no means plentiful. The engineer was compelled to achieve his object at the most moderate cost, but the very fact that he was hampered in this connection served to influence him in the accomplishment of monumental work. His timber viaducts were remarkable for the novel character of their design and their extent. In the course of 60 miles, he had to span no less than thirty-four valleys in this manner, the aggregate length of the wooden structures being about 4 miles.

The engineer adopted timber as a constructional material because it was cheaper than iron, and American oak was used extensively. Some were of great height, the St Pinnock viaduct, for instance, carrying the train 153 feet above the bottom of the valley, while others attained great lengths, the Landore viaduct measuring 1,760 feet from end to end.

These evidences of Brunel's work, however, are disappearing under the exigencies of today. Timber is being replaced by steel and granite to meet the increased weights and speeds of trains. The location through the county also is undergoing revision, the sharp curves introduced by Brunel being eased or eliminated, while the grades are being flattened. Consequently in a few years the name of Brunel in Cornwall will be naught but a memory. Fortunately, other evidences of his handiwork abound on this system notably in the Saltash, Chepstow and Maidenhead bridges, as well as the Box and Foxwood tunnels.

In Ireland, however, a far more daring expression of his skill is offered. This is the stretch of line along the seashore between Bray and Wicklow, which now forms part of the Dublin and South-Eastern Railway. This was the first stretch of iron road to be opened in the Emerald Isle, the original 1¾ miles being operated in the first instance by the system of atmospheric propulsion, whereby the train was hauled along the metals by suction.

When it was decided to connect Wicklow with Bray, the trying character of the country lying between the two points, and especially of Bray Head, demanded a master-hand to effect the location and to carry the building operations through to success. It was a matter of 16 miles, but they proved perhaps the most trying 16 miles of railway construction ever attempted in this country. It was stated that Bray Head would defy conquest, for it was approachable only through very rocky country, and it is quite possible that the gloomy outlook was responsible for tempting Brunel to achieve something bold and striking. There was no need to have carried the line in this direction, a fact which is realised today, for by making a detour inland an easier location could have been found, and the present generation would not have been called upon to pour out heavy sums of money to keep their line intact. Brunel's vanity has cost the railway company several thousands of pounds since the line was opened. It is only by superhuman effort that the railway is not devoured by the sea, over, £40,000, or $200,000, having been expended in defence works over this 16 miles of line during a period of ten years alone.

Apart from this unsatisfactory feature, the line is a constant source of anxiety. A little to the south of Bray is Bramstone tunnel and a wild ravine.

This gulch attracted the engineer. Instead of avoiding it, he bridged it with a wooden viaduct 300 feet long by 75 feet high. Before it was quite completed it was destroyed in a single night, the demolished timbers being carried out to sea. A few years later, while a train was crossing, the engine left the metals and precipitated a sensational accident. Investigation revealed the fact that it was due to the action of the waves, which, battering against the piers of the viaduct, had so vibrated the structure as to throw the rails out of gauge.

Thereupon it was decided to abandon the viaduct and drive the line directly through the rocky promontory. The traveller still can see traces of the original route in the decaying approaches to the gap formerly conquered by a timber trestle.

Still it was a grim fight with Nature for every foot of the way. A mere ledge suffices to carry the track, and this gallery is often at a level of 70 feet above the sea beneath. Here and there the line is enclosed by a roof recalling the snow shed of the Selkirks or Cascades, to protect the rails from stones bouncing down the cliffs. Curiously enough, the method in which Brunel drove his line along this forbidding wild shore recalls the staggering feats accomplished in the American mountains, and indeed a journey over this railway will provide a thrill in miniature such as results from a toil through the mountain backbone of the New World. The dislodgment of massive boulders and landslides are so frequent that flagmen have to be retained to keep a vigilant eye on the track and to warn passing trains. At places long walls have been erected high on the hillside to arrest the descent of the movements of loose rock on the one hand, while on the other the cliff face has been cut into terraces to break the force of the waves, and, together with retaining walls and groynes, seek to counteract the insidious erosion of the sea.

When Bray Head has been passed the physical character of the country changes with startling suddenness from jagged rock to clay. Here the engineer was brought to fierce grips with his adversary. The clay is honeycombed on all sides with springs, and there is a constant war between the engineer and Nature for supremacy. Building the line was exacting indeed, but the puzzles which had to be unravelled then are equalled by those attending the preservation of the road. The battle was waged relentlessly for some years, but the sea won; the engineers were compelled to re-lay their track some distance inland.

The shareholders in the railway are paying dearly for Brunel's colossal error. Indeed, it is a poor return for an outlay of over £400,000, or $2,000,000, which were sunk in this 16 miles of line. It may be wonderful engineering, but it is not business. The railway company is anxious to abandon this location and to rebuild the line along the route it should have followed in the first instance. At the present, such a result is not financially possible, but its realisation is merely a question of time.

One inspiriting phase of the railway builder's work is the race against time, and in the fulfilment of such a task, many an astonishing performance has been achieved. When one of the great American railways was pushing its way to the Pacific coast, it required a tunnel to be driven for 2 miles through the Cascades. It was a daring piece of work, and the railway company, after considering the scheme, decided that it could be accomplished cheaper and more quickly under contract than by direct labour. Upon the advice of their surveyors, they set the time for its completion at twenty-eight months. Considering the remote situation of the work the feat was considered absolutely impracticable, and no recognised contractor could be prevailed upon to incur the risk.

The company, however, was convinced that some daring spirit existed who could, and would, fulfil their requirements, so they advertised for tenders. When these were perused, it was found that one man was willing to meet the time limit and at a price far below competitors. His bid was accepted. That man was Bennett, and he lost no time in setting his carefully laid plans in motion.

He was over 3,000 miles from the country in which the tunnel was to be driven, yet before the ink on the contract was dry, he had wired to his assistant on the Pacific coast to hurry forward all requisite appliances, while he himself purchased an elaborate plant of the most modern type to be shipped to the railway point nearest the site. From this station he had to transport every ounce of material for a distance of 82 miles through the roughest and most broken mountainous country it is possible to conceive.

There was no road, so he had to blaze one through the deadfall and littered rock, fording creeks and streams and toiling through viscous mud. The wagons sank above the axles, and had to be hauled through the muskeg by block and tackle. In this way, by sheer physical effort, he gained the mountain which was to be pierced. It took him a solid six months to get his forces and artillery to the spot, leaving him scarcely twenty-two months in which to hew the passage through the solid rock.

So pressing was time that he never permitted an hour's cessation day or night. An agent on the coast recruited men by the score and dispatched them up country in large corps. As they arrived they were divided into 6-hour shifts on either side of the mountain, and in this way toil was continued unbrokenly throughout the whole 24 hours. When he had settled down to work in grim earnest wages were absorbing money at the rate of nearly £2,000, or $10,000, per week.

Preliminary to embarking upon the contract, he had prepared careful calculations showing him how much rock it was requisite to remove every day to effect completion in time, and he made up his mind to hold to this table by hook or by crook. A tunnel face is not a spot where much leeway can be made up, for only a certain number of men can be crowded upon its limited area. But he met this disadvantage by spurring the drillers to superhuman effort by the offer of an attractive bonus. In this way he was able to maintain the advance he had calculated per day until the heart of the mountain was gained, when owing to the extreme hardness of the rock the men could not help falling behind the scheduled progress. Now and again, however, when they encountered a softer stretch of material they were able to make up lost time.

The months sped by; the contracted time for completion loomed nearer and nearer. Determined not to be beaten, Bennett urged his drillers harder and harder, offering fancy wages for additional effort. The strain wore him almost to a skeleton; he scarcely slept, so haunted was he by the determination to fulfil his side of the bargain. Checking and rechecking of the finished work convinced him that the opposing parties could not be far apart in the heart of the Cascades.

One morning, the men on one side paused momentarily in their drilling. They could hear the faint muffled chink, chink of drills. It was the party advancing from the west. With a loud cheer, answered by a ghostly sepulchral hurrah, both parties bent to their tasks with redoubled energy. Before long a gaping hole was revealed in the heading. The two forces had met – the tunnel was pierced. Without hesitation they set to widening the breach out to its appointed dimensions, and at last, with a sigh of relief, threw down their tools. The tunnel was finished practically, and there were seven days or so to spare.

In another instance, a railway company required a bridge to be opened within a certain period. Its accomplishment on time meant the accretion of a large sum of money to the treasury, and accordingly a bounty of some £5,000, or $25,000, was offered to the firm building the bridge.

The latter in turn offered a portion to the men responsible for the actual work. Under the incentive of this offer, the riveters and erectors strove might and main. The odds were against them hopelessly, but general cooperation enabled the work to go forward with great speed. By maintaining this high pressure, the huge fabric assumed its definite shape in quick time and the last rivet was driven home with a resounding cheer a few minutes before the expiration of the stipulated time.

Yet railway construction has its farcical side, especially in America. Conflicting interests often clash, and then lively times ensue. In Canada it has been no unusual sight to see an existing railway rush a large gang of workmen to a point threatened with invasion by a rival. Their presence ostensibly is to improve the line in possession, but in reality the men are drafted there to thwart the competitive enterprise. This is the 'fighting gang', and it is rightly named, because the opposing forces often meet and a free fight results.

When these tactics are waged by opposing railway magnates, the struggle is often bitter and long drawn out. It was so when J. J. Hill and Harriman came to close grips in Oregon. The former great railway builder decided to carry a line down to the coast along the bank of the Columbia River. Harriman construed this act as an invasion of his preserves, and spared no effort to defeat the 'Grand Old Railway-Builder of the West', as J. Hill is called popularly. Directly Hill's proposals became known, Harriman, to secure his legal status, revived a defunct project known as the 'Wallula Pacific Railway', which had been incorporated so many years before, and yet had accomplished so little, as to be forgotten. Hill was coming down the north bank of the Columbia, and suddenly Harriman discovered that his moribund project was to follow the same course. The result was that two rival constructional forces appeared on the scene, one bent on building a line, and the other determined to prevent its realisation. A hail of rock rained from one camp to the other, and the grade was demolished as rapidly as fashioned. One day the Hill navvies were in possession, the next, through being outnumbered, they were driven out and the Harriman army held the position, only to evacuate it when the former reappeared with reinforcements. No blood was spilt, but it came perilously near it when a navvy on one side threw a piece of rock harder against an opposing workman than the latter appreciated. Injuries were numerous, and one day the aspect became so threatening that a pitched battle appeared certain. At times, however, the battle became Gilbertian. The rivals merely played catch ball with pieces of rock, tossing the missiles at one another with considerable banter and amid a rain of jokes.

For eighteen months this state of affairs prevailed, and then, the courts deciding against Harriman, he was forced to retire from the scene. Directly he did so, his gangs of navvies walked over to the opposite camp, because from their point of view, Hill's money was just as good as that of Harriman. It was immaterial to them for which side they worked, so long as they were paid for it. The result was that the two gangs which had been engaged in more or less deadly strife, now worked harmoniously side by side to carry the Hill line into Portland. Such tactics as these, however, come somewhat as an interlude to the grim tussle with Nature which is the railway builder's invariable lot.

CHAPTER 3

The Boring of
the Gotthard Tunnel

The little country of Switzerland, as is well known, is a tumbled mass of snow-clad mountain ranges. On the Italian frontier, however, this natural barrier becomes more rugged and defiant, some of the peaks towering 10,000 feet or higher into the clouds. For centuries this frontier chain so successfully walled in, the Helvetians that they could not pass into Italy without making a wearisome detour. Travelling from one country to the other before George Stephenson demonstrated the possibilities of the steam engine running on rails, therefore, was a journey not to be lightly undertaken, for it occupied weeks. An effort to ease this situation was made so far back as the thirteenth century by the blazing of a footpath over the St Gotthard, but it was a mere dangerous and dizzy trail. Little wonder, therefore, that it was not favoured by other than the more adventurous.

It was not until about a century ago that the first vehicle lumbered over this rugged hump. Then the demand for closer communication between the two countries prompted the ambitious Helvetians to embark upon a costly and momentous enterprise – the building of a post road over the mountain. They cut a roadway 18½ feet wide, with an average grade of 10 per cent, to a height of 6,936 feet up the flanks of this snow-topped giant, with its deep rifts, rushing rivers, and faced the terrors of the avalanche. It is a striking piece of work, for at places the road clings, limpet-like, to perpendicular walls, describes sharp twists and turns sudden corners. Although the people could ill afford the expense of the undertaking, they carried it to completion, confident that untold benefit would accrue from its provision.

They were right in their surmise. That mountain road changed completely the direction of the stream of traffic flowing between Switzerland and Italy. The novelty of the route, the magnificent panoramas unfolded from every foot of its length, appealed to the tourist and traveller and they bravely essayed the 'pass'. Today, that mountain road is trodden but seldom. It has fallen into desuetude; the railway has killed its utility.

So soon as the iron horse invaded the little country, it was sought to carry it into Italy via the St Gotthard; not over the mountain crest, but through its base. Every engineer nursed the ambition to overcome that frowning knot with the steel highway. For years brilliant minds lived, dreamt and died obsessed with this one great idea. Even in 1846, when the first railway was opened from Baden to Zurich, preparations were made to carry the line onward through the mountain chain. To the Swiss people, boring through a mountain for 9 miles or so appeared no more difficult than burrowing through a hillock for as many yards. It was only a question of time and expense.

An 'Alpine tunnel fever' set in with terrible malignancy, and there was fierce rivalry and jealousy created between the various railway companies, cantons and towns as to who should have the honour of completing this remarkable link. Fortunately, the government itself preserved a cool head, turned a deaf ear to entreaties, refused concessions, and discouraged any possible hope of financial aid. The last-named factor proved the greatest stumbling block, but there is no doubt that if the money could have been obtained for such an enterprise, an attempt to tunnel the Alps would have been made in the fifties.

Though the ambition was scotched, it was not killed by any means, for a few years later the same scheme was revived and more keenly discussed than ever. The French and Italian nations resuscitated the project by cooperating in the effort to pierce the Col de Frejus, popularly known as the Mont Cenis tunnel. The first stroke of the pickaxe upon this momentous enterprise was made in August, 1857, and the two chief engineers, Grattoni and Sommeiller, pledged themselves to complete the task with the assistance of the French and Italian governments. In the face of the most terrible difficulties that could be conceived, equipped with tools which appear puny and futile in comparison with those used for such work today, they cut, blasted, and excavated their way through 7½ miles of dense rock. Boring from either end, the rock-hogs broke down the last wall of rock on Christmas Day, 1870, and in September of the following year, a shorter and more direct route between the two countries was opened to traffic.

The progress of this tunnel was watched with the closest interest by the Helvetians. This piercing of an Alpine mountain was something new in railway engineering. The wiseacres croaked that it would never be completed; that Nature would spring some sudden surprise upon the engineers in the depths of the mountain which would arrest the whole enterprise. But as the two headings slowly but surely approached one another, and the engineers broke down their obstacles as they arose with commendable pluck and determination, the sceptics became silenced.

The pride of the Swiss was wounded. If the French had Italians could accomplish such a herculean and apparently impossible task, why was a similar idea beyond their powers? The 'conquest of the Alps' broke out with renewed vigour. It became more than a personal issue; it blossomed into one of economic, political and commercial importance. Consequently, before the Cenis Tunnel was opened for traffic, the preliminary arrangements for burrowing through the St Gotthard had assumed concrete shape. But it had been a wearisome enterprise. The promoters had to battle against intrigue and jealousies innumerable on the part of private individuals, companies seeking for the same concession, towns and departmental governments. But the project became one of even more than national importance; it became an international question. The provision of such a route would bring northern Europe into closer touch with Italy and her ports on the Mediterranean. That fact was realised, and when the company incorporated to carry out the work announced that the task was far too risky for private resources, the governments of the countries most intimately interested in the fulfilment of the project promised tangible assistance in the form of substantial subventions.

The path of the tunnel through the heart of the mountain was plotted by Mr. M. O. Gelpke, C.E., and this in itself was a great achievement. Fifteen stations were scattered over the mountain slopes for the manipulation of the survey instruments, and many of these were situated unavoidably in positions very difficult, and often impossible, of access. Borings were made to ascertain the rock strata which would have to be pierced by Professor Fritsch of Frankfort, and from the result of these essential investigations it was computed that the work, including the necessary railway line on either side of the great tunnel, could be completed for a sum of £7,480,000, or $37,400,000. The money was raised by guarantees of £1,800,000 ($9,000,000) from Italy, £800,000 ($4,000,000) from both Germany and Switzerland, and by the issue of shares and mortgage bonds to the extent of £2,720,000, or $13,600,000. As a further contribution to the task, the Swiss government undertook to supervise actual construction.

The financial arrangements completed, the company had to search for a man to bore the tunnel. For this purpose, tenders were sought for the whole contract. The terms of the latter were severe, as were also the technical conditions. The tunnel was to carry a double track, to have a height of 19.68 feet to the crown of the arch, and a maximum width of 26.24 feet, with a minimum width of 24.93 feet. The tunnel was to be quite straight, with the exception of a slight curve at the southern end, where, for a distance of 474 feet from the entrance, a curve of 984 feet radius was to be introduced to gain Airolo station. The rise from the northern entrance was to be about 1 in 172 to the summit level 3,781 feet above the sea, followed by a drop of 1 in 1,000 to the southern end. These gradients falling on either side from the centre were necessary for drainage, and were estimated to be just sufficient to ensure the water flowing to the portals.

Seven tenders were submitted for the enterprise, the lowest being that of L. Favre, a well-known engineer of Geneva, who had completed many notable railway works in Europe. He undertook to complete the tunnel for £2,000,000 ($10,000,000) within eight years. His nearest competitor, an Italian company, wanted 25 per cent, more, but would not guarantee completion within less than nine years. Monsieur Favre was supported by a body of influential capitalists, and the contract was awarded to him.

Having sanctioned the project, the government was determined that it should be completed, and resolved that the engineer should be held to his self-appointed time limit. The penalty it stipulated was exacting. For every day over the ninth year, Favre was to forfeit £200, or $1000, for six months, and then double that penalty per day until completion. A year was thus allowed over and above what he demanded to cope with any unforeseen contingencies that might arise during the progress of the task. Similarly, M. Favre was to receive a premium of £200, or $1,000, a day for every day he was in advance of the stipulated period. His Italian competitor, while agreeable to the forfeit, stipulated that it should not be enforced until after the eleventh year, which terms the authorities refused to entertain. To ensure securing the forfeit money should the engineer be late, Favre was compelled to deposit a sum of £320,000 ($1,600,000) with the government before a stone was moved.

No undertaking of such a magnitude as this tunnel, although protected adequately by severe restrictions, ever has been carried out in the face of so many vicissitudes; no engineer ever has been so harassed as was M. Favre. From the moment the tender was signed and sealed, troubles commenced, some incidental to the task, others purposely thrown in his way by jealous outside interests. In the first place, the government undertook, according to the terms of the contract, to have the approaches to the tunnel completed so that he could commence operations without delay. This was not done. Further opposition was then encountered from another and unexpected quarter, which assumed such proportions as to jeopardise the whole scheme.

Italy, having contributed about a sixth of the cost, and who therefore had an important voice in the matter, demanded that half the work should be granted to the Italian engineers who had been engaged upon the Mont Cenis tunnel. This was a bitter question, and it took M. Favre two weary months to adjust it.

These hindrances at last settled satisfactorily, work was commenced on the northern side of the Alps at Göschenen on 4 June 1872, and at Airolo, the southern portal, on 2 July of the following year. The preliminary preparations were of a gigantic character. Though M. Favre had sublet the constructional contract for the tunnel itself, he was primarily responsible and nursed it as the engineer-in-chief. Huge plants had to be installed at either end for supplying the various demands for power for a thousand-and-one purposes. At the northern end water turbines were laid down, driven from the river Reuss, a head of water of 279 feet being available. At the Airolo end a similar installation was established and operated under a water head of 541 feet from the Tremola. Subsequently, it was found that this latter supply was inadequate. But M. Favre was a man of infinite resource. He promptly built a viaduct 12,000 feet in length, tapping the Tessin River, and thus overcame the water power difficulty. Small towns sprang up at either end around the respective portals to house the machinery, the workmen, and innumerable other details.

As tunnel-boring operations upon such a scale as this were in their infancy, this engineer-in-chief perforcedly had to break a great deal of new ground to carry out considerable pioneer work. Hitherto, the usual tools at the service of the excavators were the pickaxe, shovel, chisel, and sledgehammer, but such implements as these in a work of this magnitude were akin to forging a mighty crank shaft with a blacksmith's hammer. New forces had to be created. The Mont Cenis had demonstrated this fact, and in the course of its realisation, a new tool appeared. This was the mechanical percussion rock drill, operated by compressed air at a pressure of 112 pounds and upwards per square inch. To furnish the requisite energy to the tools, elaborate air-compressing plants had to be laid down. These were designed by Professor Colladon, and they were capable of compressing 1,596 cubic yards of air to a pressure of 8 atmospheres every minute, the power being stored in huge cylindrical reservoirs, not unlike mammoth steam boilers, from which the conduits extending to the working faces on either side were charged.

The scene in the tunnel was impressive in the extreme. At the working face a little gallery was bored, about 8 feet wide by the same in height, at the roof of the tunnel. The drilling machines were mounted on travelling carriages, with their perforating chisels jutting ugly and business-like from the front.

With the pent-up force of 8 atmospheres behind them, they rapped against the solid rock and slowly but surely made a perforation. At frequent intervals there was a slight stop, the chisel point was withdrawn and a jet of water, drawn from a tender hauled up in the rear, was directed into the hole, when the chisel instantly resumed its monotonous round. At intervals, a chisel, with its cutting edge blunted from continual hammering at the iron-like mass, was taken out, thrown on one side, and another inserted in its place, to continue the attack on the rock. Progress was laboriously slow, or comparatively rapid, according to the nature of the material encountered. When the rock was of a granitic nature, then advance was only at the rate of an inch or two per hour; on the other hand, when soft, clayey material was tapped, then the chisels bored their way at the rate of as many feet in the same time.

Three men attended to each machine, and by means of levers and wheels the height of a drill could be adjusted to a nicety. Movement was difficult, for the space was cramped. In the murky gloom, the outlines of the men could be faintly discerned. The fitful glimmer of the oil- lamp which each carried – electric lighting had still to be invented – fell upon their semi-nude bodies and swarthy faces. The streaming perspiration mingling with the grime and dust, which strayed over their skin in fantastic streaks, gave the men a fiendish appearance. The temperature was that of an oven. As the men drew nearer and nearer to the heart of old Gotthard, the heat rose until the men laboured in an atmosphere of 90° Fahrenheit or more. The only sounds were those of the hammering of the drills as they bored into the rock, and the hissing of the escaping air after it had completed its allotted task in operating the chisels.

At long intervals there came a heavy silence. The holes had been bored to the requisite depth. The machine was drawn far back into the boring. Explosives were slipped into the holes and tamped home. From a safe distance the charges were fired. A dull, smothered roar, a rending and crumbling, and another gap was torn in the bowels of this monarch of the Alps. The excavators hurried forward, cleared away the tumbled debris, and brought the lumbering drill carriage up to the fresh working surface.

Day in and day out, week after week, month by month, this round continued. It was monotonous, and the work was hard. The stifling atmosphere and the conditions told severely on the physique of the workmen. Congestion of the brain, irregular action of the heart, anaemia, or one of numerous other obscure maladies, was the reward for their labour. Their faces assumed a deathly pallor; working in cramped positions gave them an unsightly stoop, and deprived their legs of movement, so they tottered rather than walked as they returned from the scene of their toil at the end of the shift.

The pay was wretched, ranging from ½ crown to 5 shillings (from 60 to 125 cents) per day of 8 hours, out of which they had to board themselves! Needless to say, but few Englishmen or western Europeans figured on the payroll, for none would accept such starvation pay for such terrible work. The labourers were Italians for the most part, and yet nearly one and all, by subsisting on miserable food, consisting for the most part of a kind of meal porridge, cheap and yet limited in quantity, saved a part of their earnings and sent it home to their needy families in sunny Italy. The average number of men employed was about 4,000, half at either end, but at times it ran up to as high as 7,000. The mountain claimed 310 lives, killed by accident alone, and 877 injured, before it was conquered, but, considering the conditions, it is remarkable that the casualty roll was not heavier.

In the wake of the small heading gallery came the other gangs. These rigged up the timber and other supports to the roof and excavated the small opening to the full dimensions of the tunnel. Last of all came the masons, setting the masonry lining, from 18 to 30 inches thick, in position, for the tunnel is lined throughout. In passing through the granite rock there was but little fear of a collapse of the roof, but in the treacherous clay advance had to be made warily, and heavy timbering resorted to, in order to prevent the soft soil caving in and burying all in its sticky embrace.

The material for the headings and lining, as well as the workmen and tools, were carried to and fro upon a small railway, the locomotives of which were driven by compressed air – steam was impracticable, because it would have fouled the workings, while on the short distance between the inner end of the railway and the working face, haulage was done by horses. The privations suffered by the navvies were only equalled by those experienced by the animals, the mortality of which ran up to as high as 25 per cent, of the number employed.

Water was a constant menace, and at times retarded progress seriously. On the south side it was particularly troublesome. Time after time the drills or detonating charges would tap one of these subterranean streams, and the water would pour out in a cascade. These rivulets were of varying volume, but in one stretch, where the rock was extremely friable, it was considered too dangerous to use the mechanical drilling machine, so the men had to cut their way forward by hand. In so doing, they released a vast underground pocket of water, which rushed out at the rate of over 3,000 gallons per minute. At one spot it was only by superhuman effort that headway was made, for the men were half submerged in these torrential outbursts, escape from which was only possible by penetrating farther into the mountain.

In 1876 another terrible calamity overtook Louis Favre. It was discovered suddenly that the railway, far from costing the estimated sum, would approximate over £1,500,000, or $57,500,000. Somebody had blundered, and badly too. A deficit of over £4,000,000, or $20,000,000, appeared certain. What was to be done? The development of such a contingency never could have happened at a more inopportune moment. Times were hard; money was scarce; financial crashes loomed in every quarter of the Continent; to make matters worse, war was raging. Never in the history of engineering had such an extraordinary and unaccountable mistake been made in the estimates.

The discovery came as a thunderclap. The stock of the company ran down like a thermometer plunged into ice. Those who had supported the enterprise in the face of hostile criticism began to doubt the wisdom of their optimism. A gloom settled everywhere. It appeared as if the gigantic achievement would become numbered among the great unpaid; would be another contribution to those unfinished enterprises characterised as follies.

But Monsieur Favre kept going. There was the daily penalty staring him in the face if he did not finish within time. Any prolonged delay spelled ruin to him and to those who had financed his task. To make matters worse, the Swiss departments who had the most to gain from the completion of the railway steadfastly refused to extend the slightest assistance.

Matters reached a crisis. Either the money must be found, or that already spent must lie buried in the mountain. An International Conference was called to consider the situation, where, as prominent cities and railways who hoped to reap something from the completion of the tunnel promised support, Germany, Switzerland and Italy agreed to increase their subventions. Much of the projected work originally contemplated was postponed indefinitely in order to reduce the first cost.

This readjustment of the financial situation enabled work to be resumed energetically. But Favre was harassed sorely still. Payments for work became irregular, and every possible obstacle that could be placed in his way was forced to the front by intriguing opponents. Efforts were made even to create a rupture between him and the International Society, but Favre's unflagging perseverance and determination resisted all such machinations, and he plodded along resolutely.

However, these worries and his feverish anxiety to succeed in his enterprise told upon his health. He never lived to see his great achievement completed. On 19 July 1879, while inspecting the progress of the work at the headings, he was seized with an apoplectic fit, to which he succumbed in a few hours. Literally in harness, this guiding spirit and clever engineer passed beyond the veil when the tunnel, the crowning effort of his life, was rapidly approaching completion.

His mantle fell upon his right-hand assistant, M. Hellwag, an accomplished German engineer, and he pushed forward the scheme with an energy characteristic of his late chief. But friction again rose. Swiss engineers were jealous of this appointment, and at last in sheer disgust the new engineer-in-chief threw up the work. He was hounded from his post, despite the fact that on another section of the railway he had overcome ingeniously the negotiation of sharp ascents within short distances, which otherwise appeared impossible, by the invention of a spiral tunnel, wherein the railway burrows into the mountainside, describes therein a complete circle, and emerges again immediately above the portal by which it entered.

On Saturday 27 February 1880, while the workmen on the Göschenen side were tearing the vitals out of the peak, they were surprised to find large masses of rock falling about their ears without any effort on their part. They stopped. The situation seemed uncanny. They listened intently, and then heard the familiar sound of a muffled roar, indicating blasting in the heading. The workmen on the Airolo side were upon them. Terrified lest the next concussion might bury them beneath a mass of rock, they hurriedly retreated and waited. Presently, one espied the point of a chisel ploughing through the rock towards him. He grasped its extremity, but as quickly dropped it, for it was so hot that it burned his hand. Frantically these men rapped upon the last remaining wall of rock to inform their comrades on the other side that they were through. With lightning-like rapidity the news flashed through the Göschenen workings that the men from the Airolo side might be seen at any minute, and that the task of eight weary years was consummated practically.

As quickly the news flashed from Göschenen to the Airolo portal to cease work, since it was decided that the last blast tearing away the final thickness of rock should be the occasion of great jubilation. The whole country was excited. Officials hurried to the scene, and the countryside from far and near flocked to the two mouths of the tunnel. There was no sleep for anyone in the constructional camps that Saturday night. The men were in a perfect state of frenzy. In the darkness, the preparations for the culminating move were hurried forward. It was arranged that as the men on the Airolo heading had first pierced the last partition of rock, they should have the honour of blowing the gap which would afford access from one side of the mountain chain to the other through its base.

At seven o'clock on the Sunday morning, a train started from each end laden with invited guests to witness the final operation. Amid many huzzas they disappeared into the dark, yawning mouths of the great bore. When each party reached the heading, the machines were already at work. Only a foot of rock stood between those who had journeyed up from Airolo and the others who had travelled from Göschenen. The distinction of making the breach 1,000 feet under the village of Andermatt nestling in the sunshine on the mountain slopes, and with the little lake of Sella 3,000 feet above one's head, was given to two Piedmontese workmen, Neccaraviglia and Chisso, who had toiled in the Cenis, and afterwards in the Gotthard, since its very commencement. The last charges were rammed home, and at 11.45 on the Sunday morning eight rumbling detonations heralded the piercing of St Gotthard. Ere the smoke had cleared away, the men sprang forward. There was the final breach, about 3 feet in diameter. Engineer Bossi sprang through the gap, and emotionally embraced his confrere on the other side, followed by his workmen, who shook hands with their comrades. It was a strange scene in the depths of the Alps, and the wild vivas of those assembled, to the memory of Louis Favre, reverberated weirdly down the shaft on either side.

The excavations of the works to the full dimensions and the lining up of the last section proceeded with great rapidity, and on 22 May 1882, amid great festivity, the tunnel was declared open. It had taken ten years to complete, but had Favre been left to his own devices, and had he not been exposed to financial harassing and intrigue, and had not his successor Hellwag been driven from his post, it would have been finished in the time the engineer contemplated. At that time Favre's skill, pluck and unflagging devotion to his task were not appreciated, but recognition of his genius was afterwards extended by the erection of a monument to his memory at the Airolo entrance to the tunnel. It is safe to assert that it was due to his enterprise and grim determination in the face of adversity that the St Gotthard tunnel became an accomplished fact, and resulted in the reduction of the journey between Northern Europe and Italy by 36 hours.

In addition to the tunnel, 172 miles of line had to be built to connect the Swiss with the Italian railway systems. From the body of this frowning clump 31,800,000 cubic feet of rock were torn by means of 2,200,000 pounds of dynamite.

The remaining sections of the railway named after the tunnel abound in interesting features from the technical point of view, the most notable, possibly, being the remarkable spiral tunnels to which reference has been made, and the successful application of which in this instance has been reproduced upon other railways where similar conditions prevail. The best examples, possibly, are those by which the Biaschina gorge is negotiated, since here there are two of these tunnels side by side, the railway almost describing a figure eight in corkscrewing from one level to the other. Exclusive of the Gotthard, there are no less than seventy-six tunnels and galleries, aggregating 29 miles, as well as 1,384 other structures, 324 being bridges and viaducts over 39 feet in length. In one stretch of 7 miles, in skirting the south-eastern arm of the Lake of Lucerne, the railway passes through nine tunnels, ranging from a mere 85-feet burrow to others 6,512 feet in length. Among the Gotthard fastnesses the railway work becomes bolder, the bridges are lofty, while the line zigzags in a remarkable manner. It is a case of tunnel, cut and bridge all the way. Up to 1880, when the railway was finished practically, constructional work provided regular employment for 10,757 men.

So rapidly did the volume of traffic upon the railway swell, however, that it became extremely difficult to handle it, as there was only a single line, except in the tunnel and at one or two other points. The provision of another track became imperative, and in 1886 it was commenced. This was not a simple matter, as the new work had to be carried out without interrupting traffic in any way – that is, so far as the main through service was concerned. With the exception of the Gotthard and four smaller tunnels, all the other structures had to be excavated out to carry the second pair of metals, while, similarly, all bridges had to be increased in width. In order to finish the work as rapidly as possible, the task was divided up into a number of small, separate contracts, each covering a few miles. Vehicles for the conveyance of constructional material were provided and supplies were hauled free of charge by the railway, while explosives for blasting were sold at cost price.

The most difficult works were carried out by the company itself by its own engineers and labour. In this comprehensive widening system, over 100,000 cubic yards of rock which had been excavated from the St Gotthard and dumped in the vicinity of Airolo were reclaimed, to be used in the building of embankments, revetments and retaining walls. The tunnel widening was carried out almost exclusively at night and on Sundays, since the smoke from passing trains would have impeded such work during the day. The quickest methods of widening were adopted, and in the approach to the Bristen tunnel an excellent expression of this is afforded. Instead of trimming back the mountainside to provide space for the second pair of rails, a gallery was built projecting from the mountain and supported on heavy masonry pillars, giving the appearance of a colonnade.

In the handling of unavoidable night trains an elaborate protection system was adopted in connection with the tunnels, to prevent disaster to the trains themselves or to the working gangs. No trains were permitted to enter a tunnel until assurance had been made doubly sure that there was no constructional train standing on the only line to court collision, and that the workmen were safe. Each working squad was covered amply by electric and other signalling devices. Similarly, all metallic structures that required moving were handled on Sundays, when traffic was at its lowest ebb, between the scheduled movements of passing trains, so that the latter might not be delayed. It was estimated that this work would occupy nine years, but in reality it was accomplished in five and a half years, and the total cost of widening the whole mileage to a double line was only £500,000, or $2,500,000.

CHAPTER 4

The Railway Invasion of Canada

The news of the victory of Stephenson's 'Rocket' in the historic railway locomotive contest at Rainhill on the Liverpool and Manchester railway in 1829 scarcely had filtered round the world, when the idea of transporting passengers and merchandise by steam power along two parallel rails occupied the earnest attention of enterprising spirits in Canada. They realised that the new method of locomotion was certain to play an important part in the opening up of British North America. As a result of deliberations, a small body of prominent business men in Montreal applied for a charter to construct a railway from La Prairie to St John's in the province of Quebec, which was granted in 1832 under the seal of William IV.

It was an unpretentious enterprise, for the projected line was only some 14 miles in length. It was named the Champlain and St Lawrence railway, the idea being to link Lake Champlain, whence New York could be reached by water, with the St Lawrence. The first section of the line was opened in 1836, though it was not operated by steam. The rails were of wood, and the vehicles were hauled by horses. This system obtained for only one year, however. The first winter sufficed to demonstrate to those concerned with the enterprise that such primitive methods were far from satisfactory. Consequently, the 'wooden flanges', as the rails constituting the track were called, were torn up to make way for iron rails, and the steam- engine took the place of the animal motor.

A year or two later, the objective of the promoters was attained. Lake Champlain was brought into communication with the St Lawrence at Montreal by a railway some 50 miles in length, the inland sheet of water being tapped at Rouses's Point at the head of the lake in United States territory. It is stated that Jay Gould, who afterwards became one of the greatest railway builders and magnates in the United States, gained his first insight of the construction of railways upon this line, by being associated with the location survey. From this humble beginning was woven the huge railway network of Canada, which now gridirons the country in all directions, and aggregates some 25,000 miles.

Other projects were formulated in rapid succession for a comprehensive invasion of the eastern corner of the country. Foremost among these was the Grand Trunk Railway Company, conceived in 1852, to build a trunk road between the Atlantic seaboard and the Great Lakes, which at that time was practically the western commercial limit of the Dominion. It was an English enterprise, and, moreover, was strongly imperial from the sentimental point of view, for it was planned to thread Canadian territory entirely.

The famous firm of railway constructional engineers, Messrs Peto, Betts & Brassey, fresh from their triumphs on the Continent, were willing to carry out the work. They had an extensive accumulation of plant lying idle, and at the time were seeking for fresh worlds to conquer. Canada presented just the opportunity they desired, and they were ready to provide all the railways that Canada would require for some years to come. The faith in this firm of constructional engineers was so great that British financiers were open to provide any amount of money that might be required.

The negotiations were prolonged, as rival interests opposed the scheme vehemently. The preliminaries passed through many vicissitudes, but the compact between the English financiers and the Canadian authorities was ratified and sealed, at last, for the construction of a main line between Montreal and Hamilton, a distance of about 373 miles, which the provincial government undertook to finance to the extent of £3,000, or $15,000, per mile. Hamilton was selected as the western terminal point because therefrom another line extended to the Lakes, while a railway was creeping up from Portland on the Atlantic coast to Montreal. By the construction of this central section, 964 miles of through continuous railway would be provided for the benefit of the population.

But the undertaking proved to be one of the most difficult that the engineers, despite their wide and varied experience, had been called upon to fulfil up to this time. The country traversed was very sparsely populated, the forests were dense, and in winter, under the combined adversities of snow, ice and intense cold, the situation was terrible. Labour was scarce, wages were high, and material was found to be expensive. In the end, it was found that the average cost per mile approximated £8,000, or $40,000, so that to link Montreal with Toronto entailed an expenditure of £2,664,000, or $13,320,000. Moreover, it was one of the largest contracts that the engineers ever had carried out, while the physical conditions harassed them to such an extent that when they balanced up their books, they found they had incurred a loss of about £1,000,000, or $5,000,000. The wide gauge of 5 feet 6 inches was adopted, and this factor developed into as keen a bone of dissension in Canada as it did in Great Britain, and as in the latter country it was finally abolished, so in Canada it was abandoned in favour of the standard gauge of 4 feet 8½ inches, though the conversion cost the Grand Trunk railway a matter of £1,000,000 ($5,000,000).

Yet in building this line the contractors set up an engineering monument which for years ranked as the 'eighth wonder of the world'. Montreal was on the north bank of the St Lawrence, while the link connecting the metropolis with the Atlantic seaboard followed the southern bank of the river. The two sections of line were interrupted by the rolling waterway, which at this point is nearly 2 miles wide. The spanning of this gap, so as to bring Montreal into direct railway touch with the coast, had been one of the great obstacles to the incorporation of the railway in the first instance, but Messrs Peto, Betts & Brassey undertook to forge this link. At that time it was so formidable an undertaking as to be thought absolutely incapable of realisation. Indeed, when a suggestion for bridging the St Lawrence at this point was advanced for the first time, it was laughed to scorn.

However, its construction constituted a vital part of the contract. Accordingly, the contractors lost no time in attacking the undertaking when they secured a foothold in the dominion. The river was surveyed minutely up and down for a considerable distance, while detailed soundings were made to discover the extent and nature of the foundations requisite for the piers. After infinite labour a suitable site was discovered, and a great measure of credit for the location is due to Alexander M. Ross, who was one of the engineers to the undertaking, George Stephenson acting as consulting engineer. Ross carried carefully prepared and detailed plans of the structure he had formulated to his co-adjutator in England, and Stephenson admitted, when first submitted to his notice, that 'the idea was certainly startling'. However, he complimented Ross upon his daring, and as the latter engineer had won his spurs in England before he departed to Canada on behalf of the group of capitalists financing the Grand Trunk railway, his work received greater consideration from the eminent engineer than might have been the case otherwise. The result was that when Stephenson went to Canada to consider the subject on the spot he concurred with Ross in the general scheme and the design was elaborated conjointly.

When the location was settled definitely, the project was assailed vigorously by bridge designers in America, but this animosity was inflamed from the fact that they had prepared alternative proposals for bridging the waterway at a different spot. The rival engineers emphasised the danger from ice, and commented strongly upon the risk, in fact serious danger, arising from this cause, to the full £50 brunt of which Stephenson's bridge would be submitted. Some critics even went so far as to state that the structure never would be completed, or if so, would come down under the first packing of the ice. Stephenson, however, treated his American detractors with contempt, and, to the mind of the latter worthies, appeared to fly deliberately in the face of Fate by concurring with Ross's recommendations. That was nearly sixty years ago, but the piers have given no sign of collapsing yet.

The resident engineer and superintendent of the constructional work, Mr James Hodges, realising the monumental character of the undertaking – for it was a larger bridge-building scheme than ever had been attempted up to this time – spent many hours together wrestling with difficulties as they developed, for the unexpected confronted them at every turn. The ice was one of their greatest perplexities, because during the winter the river is frozen so solidly that it will support the weight of a train, and, indeed, a track has been laid across the waterway in winter to maintain communication between the two banks. When the ice broke up, the floes became jammed and piled against the temporary works around the piers in an inextricable mass to such an extent that it demanded unremitting vigilance to guard against a collapse of the dams under the enormous pressure exerted upon them.

The depth of the river and the current were two other factors which had to be taken into serious consideration, for some of the piers are sunk in 22 feet of water, while the velocity of the current is about 7 miles an hour. The working season was very short, averaging about twenty-six weeks during the year, and during this period every available mail had to be crowded on to the work. When construction was in full swing, between 2,000 and 3,000 men found employment.

The bridge consisted of a huge rectangular tube, similar to that spanning the Menai Straits, carrying a single track. From end to end, it measured 6,592 feet by 16 feet wide, 18 feet in height, and weighed 9,044 tons. It was divided into twenty-five spans, twenty-four of which were of 242 feet each, while one was of 330 feet. The piers were built massively in masonry, the stone being obtained from quarries in convenient proximity. The ironwork was prepared in England, each piece being marked carefully for its position in the structure. The bridge had a gradual slope upwards from either bank to the centre, where the height from the bed of the river to the top of the tube was 108 feet. For its erection, 2,250,000 feet of timber were required in connection with the temporary work, the piers and abutments demanded the use of some 3,000,000 feet of masonry, and 2,500,000 rivets were used to secure the component parts of the ironwork together. In addition to the bridge proper, some 2,500 feet of approaches on either side had to be fashioned, so that the total length of the work was 9,144 feet. The contracted price for the structure was £1,400,000, or $7,000,000, but it was completed for £100,000 ($500,000) less. Of this total, the masonry and temporary work absorbed £800,000, or $4,000,000, and the ironwork £400,000 ($2,000,000).

While the work was in progress, the railway company found increasing traffic, as the sections of completed line were opened, so emphasised the urgency of securing through communication across the river that the contractors were approached, and a bonus of £60,000 ($300,000) was offered to them if they would complete the work a year earlier than was stipulated in the contract. The engineers redoubled their efforts, and on 17 December 1859, the great bridge was opened, though the official ceremony took place five months later, when King Edward VII, then Prince of Wales, opened the Victoria Bridge, as it was christened, in the name of Queen Victoria, during his visit to the dominion.

Stephenson died before his great work was completed. For a quarter of a century or more, it constituted one of the sights of the North American continent. As the country became more settled and the volume of traffic flowing to and fro across the river increased, the railway experienced a very great difficulty in handling it over a single line. At last the inadequacy reached such a point that some improvement was imperative. A second bridge would have been too costly, and after considerable reflection it was decided to replace the tubular bridge by one of larger dimensions.

A minute examination of the existing structure was made, and it speaks volumes for the work of Stephenson and Ross, as well as of the contractors, that the bridge appeared as sound and as fit for another century or more as it did on the day it was first opened. The piers had been built so solidly that they did not show the slightest trace of the terrible bufferings and pressure to which they had been subjected by the ice during some fifty winters.

Consequently, it was decided to remove the tubular structure and to erect in its place an open truss bridge, 66 feet 8 inches wide, carrying a double track, a roadway for an electric tramline, space for vehicular traffic, and a pavement for pedestrians. The engineers designing the new structure came to the conclusion that the striking stability and condition of the masonry piers would carry the new bridge with but slight alteration. As a result of this conclusion, it was decided to erect the new structure around the old bridge, cutting away the latter span by span, so that there was no interruption to the train service.

This appeared to be a simple expedient, but when the engineers commenced operations on Stephenson's handiwork, they found that it was built of far tougher material than they had expected. The rivets defied withdrawal, so excellently had they been driven home, and one of the engineers showed me one of these securing pieces, which he had preserved as a memento of British handiwork of some seventy years ago. As a matter of fact, as he related, it was far easier to build the new structure than it was to destroy the old, and the cutting away of the old tubular bridge span by span was found to be an exceedingly laborious task.

However, it was achieved, and there was not the slightest interruption in the traffic, which testifies to the skill and care with which the engineers laid their plans. Nor was it attended by any untoward incident, though what might have proved a terrible accident was averted very narrowly during reconstruction, as was related to me by one of the engineers. It was Sunday morning, and they were rebuilding the central part of the bridge. Special men had been stationed at each approach to the bridge, and elaborate instructions had been drawn up for controlling the passage of trains by flag signalling. Sunday was selected for the most difficult portions of the work, as on that day the trains were few and far between.

On this Sunday morning the work had advanced so satisfactorily that the old tubular span had been removed, and there was a wide gap in the continuity of the ironwork carrying the metals, showing the murky river swinging along at a merry pace below. Everything was ready for completing the new span, when one of the engineers, happening to glance shoreward, observed a train entering the bridge and coming along at a brisk speed. Something had gone wrong; the flagman had misunderstood instructions or had given a wrong signal. The train was speeding to its doom, for there was the yawning gulf. But the engineer never lost his presence of mind. Realising the situation, he threw down his instruments, and ran along the track towards the advancing train waving his arms frantically and yelling like one bereft. The engine driver, unlike the majority of his ilk on an American railway, concluded that something must be amiss, and applied his brakes sharply, pulling up a short distance from the brink of the abyss. It was a narrow escape; had the engineer hesitated a minute, disaster swift and sudden would have overwhelmed that train.

When the new bridge, with its 22,000 tons of steel, was completed for traffic it was renamed, but as the reconstruction coincided with the jubilee of Queen Victoria's reign, the revision comprised merely the perpetuation of that auspicious event, and today the structure is known as the Victoria Jubilee Bridge. From first to last, the structure has cost £1,800,000 ($9,000,000), of which reconstruction absorbed about £400,000 ($2,000,000).

As the Grand Trunk increased in importance, subsidiary and tributary railways were absorbed. Nor was the original idea of a trunk line overlooked. This end was achieved by pushing towards Chicago, the busy centre of the middle states. Continuity of rail in this case, however, was interrupted by the St Clair River, the narrow strait which connects Lakes Huron and Ontario. In the early days, communication was maintained by means of ferry boats, which handled complete trains, but as the river is extremely erratic, with strong currents varying in velocity according to the direction of the wind, and is congested with shipping, the ferry service possessed many shortcomings. When the strait was obstructed with floating ice, the situation became far more serious.

Accordingly, in order to remove these disabilities, a bold solution was elaborated in the form of a tunnel beneath the waterway connecting Sarnia on the Canadian with Port Huron on the United States side of the St Clair River. It certainly was an audacious remedy for a perplexing problem. The river is 46 feet deep and is nearly ½ mile wide, so that the tunnel had to be planned at a great depth. However, no better alternative could be offered, for a bridge was quite out of the question, so in 1886 the St Clair Tunnel Company was formed as a subsidiary undertaking of the railway, to complete a subaqueous link of communication, with Mr Joseph Hobson as chief engineer.

As the topography of the land on either side is tolerably flat, the question of the approaches had to be settled, and a heavy grade at either end could not be avoided. Technical difficulties were encountered at the very start. A trial shaft was sunk on the Canadian side to a depth of 98 feet, while another shaft on the American side was carried down to 92 feet. The preliminary shafts were elliptical in shape, measuring 4 feet by 8 feet in diameters.

When the requisite depths were obtained, galleries were driven at right angles beneath the river. These efforts proving satisfactory, it was decided to build the complete tunnel from either bank from shafts, as in the case of the Blackwall tunnel. The shafts were each 23 feet in diameter, and they were so built that there was a circular ring, the lower face of which carried a knife-edge digging into the ground. The soil was excavated from beneath this knife-edge, and as the brick wall lining of the shaft was built upon the upper surface of the knife ring, it was considered that the superimposed weight would drive the knife downwards as the earth beneath was removed.

But these carefully laid schemes and anticipations went astray. Exasperating failures and mishaps occurred, and at last the engineer changed his plans; the shaft method was abandoned. Instead, he decided to drive the tunnel from either end through the approaches. For this purpose, the plant and machinery were removed inland from the shafts for a distance of 1,900 feet on the Canadian, and 1,800 feet on the American bank respectively. Two huge cuttings were driven downhill until the tunnel level was gained, when the burrow beneath the river was commenced. The tunnel itself consists of a circular iron tube or pipe of sufficient diameter to carry a single track. It is 19 feet 10 inches in diameter, is built up of cast-iron rings, and weighs complete 56,000,000 pounds, or about 25,450 tons. Boring was effected from either end by means of the hydraulic shield, and in less than three years the task was finished.

The length of tunnel beneath the water is 2,290 feet, while that under dry land represents another 3,748 feet, making a total length of 6,932 feet. To this must be added 5,580 feet of approaches, which brings the total extent of the work to nearly 12,000 feet, or 2½ miles. It cost £540,000, or $2,700,000, and has always ranked as a noteworthy achievement in this particular branch of engineering.

Owing to the steepness of the approaches on either side, special locomotives had to be built to handle the traffic through this artery. They were powerful creations of the railway engine designer, and when they appeared were the largest steam locomotives in the world. They could haul a train weighing 760 tons, though at times the pace was slow.

But traffic between the United States and Canada increased by leaps and bounds, owing to the provision of this tunnel, with the result that in a very few years the railway authorities found that the tube was quite overtaxed. A solemn conclave was held as to the best ways and means of meeting this development. The track could not be doubled, so the question was how to increase the existing hauling capacity of a single engine. Steam could not meet the question, so was ruled out of court. Then an engineer suggested electrification, and advanced a report to show how the weight of each train might be increased by nearly 25 per cent, with quicker working, and consequently would facilitate the passage of a greater number of trains in a given time.

This engineer, Mr Bion Arnold, was authorised to proceed with his scheme and to complete his plans for the electrification of the tunnel. He did so, and as a result a specification was drawn up requiring the haulage of a train weighing 1,000 tons over the 2¼ miles in 15 minutes, with a maximum speed of 25 miles and a minimum speed of 10 miles per hour respectively. When the plans were made known it was realised that the project comprised the most ambitious electrical undertaking that ever had been attempted up to that time in railway operations, especially as it was insisted that the electrical system should be of a type which constituted its first application to heavy steam railway working. This is what is known as the single phase alternating current system with overhead conductor.

The invitation for tenders was awaited with keen anticipation throughout the world, as it was conceded to offer a unique opportunity to the electrical engineer. Consequently, keen competition was evinced to secure the honour of carrying out such a remarkable undertaking. The contract was secured by the Westinghouse Electric & Manufacturing Company, and was carried to a successful conclusion at a cost of £100,000 ($500,000). The locomotives now used on this service are among the most powerful in the world. They weigh 135 tons, and develop about 2,000 horse-power, which enables them to haul a 1,000-ton train up the heavy approach grades at a minimum speed of 10 miles per hour. Moreover, since electricity was adopted, the tunnel has been kept free from the dense clouds of smoke and steam which originally converted the tube into a veritable inferno, and, what is far more important from the railway company's point of view, the electrical system is able to meet three times the volume of traffic that exists today, so that there is ample provision for the future. As it is, the 2¼ miles of line beneath the teeming St Clair River is the heaviest electrically worked section of railway in the world.

Another link with the United States, however, was incumbent to bring the manufacturing centres around Buffalo into closer communication with the dominion. Yet there was only one point where this link could be provided – across the gorge through which the Niagara River, after tumbling over the lofty cliff, seethes and boils on its way to Lake Ontario. A suspension bridge met the exigencies of highway traffic for some years, but here again improvement was demanded. Accordingly, a new bridge was planned, and this constitutes one of the most graceful structures spanning that fearful rift.

The old bridge fulfilled its services faithfully for forty years, and when demolished was found to be possessed of several years of life. The new bridge is a splendid work, and its close proximity to the Falls offers a striking comparison between the handiwork of Nature and that of the engineer. The bridge leaps across the gorge in a single span, and when one is speeding over the structure in the train, one is at an elevation of 226 feet above the raging waters below. The span is of no less than 550 feet, and the ends are secured to massive anchorages sunk into the face of the cliffs. It is wrought throughout of steel, and is approached from either side over a single truss span 115 feet long, giving a total length of 780 feet.

But the bridge serves a dual purpose. The upper level or deck, 30 feet in width, carries two tracks for the railway's need, but below this is another deck, 57 feet wide, which has a central carriageway flanked on either hand by a broad pavement, so that the bridge provides vehicular and pedestrian accommodation between the opposite banks. In order to provide this improved connection between the two nations, a sum of about £100,000 ($500,000) had to be expended. The improved facilities it offered so appealed to the public on both shores that they celebrated its opening in 1897 by a three days' carnival.

As time sped by, the Grand Trunk railway gradually but surely swallowed its competitors, until at last it was left in undisputed possession of the province of Ontario, from the railway point of view. Today, it has over 8,000 miles of intricate steel ribbon stretched between the Great Lakes and the Atlantic coast, while between Montreal and Chicago the fastest trains in the Dominion hurtle to and fro over a double track 840½ miles in length, which is the longest continuous stretch of double track under one management in the world, and upon which some exhilarating speeds are attained.

When the British capitalists committed themselves to an expenditure of over £9,000,000, or $45,000,000, for the construction of less than 500 miles of line through virgin territory, it is doubtful whether in their rosiest dreams they ever anticipated that it would grow into a huge organisation aggregating a third of the railway mileage of British North America within sixty years.

Development is still being maintained; new territories are being conquered. A new long and sinuous arm, 3,556 miles from end to end, is being stretched out from the Atlantic to the Pacific Ocean, to bring the eastern into direct touch with the western seaboard. The whole has grown from the insignificant little wooden road that was laid between La Prairie and St John's in the province of Quebec eighty years ago.

CHAPTER 5

The First Trans-Continental
Across the United States

There were difficulties from end to end: from high and steep mountains; from snows; from deserts where there was a scarcity of water, and from gorges and flats where there was an excess; difficulties from cold and heat; from a scarcity of timber and from obstructions of rock; difficulties in keeping a large force on a long line; from Indians; and from want of labour.

This was the terse story related to the United States Congress by Collis P. Huntington, one of the moving spirits of what, at that time, was a tremendous undertaking – the construction of the first railway across North America, whereby the Atlantic was linked with the Pacific by a bond of steel. But that concise statement concealed one of the most romantic stories in the history of railway engineering: of grim battles every hour either against the hostile forces of nature or of mankind.

It was in 1863 that the first sod was turned in the construction of the first line, which was destined to bring San Francisco within 120 hours' journey of New York, and which changed completely the whole stream of traffic flowing round one half of the northern hemisphere. But for some years before the spade was driven into the earth to signal the commencement of this enterprise, the idea had been contemplated and discussed in a more or less academic manner. It was such a vast scheme, the commercial possibilities of success appeared so slender that the most daring financiers of that day shrank from fathering it. Capitalists concluded that they might just as well pour their money down a well as to sink it in such a project as this.

The public, however, regarded the idea from a totally different standpoint. East wanted to shake hands with the west over the mighty mountains and vast plains. To pass from New York to San Francisco, or in the reverse direction, in those days was a perilous journey. One either had to make a protracted and dangerous voyage down one side of the American continent, round Cape Horn, and pass up the opposite coastline for some 10,000 miles; to brave the peril of traversing the fever-ridden Central American Isthmus; or to embark upon an overland journey of some 3,000 miles through country where long stretches of parched, waterless desert gave way to lofty, snow-capped mountains, with the Indians in open warfare.

When California seethed in the famous Gold Rush, and adventurers flocked to this magnetic hub from all parts of the world, the absence of a connecting link was experienced to an acute degree. The gold-fever-stricken pioneers had to gain their objective as best they could, and with the best means of locomotion they could afford. In a single year, 100,000 gold-seekers trailed across the continent.

The traffic produced by the discovery of gold set Collis P. Huntington thinking. Here was a heavy volume of traffic slipping through the fingers. Why should it not be handled by a railway? This was his argument, and as he was a dreamer of commercial conquest, though not in an idle manner, he decided to remedy the deficiency. Looking into the future, he saw that a line not only would meet the immediate demands born of the gold rush, but that it would develop into a great highway between Europe and the East, as well as the Antipodes. He discussed the idea with kindred spirits, Leland Stanford and Thomas C. Durant, and they became enthused with the project. But the question was how to obtain the money requisite for construction? To appeal to the public was useless, and no assistance could be anticipated from the financial world. So they approached the government, and their endeavours proved so successful that the country decided to subsidise the undertaking.

When the government's sympathy had been secured in a practical manner, the next step was to discover an engineer who could superintend the survey and conduct constructional operations. The country did not possess many Stephensons, and the work in contemplation was of such an unprecedented character that no ordinary engineer would prove equal to the task. Happily, however, there was in San Francisco a railway engineering genius whose ability was being wasted for lack of opportunity. This man was Theodore D. Judah. He was a born engineer, and his skill in railway engineering had achieved a peculiar distinction up and down the Pacific coast. This work was his sole hobby, and the greater the difficulties to be overcome, the more enthusiastically and determinedly he threw himself into the task. His efforts in this direction were so strenuous that he was regarded generally as a crank, and his great dreams of railway conquest provided a continual source of amusement. He was always diving into the mountains, reconnoitring the passes with a view to their suitability for carrying the steel highway, and openly admitting that his greatest ambition in life was to be given the chance to lift the metals over the gaunt sierras frowning upon the Pacific coast, and to drop them on to the plains rolling eastwards from the opposite slopes.

On one occasion, he resigned his position upon a new railway line that was being built around San Francisco, and, unaccompanied, forced his way through the rocky barrier, making a mental note of the configuration of the country as he proceeded in case of something turning up, laboured across Nevada's dreary wastes of alkali, skirted Salt Lake, and at last gained the Missouri. As a result of his frequent peregrinations among the mountains, his eye became trained expertly in spying out the suitability of the country for the iron road, and he became known under the sobriquet of 'The Railway Pathfinder'. It was a picturesque nickname, but it was one which described his personality to the full. That his wanderings were not in vain is proved by the fact that nearly every pass through the mountains which he stated to be adapted to carry a railway has been pressed into this service since, in order to gain the Pacific coast.

Indeed, the pioneer trans-continental railway owes its birth to Judah. For years he had advocated the project, and emphasised its practicability. When Huntington and his colleagues were ready to commence operations, they sent for Judah, convinced that he was the very man for whom they were searching, to plot the path for the line and to take command of the forces in the field. The Railway Pathfinder, realising that the ambition of his life was within reach at last, hurried eastwards. There was a short consultation which sufficed to prove to the promoters that Judah was the man to carry the enterprise to success, and there and then he was placed in supreme control of the construction. The difficulties among the mountains were what the promoters feared the most, but the pathfinder regarded them so lightly that their apprehensions vanished. He had spent so many months among their silent fastnesses that he knew the range through and through. His plans were daring and feasible, his reasoning lucid, and his enthusiasm infectious. In order that the directing hand in the field might not be trammelled or harassed by business or administration details, a special emissary was deputed to attend to these secondary but vital essentials, so that Judah might be able to concentrate his energies and ability entirely to plotting and pushing the line forwards.

According to the arrangement with the government, the railway was to commence from the eastern bank of the Missouri River at Council Bluffs. The selection of the eastern bank as the starting point involved the erection of a huge bridge as the first step in the undertaking. Such an idea appears somewhat curious at first sight, as one would have thought, naturally, that the western bank would have been selected as the obvious eastern terminal. But the government recognised one point. The railways were spreading their tentacles slowly but surely from the Atlantic coast towards the Missouri River. When they gained its banks, a break in the through rail communication would develop, as the eastern railways were in their infancy, and far too poor to undertake the construction of an expensive bridge across this wide waterway to link up with the line stretching to San Francisco.

Construction was commenced from both ends of the line. San Francisco was the Pacific terminal, but as the Golden Gate was connected already with Sacramento, the capital some miles inland, the latter place was the point to which the constructional forces were dispatched. The arm driven eastwards from the Pacific was known as the Union Pacific railway, while that forced westwards from Council Bluffs was designated as the Central Pacific. The two arms were to meet about half-way across the continent.

Judah hurried to California and was soon in the turmoil of his task. The great difficulty on this section was in regard to the supply of the constructional material. Everything had to be sent round by water via the most southerly point of the continent, and as this was a voyage occupying several weeks, extreme care had to be observed to send forward supplies in a steady, constant stream, so that no delays might arise from lack of material. But storms raged, while the negotiation of Cape Horn is a difficult feat at the best of times. The boats were caught in the terrible embrace of wind and wave, and, upon emerging from the conflict, struggled, battered and torn, into the nearest port for repairs. Despite these heavy drawbacks, which no human foresight could determine or avoid, practically no dearth of supplies ever was experienced at the railhead among the mountains. In fact, Judah prosecuted his task so vigorously that before many months had passed the first railway conquest of the sierras, considered invulnerable for so long, was announced far and wide.

How was it accomplished? The pathfinder followed the easiest path open to him. Distances between points might have been shortened, but time was money. The builders had urged this emphatically upon Judah, so that opportunity to indulge in stupendous engineering feats was denied him. Yet the very conditions which were imposed enabled the pathfinder to display some masterstrokes of genius unconsciously. So long as a natural path for the metals was available, he followed it. If his advance were disputed by an obstacle, he either removed or ran round it. The hump was levelled and the depression was filled. The rivers were followed so far as practicable along their puzzling meanderings. He lifted the track several thousand feet towards the clouds to gain the railway summit of the range, and then dropped over the other side. In one place among the snow-clad peaks he had to hew a narrow shelf out of the solid rocky mass to wind round the huge shoulder of a mountain. The wall of rock sheered up on one side to a dizzy height; on the other way, it dropped for over a thousand feet into the river surging below.

The San Francisco division teemed with complex and highly troublesome perplexities, but one and all arose from the resistance of Nature. Yet they were slight in comparison with those which the engineers experienced as they pushed forwards from the Missouri River. Here it was the hostility of man which harassed them. The Indians, driven from the eastern states by the march of civilisation, resisted its further approach into their domain. Fierce opposition was anticipated, but the results proved far more serious than the most gloomy forebodings. At every turn, the savages swept down upon the little band toiling in the solitude of the wilderness, and these organised onslaughts became fiercer and fiercer as the base of operations was left farther and farther to the rear. For every spike that was driven, clinching a rail to its wooden cushion beneath, an arrow sped from an Indian bow, to be answered by the sharp crack of a rifle from the railway building forces. History does not record how many navvies fell victims to the noiseless weapon of the savages, or how many Indians entered the Happy Hunting Ground by way of a bullet. Yet the total of lives would outnumber the spikes driven to secure the metals for the 1,800 miles between the Missouri River and the Golden Horn. A conclave with the Red Men was urgent before the engineers stirred from the bank of the Missouri. Council Bluffs is a famous spot in the history of the New World, because here the Indians were wont for centuries to meet to settle tribal disputes. It was here that Collis P. Huntington and his colleagues met the Red Men to discuss the terms and treaty for the acquisition of the necessary land to found the city of Omaha.

At that day, the nearest point to which the railway had advanced towards the river from the east was Des Moines. The first locomotive required for constructional purposes upon the Central Pacific, and which weighed some 60 tons, had to be hauled across country on the deck of a trolley by teams of horses. When the trans-continental railway was taken in hand, however, the eastern railways were pushed forward with great speed to reach Council Bluffs, in order to carry the thousands of tons of supplies of every description requisite for building purposes.

The scarcity of one commodity was felt severely. In this country one may travel for miles and not see a single tree. This hit the railway hard. Every baulk of timber, whether it was required for a fire, a shack, or a sleeper, had to be brought over enormous distances. By the time a sleeper was laid, it often cost as much as $2.50, or 10 shillings!

The route between east and west is popularly known as the 'Overland Route'. How it received this name is a little story in itself. Among those who arrived at San Francisco in the glorious days of '47 to make money out of the gold rush was a Dutchman, whose topsy-turvy English was characteristic of a foreigner possessing only an imperfect acquaintance with our tongue. He opened a saloon, which became a most popular resort. Whenever a stranger entered the rendezvous, Boniface's curiosity was aroused. The new arrival was asked inevitably by which of the three routes he had gained the Golden Gate. 'Did you come the Horn around, the Isthmus across, or the land over?' the Dutchman inquired. 'The land-over' signifying the wagon-trail across the states, so appealed to the fancy of the railway builders that they always referred to the trans-continental as 'the land-over route', which in course of time became twisted into the more correct designation under which it is known to this day.

The level character of the country west of the Missouri River lent itself favourably to rapid construction, as well as easy alignment. At one place it was found possible to lay the track as straight as an arrow for 41 miles. The grade grew quickly, and the rails advanced in a continuous black-grey line across the prairie with striking rapidity, when the Indians refrained from endeavouring to arrest its progress. However, the raids of the Red Men became so devastating eventually that it appeared as if work must be brought to a standstill.

At the critical moment another man appeared on the scene, and his efforts contributed very materially to the completion of the line. This was Major Frank J. North, one of the most daring frontiersmen that those troublous times with the Indians produced in America. He was Fenimore Cooper's mythical 'Pathfinder' in the flesh, and he came to be just as greatly feared by the Red Men. When the railway engineers failed to make headway against the Indians, he offered his services, which, needless to say, were accepted gladly. From that moment the protection of the grade became his one object in life, and his capture became the one absorbing ambition of the Indians. He had roamed the plains for years, leading a rough-and-ready frontier life, had become familiarised with the Indians, their habits, customs and ways; could anticipate their every movement and knew how to counteract their subterfuges. He was versed thoroughly in their ways of warfare, was a born fighter, and was possessed of indomitable energy and pluck.

In order to protect the railway builders, he raised four companies of friendly Pawnee Indians. With these trusty scouts he would creep out stealthily at night from the constructional camp, make his way with impunity to the tepees of the Cheyennes or Sioux, and ascertain their projected operations. Sometimes he would surprise an Indian camp, and scatter the inmates who were on the warpath to the four winds. His marauding expeditions became so audacious that the natives were compelled to withdraw a respectable distance from the grade. He became so universally detested among the foe that the mention of North's name was sufficient to provoke the most dismal howls of execration and vicious snarls of vengeance.

At times he was absent so many days from the railhead camp that the engineers wondered gravely whether or not he had met an untimely end. Then when they were on the point of giving up hope of seeing him again, he would trot unconcernedly into camp, with his Pawnee shadows, as if returning from a hunt, but his general appearance and self-satisfied air told the navvies that he 'had been at the Indians again'. He provoked the hostile Red Men to such an extreme pitch that they turned out in tremendous force sworn to his capture or death. Four times a pitched battle was fought, with tremendous losses; four times the Indians drew off, leaving North flushed with victory. At last the enemy became so disheartened that it withdrew, retreated for miles from the line, and there was a sullen interval in the conflict.

North, however, was not to be lulled into a false sense of security. He divined that some ulterior move was projected. So it proved. The Indians, instead of concentrating their energies upon the destruction of the forces at the railhead, decided to attack the long line of communication at various points, to surprise and destroy the supply trains. A guerilla war broke out, and this baffled North, for he could not bring them to a pitched battle.

The Indians clung like limpets to the grade, and woe betide any stragglers who fell into their hands, for they were cruelly tortured and put to death. Time after time, as the supply train was puffing along slowly, the plain on either side suddenly would reveal hordes of ferocious savages, who had crept through the tall grass unobserved to within a few feet of the track. The men on the train secured any shelter possible behind the transported goods, and blazed away furiously. Brisk skirmishes and opportunities to display marksmanship occurred nearly every day to relieve the tedium of swinging hammer, pickaxe and shovel. Major North happened to be attacked in this way one day, though the enemy were unaware of his presence. But they were so dismayed at the spirited reception that they received that they broke and fled, with North in pursuit. He chased them for hours, and inflicted such losses that the tribe surrendered. A few days later, a large number of the vanquished enlisted under the railway builder's banner, assisted in the building of the grade, and became law-abiding citizens.

There was one point which was a tempting prize to the Cheyennes. This was a depot 372 miles west of Omaha. Its safety was entrusted to North's friendly Indians, and they proved too watchful to enable a raid to be made with success. The Cheyennes were determined to secure its capture, and, quietly gathering reinforcements, one day made a supreme attempt to rush it with a thousand men. It was a desperate battle that ensued, but the defenders, being entrenched, secured the advantage, and after fighting desperately for several hours were left in possession of the hundreds of tons of supplies.

These tactics had to be pursued for some 500 miles, but the engineers in time became wearied at the daily round of working and fighting. Besides, they were approaching the Rocky Mountains, where the physical difficulties would be so great as to command their entire concentration in order to lift the metals over an obstacle 8,000 feet above the sea. It was realised, also, that the broken slopes would, give the Indians every advantage to prosecute their guerrilla warfare to distinct advantage. The outlook was so depressing that a halt was called. The situation was urged upon the government, and, as a result, General Grant decided to interview the Indians in person, with a view to placating them. He made a hazardous and exciting journey along the railway to the heart of the enemy's country. There, with pow-wow and peace-pipe, an honourable treaty was drawn up; the Indians promised to abandon their opposition, and to permit the railway to go forward.

Another difficulty the builders had to battle against was the scarcity of labour. The Californian Gold Fields were too magnetising to cause the men to stay long on the grade. They preferred to woo the fickle goddess of fortune in a scramble for the yellow metal, to a steady, daily round of toil at a regular wage. As a last resource, the sheet-anchor of the railway builder had to be called in – the Chinaman. The Orientals stuck to the work, and under their efforts the line progressed with greater speed than had been possible before their advent. At one time, the rails were laid so speedily that the teams could not bring up supplies fast enough to meet the needs of the graders and track-layers.

The permanent way was crude. It was a pioneer line in very truth. The earth was thrown up roughly, the sleepers were dumped on its crown, and the rails were hastily spiked to their bed. The line was little better than what one sees hastily improvised for the transportation of spoil on large engineering works. It writhed and twisted among obstructions in a fantastic manner, for the engineers, having neither funds nor time at their disposal, merely ran round or over humps, whichever method was the quicker. Speed and comfort were negligible considerations. The line, once communication with the coast was established, could be overhauled and strengthened later at leisure. Consequently, travelling was rough, the oscillation was severe, and the danger of derailment always existent. It was these conditions that prompted a phlegmatic Englishman, who essayed the journey shortly after the line was opened, to remark that 'the train travelled more smoothly when it was off the rails!'

Some idea of the speed with which work was prosecuted, the innumerable drawbacks notwithstanding, may be gathered from the fact that the whole 1,800 miles of line was built and opened to traffic within six years from the turning of the first spadeful of earth at Sacramento. For the greater part of this distance, the monthly average was 50 miles – truly a magnificent feat. In order to maintain this high pressure, 25,000 men and 5,000 cattle teams were required, and the total cost of the work was $115,000,000, or, roughly, £23,000,000.

The dawn of the year 1869 saw the two advancing arms racing towards the Great Salt Lake. The Central Pacific, upon encountering this inland sea, debouched to the north and plunged into the broken Promontory Range. Here, at an altitude of 5,000 feet, the two arms met, and, amid the wild huzzas of over a thousand people, the last gap was closed, and golden spikes were driven into a sleeper of polished laurel by Leland Stanford and Thomas Durant, the presidents of the respective divisions, to admit the passage of a train, waiting close by with steam up, to pass from the Central to the Union Pacific railway. The precise point at which the opposing armies met is indicated by a board standing beside the track, the inscription on which runs:

Last Spike,
Completing First Trans-Continental Railroad Driven at this Point,
10 May 1869.

The occasion was one of great rejoicing, especially among the citizens of San Francisco. The town went mad with excitement. The festivities commenced two days before the golden spike was driven, and was continued for two days afterwards. Literature contributed its quota to the commemoration of the historic event in the form of a poem from Bret Harte.

In crossing the prairie stretches, the railway constructional forces were indebted appreciably for their support to the buffalo, which roamed the plains in tens of thousands. The slaughter of this animal was tremendous to provide fresh meat for the camps, and hides for the clothing of the workmen against the blasts and severe cold of winter. Their existence was providential, especially when the Indians succeeded in capturing and destroying the supply trains bringing up provisions. Water often was a serious problem. For stretches of over a hundred miles at a time not a drop could be obtained from the parched land, and specially built cars had to be pressed into service to transport this indispensable commodity.

Some idea of the solitude of the country may be gathered from the fact that during a continuous 600 miles not a single white man or homestead was seen. Before the line was completed, a pony express plied between Sacramento and Salt Lake City and the journey under normal conditions occupied three and a half days. Today, the distance is covered in about one third of the time.

In the course of a few years, the traffic on the Overland Route assumed such proportions as to be beyond the capacity of the ill-laid track. The grades were too heavy and the curves too sharp, while rails and bridges were too light. Extensive reconstruction was taken in hand. Banks were abolished, curves were straightened, bridges were rebuilt, the permanent way was re-ballasted, short sections were cut out here, or introduced there, to reduce the mileage – in short, the whole line was rebuilt practically at an expenditure of millions to bring the great highway up to the model of present-day practice.

One of the most important of these improvement works was that known as the Lucin Cut-off. This was a daring piece of engineering forced upon the railway by rival lines, which, possessing easier grades and a better alignment, could haul heavier loads at a speed beyond the capacity of the pioneer road. This adverse factor was experienced very severely around the north end of Salt Lake, where the line plunges into the rugged and broken Promontory Range, to overcome which such heavy grades had to be introduced as to reduce the speed of trains to a crawl of 12 miles per hour.

At first it appeared impracticable to ease this situation, but the chief engineer was called in and urged to find a means of extricating the company from the predicament. After several months' survey around this sheet of water, he prepared plans which he submitted to his directors. They were extremely audacious. He suggested the abandonment of 373 miles of the old line completely, as it was beyond improvement. In its place he proposed 326 miles of new track, which not only showed a saving of 57 miles in distance, but gave no ruling grade exceeding 21.12 feet per mile. At one point he was baulked by the configuration of the country in the Pequop range, where a grade of 74 feet to the mile was found unavoidable. Moreover, he showed a saving of over ½ mile in vertical height, the climb on the westward run being cut down from 4,550 feet to 1535 feet, and on the eastward journey from 4,456½ feet to 1,444 feet.

The salient feature of the scheme, however, challenged particular attention. Instead of running around Salt Lake he advocated a route across it, giving a line as direct as the bird flies from shore to shore, supported on earthen embankments where such could be erected, and in other places upon a timber viaduct. Some idea of what this scheme represented may be gathered from the construction of a bridge from Dover to Calais – a project that has been promulgated – for the distance was about the same.

The engineer was prompted in his belief as to the practicability of the suggestion from his personal investigations. Popular fancy had clothed this stretch of salt water in many legends, one of which was that its depths were unfathomable. This fallacy was scattered to the winds when soundings were taken, for the water was found to be comparatively shallow at the point it was contemplated to cross the lake. Collis P. Huntington hesitated from embarking upon the scheme when it was first unfolded, partly on account of its estimated cost, but more because of its unusual character.

However, when E. H. Harriman secured the control of the line, he entertained no qualms. His engineer said it was feasible, so it must be done to avoid that laborious haul over the hills to the north. Work commenced forthwith, and was pursued with great vigour. When the bank of the lake was gained, the engineer pushed the earthen embankment as far into the water as he could, so as to reduce the extent of the trestling. The distance from shore to shore was 27 miles, but as he took advantage of a peninsula which juts well into the water from the north bank, four miles of the line were built on dry land.

To commence the embankment from the water's edge, an ingenious expedient was adopted. Heavy planks loaded with weighty bags of sand were floated out on the proposed location, and upon this novel permanent way the temporary rails for the ballast cars were laid, and the spoil dumped into the lake until the embankment appeared above water level. Then the section of floating track was pushed still farther ahead, and the same cycle of operations repeated until the limit of the earthwork was gained. As the embankment grew in height, the light rails were replaced by a heavier type, over which rumbled cars carrying 40 tons of ballast a-piece, and which was pitched pell-mell into the water on either side. The embankment was then left for a while to permit settling to take place. In time it became as solid as a jetty.

The trestle section proved the most trying, not so much on account of the technical questions involved, but owing to the difficulty in obtaining timber. The wood had to be brought hundreds of miles from the forests of Texas and the north-west. Extensive stretches of trees were purchased and saw-mills were erected to cut the logs to the desired dimensions on the spot. Upon arrival at Salt Lake the wood was dumped into the water, large log booms being formed, so that the material might become seasoned thoroughly.

Work was delayed considerably by the lack of supplies of timber, from storms which swept this inland sea, and which at times wrought considerable damage. At one or two places, although careful soundings were taken, the lake bed proved fickle. When the pile-drivers were set to work, banging the massive uprights into the solid earth, progress would be painfully slow for a time, and then suddenly the pile would descend with uncanny rapidity. The cause was discovered readily. The lake bed is covered with a thick crust of salt and soda deposits, the accumulation of centuries, packed so hard as to give the semblance of being solid rock when sounded. Yet it was only a shell or crust covering unstable soil below. Driving the piles broke up this rind, and then a solid foundation could not be found.

Attempts to remedy this state of affairs were made by pitching rock into the water to provide a solid floor to support the timber uprights. This method proved so slow and expensive that the engineer devised another solution of the difficulty. He ran out a light trestle and dumped rubble overboard around its foundations until the woodwork was buried completely, and a solid earthen embankment was produced to carry the rails.

The actual extent of timber trestling aggregates 12 miles, and this erection spans the lake practically at its narrowest central part. Some of the pile drivers were carried on floating pontoons, while others were mounted on the track above, the permanent way being pushed forward as rapidly as the timber work was completed. Owing to the depth of the water, some of the upright members are as much as no feet in length. They are disposed in rows of five at right angles to the track, and connected by massive longitudinal members, on which is laid 3-inch planking, superimposed with a layer of ballast. It was while building the timber work that the greatest depth of water was reached – from 30 to 34 feet.

The trestle was erected with striking rapidity, the record being the completion of no less than 5,317 feet of track in six working days. Had it been possible to bring the timber up more quickly, a greater length of line could have been laid in the time. At rail level, the viaduct is 16 feet in width, and the track is so smooth and solid that the 'Overland Limited' can hurtle along at full speed without producing the slightest vibration.

By the time the viaduct was completed, 38,256 piles had been used. This represented no less than 2,824,700 lineal feet of timber which had been torn from the forests. If these logs had been placed end to end they would have formed a continuous line for nearly 535 miles.

So straight did the engineer plot and build the Lucin Cut-off, that even if he had complied with Euclid's definition of a straight line, it would have been necessary only to have deducted 1,708 feet from the 102.91 miles of track which he laid. In addition, he abolished 3,919 degrees of curves. To understand what this means, it is only necessary to remember that each degree represents a segment of the circle. By dividing the above total by 360, the number of degrees to the circle, a result of 11.88 circles is obtained. In other words, on the old route between Lucin and Ogden, the train not only traversed the distance between the two points, but described nearly 12 circles as well. For 36 miles the track is dead level and for another 30 miles the rise is so slight that one has to walk ½ mile to rise his own height. By the time the task was completed a round £1,000,000, or $5,000,000, had been expended. It appears a huge outlay to reduce working expenses and to increase revenue, but it affords a striking illustration of the boldness of guiding railway spirits in America.

CHAPTER 6

The Longest 'Toy' Railway

The Principality is a land of many surprises to the visitor, for it possesses innumerable attractions. Yet it is doubtful whether any feature arouses more interest in North Wales than the strange little railway which runs from Portmadoc for a distance of 13¼ miles among the mountains. Certain it is that no tourist would think of omitting a journey over what is known colloquially as the Festiniog 'Toy' Railway, for it is one of the great sights of North Wales.

For several years it held a unique position among the great systems of the world as the narrowest gauge line in operation. The metals are laid only 23¼ inches apart – less than half the distance between the rails forming the roads of the greater proportion of steel highways bounding the globe – and yet it has a traffic which many a more important railway would have just cause to envy. Visitors disembarking from the London and North-Western express at Portmadoc, and seeing the diminutive engine and trucks drawn up alongside on their own road and completely dwarfed by the towering rolling stock of the standard-gauge line, cannot repress a smile, for the engines, cars, trucks and wagons are no larger than are used upon the larger-sized model railways devised today for the amusement and education of the young.

Yet it is a complete pocket edition of the familiar railway, and its capacity is amazing. The engine provokes interest, for it is no taller than an average-sized person. Its coupled wheels are only 28 inches in diameter, while the cylinders measure but 8¼ inches in diameter and have a stroke of only 13 inches. The cars and wagons are on the same scale, and the first impression of the diminutive iron horse awakens doubts as to whether it is safe to trust oneself to its care. But see that self-same engine busy at work hauling a train of seven passenger coaches, a guard's van, ten goods wagons and 100 or more empty slate trucks, stretching out for a length of 1,200 feet and representing a total load of no tons, out of Portmadoc, bound for the quarries, and disdain gives way to complete admiration.

The locomotive 'Little Wonder', despite its age, for it dates back from 1869, completely justifies its appellation, for it handles the above load on the steepest grades with ease, and attains a speed of 30 miles an hour where the physical conditions are suited to fast travelling. The work it has to fulfil is not to be despised by any means, for the country through which the line extends is amongst the most rugged in the country. In the course of the 13¼ miles it has to overcome a difference of 700 feet in altitude, which means a pull against the collar for the whole way from Portmadoc, though the gradients are of varying severity. Yet even the easiest climb is 1 in 186, while the steepest rise is 1 in 68.6, with a bank of no less than 1 in 36 on one of the spur lines. The curves likewise are startling in their sharpness and frequency, and at times when the engine is loaded to its utmost capacity, the train may be seen writhing like a gigantic black snake along three curves at the same time.

The permanent way was originally laid in 1839, the enterprise having been carried out for the conveyance of slate from the quarries to Portmadoc. On the downward journey the laden trucks travelled by gravity, the empties being hauled back by horses. In the late fifties, however, the chief engineer, Mr. C. E. Spooner, realising the far-reaching advantages arising from the use of power, suggested that the tramway should be converted into a railway, and in 1863 his suggestion was adopted. In the early days travelling was exciting, for the bridges and tunnels were so low that the engine driver, stoker and other officials on the line had to duck their heads when they reached these obstacles, since to stand upright in one of the vehicles was certain to court a violent end by collision with these structures. These, however, have been altered so that one need entertain no more apprehension concerning safety on this line than when travelling upon a standard-gauge road. Visitors, realising the fact that by its means they could be conveyed comfortably to some of the wildest and most beautiful corners of the Principality, sought its transportation assistance, and in 1864, passengers were first carried as an experiment, but free of charge. The Board of Trade did not decline to sanction its operation in the interests of the public, but possibly somewhat dubious of the wisdom of their action, hedged in the privilege with certain restrictions, the most important of which was limitation of speed. When, however, it was proved that there was no danger in travelling over this two-foot line at 30 miles an hour, this latter ban was removed.

The line possesses several features of technical interest, and, being a single track, is operated upon the staff system, with every device to secure absolute safety in operation in the form of signalling and telegraphing facilities. Moreover, travelling is comfortable, for although the gauge is less than two feet, the cars, designed by the engineer, are built on the bogie principle and have seating accommodation for fifty passengers. A trip over the line certainly constitutes an experience.

The complete success which attended the conversion of this railway from equine to steam power in 1864 stimulated the wider adoption of the narrow-gauge system, though as a rule this term is somewhat elastic, inasmuch as it signifies that such a railway has a gauge less than the standard width of 4 feet 8½ inches, and is particularly associated with the 39-inch or 42-inch gauge. Still several 'two-foot' lines were laid down, especially in France and India, so that the Festiniog experiment has proved a very profitable 'toy' to more countries than one. In fact, not far distant from the pioneer toy railway is another – the North Wales Narrow Gauge railway – which connects Dinas, near Carnarvon, with Snowdon Station.

These railway systems, however, are of short length, and when one remembers the broken character of the country which they serve, their *raison d'être* is obvious. But the application of the idea to a trunk line 360 miles in length appears quite impracticable. Yet it has been accomplished, and its realisation has opened up a corner of Africa which formerly was almost impassable, and which, but for its fulfilment, would have left the country traversed in the hands of hostile natives.

This 'toy' railway upon a large scale is the Otavi Line, which connects Tsumeb, buried 368 miles in the heart of the wilderness of German South-West Africa, with the coast at Swakopmund. Today it ranks as the longest narrowest gauge line in the world, the metals, as in the case of the Festiniog railway, being laid only 600 millimetres, or approximately 2 feet apart.

In the late eighties, prospecting parties who had heard of the mineral wealth lying dormant in this inhospitable and inaccessible country, set out to ascertain whether rumour could be verified to a sufficient extent to ensure the riches of the rocks being exploited commercially. They suffered great privations and hardships in their toil across the waterless veldt, but when they gained the Otavi country, they found that their journey was more than repaid by enormous discoveries of copper. They collected detailed information concerning the extent of these deposits, and when they returned to Europe it was decided to develop the new 'Copperado' without further delay.

However, there was one critical point. How could the mineral, after being mined, be transported to the coast for shipment? The intervening country was among the most sterile to be found in the continent south of the Sahara. The mining companies concerned at once suggested a railway as the only solution of the problem. But they realised very readily, from the reports of their emissaries who had ventured to Otavi, that such an undertaking was beset with difficulties innumerable, while the construction of a line upon the standard gauge would prove ruinously expensive. In order to secure extrication from their plight, the companies approached the firm of Arthur Koppel of Berlin. The latter company dispatched a corps of its own surveyors to the country to spy out the desert between the coast and the mines, in order to find the best location and to report generally upon the engineering features of the scheme.

When the surveyors returned to civilisation they unhesitatingly recommended a light narrow-gauge railway, such as they had built in several parts of the world where similar conditions prevailed. They advocated the 600-millimetre or 2-foot gauge because it not only would meet all traffic requirements for many years to come, but its initial cost would be so much cheaper, and it could be built so much more quickly than a wider or standard gauge. The recommendation was debated at great length, and after discussing the relative estimated capital and operating costs of lines of different gauges, the overwhelming advantages presented by the 'toy-line' gauge were found to outweigh any arguments that could be raised against it. The mining companies merely demanded the line as a link between the copper country and the coast for their own purposes. The country lying between the coast and the mines held out no attractions for any economic development, so that all the requisitions likely to be made by the mining companies could be met adequately by such a railway. Consequently the recommendation of the engineers was accepted, and they were entrusted with the completion of the undertaking.

When the mining companies expressed their decision they did not anticipate the extraordinary traffic which the railway would be called upon to fulfil a little later. These were duties which not only taxed the capacity of the diminutive railway to a supreme degree, but were of a character which justified the confidence of the engineers and practically saved the colony to the German Empire.

This reproduction of the Festiniog toy railway was commenced without loss of time. In 1903, constructional engineers with a boatload of constructional material were dispatched to South Africa, and the grade was commenced from Swakopmund, at a point 40 feet above the sea level, the location extending in a north-easterly direction to Otavi, 300 miles distant in the interior.

The first sod was turned in October, and the constructional engineers bent to their task with great zest. But scarcely had they got into their stride when the Hereros rebellion broke out. This was an unexpected development, and as the natives had been recruited in large numbers to build the permanent way, the engineers were faced with a grave situation. At the first signs of the insurrection, the greater majority of the natives threw down their tools and stampeded from the line to their towns and villages to take up arms. The governor of the colony strove to arrest this wholesale desertion by recourse to drastic measures – he seized as many men working on the grade as he could and placed them safely under lock and key. The result was that the little band of white engineers was left with scarcely a navvy to assist them.

However, they struggled on as best they could, but progress was painfully slow. At first the insurrection was belittled – regarded as a flash in the pan – and the engineers anticipated confidently the early return of their workmen. But these illusions were dispelled rudely when it became realised at last that the country was up in arms from end to end. There was only one way out of the desperate situation, and that was to import labour from Europe. Such a step upset the preliminary estimates for the undertaking to a pronounced degree, for the native labour had been taken into the calculation when framing the cost of the work. To bring white labour from Europe increased the capital outlay very appreciably. However, there was no alternative, and accordingly an Italian contractor arrived on the scene with a small army of 300 Italians, and work resumed its former busy aspect.

However, peace did not reign for long. The Italian workmen saw that they held the advantage over the engineers, that there was no competitive labour, and accordingly they struck for higher pay. The engineers, caught on the horns of a dilemma, had to surrender, and the Italians picked up their tools. Then another cause of dissatisfaction manifested itself. The workmen concluded that they were being driven too hard, so they declined to perform a full day's labour. They held the whip-hand and emphasised its potency so frequently, and the friction between employers and employed became so keen, that it appeared more than once as if the contract would have to be suspended until the rebellion was quelled.

While these disputes and continual bickerings were at their height, further complication was provoked. The German military authorities, finding the subjugation of the Hereros a far heavier task than they had anticipated, wished to penetrate into the heart of the country so as to strike a supreme blow upon the enemy's stronghold. They had their own line extending from Swakopmund to Windhuk, but owing to its heavy grades and light construction it had broken down completely under the strain of the heavy military traffic. The authorities strove to alleviate this situation by utilising bullock-carts to transport troops and commissariat up-country, but this alternative failed lamentably. This service was so slow, and the absence of water by the wayside was felt to a serious degree. In their extremity the German government appealed to the engineers of the Otavi line. They besought them to spare no effort to drive the railway forward speedily, first to Ouguati, 109¾ miles from the coast, and then to Omaruru, 145 miles beyond the former point. As an inducement, the builders were offered a heavy premium.

The engineers agreed to meet official demands, and to expedite the constructional work, a further army of 750 Italians and 500 Ovambo coolies was sent to reinforce the forces on the grade. To tempt the Italian workmen to strive their utmost, they offered a fixed minimum wage as an incentive. However, it was not long before trouble arose once more. The new arrivals fraternised with their compatriots already on the scene, and learned how the engineers had been forced to pay higher and higher wages by recourse to strikes. The Italians came to the conclusion that concerted action would be highly successful because several weeks would elapse before their places could be taken by other imported labour, while they regarded the Ovambo coolies, who proved industrious workmen, with supreme contempt. Every conceivable obstacle was thrown in the way of the engineers. Work was stopped upon the slightest provocation, and apparent grievances were aired with monotonous frequency.

When at last they were placated and the workmen did settle down to their tasks, they proceeded in a lackadaisical manner, and the day's work was only a quarter of what might have been accomplished. Under ordinary circumstances each Italian could have coped with 10 cubic yards of earthwork per day, but they handled only about 2¾ cubic yards! This rendered them distinctly inferior to the Ovambos, who, though not comparable with the Europeans from the physical point of view, plodded along steadily, and handled on the average from 3½ to 4 cubic yards per day. The Italians had no complaint concerning their scale of payment, for they received from 5s to 10s – $1.25 to $2.00 – per day, while the coolies, who did twice the work, received but 2s 6d or 60 cents a day, together with food and housing accommodation.

One day, matters reached a climax. The white workmen struck in a body, and declined to move a hand unless they received another increase in wages. The engineers, who had been groaning under the extortionate demands of the blackmailing Italians for several weeks past, now took a firm stand. They declined point-blank to entertain the proposal. Moreover, they commenced to take the law into their own hands and to adopt stern measures. Several of the leading recalcitrants were straightway dismissed for breach of contract. This situation lasted for eight weeks, and at times the outlook became extremely threatening, for the Italians chafed under the unexpected opposition they had encountered. Suddenly the dispute collapsed and the Italians sullenly returned to their work.

Coupled with this distressing condition of affairs at the railhead, the engineers experienced grave difficulties at Swakopmund. They could not get the constructional and other material unloaded from their ships. This harbour is notoriously a bad one, and being congested with military traffic, method and order had given way to complete chaos. Weeks elapsed before an incoming ship could discharge its cargo for the railway, and then the engineers only secured their requirements by building a special mole because the anchorage was silting up with sand.

In the spring of 1905, matters took a more hopeful turn. The sullen Italians were spurred on by the granting of premiums, and under this inducement more rapid progress was effected. The white workmen were forced to their tasks by the appearance of severe competition. Many of the Hereros grew tired of fighting and surrendered to the authorities. When asked if they would be content to work upon the railway they accepted the offer with alacrity, and the Italians saw that they were in serious danger of being displaced entirely. The fair treatment that was meted out to the natives who had surrendered became noised far and wide through the country, with the result that large numbers of Hereros, who had grasped the hopelessness of their opposition, made their way to the railhead and threw down their arms and offered to take up the pick and shovel. It was a curious sight, for here were large numbers of the natives, against whom war was being waged, voluntarily assisting in the advance of the very force that was being driven forward to bring about the complete subjugation of their race. Curious to relate, moreover, the engineers found that their former implacable foes, when properly treated, developed into splendid conscientious workmen, and far easier to control than the much-vaunted white labour.

After leaving the coast, the railway makes practically a continuous and steady climb to a maximum height of some 5,218 feet in the course of its 360 miles. Notwithstanding this extreme difference in altitude, it was found possible to keep the banks easy, the sharpest gradient being 1 in 50. The country traversed is most inhospitable, the first 145 miles being through a wild desert, and wide stretches of scrub-covered country broken with kopjes.

Extensive bridging was found necessary to carry the track across gullies and rivulets, there being in all 110 of these structures. They are built throughout of steel, the deck-plate girder type being the most generally favoured, and the most important work of this class has a length of 333 feet, built up in five spans. The curves were kept as easy as possible, the standard radius being about 500 feet. Here and there, however, owing to the cramped conditions of the route open to the track, it was found requisite to reduce the radius to some 270 feet in order to avoid heavy and expensive cutting through rocks and hills.

Some idea of the extent to which the engineers were delayed by their repeated differences with the Italian workmen may be gathered from the fact that although 23 months were occupied in carrying the rails from Swakopmund to Omaruru, a matter of 145 miles, the second section, from the latter point to Tsumeb, the present terminus, a matter of 215 miles, required but another year. When the railway was rushed onwards from Omaruru, although the country to be crossed was somewhat easier from the physical point of view, and lent itself to more rapid construction, acceleration was attributable in the main to the ample supply of labour available and absence of trouble with the workmen engaged.

Another grave difficulty against which the builders had to struggle was water. In fact, it might be said that the scarcity of this commodity was more perplexing than those governing the labour, strikes notwithstanding. It was not merely securing sufficient supplies for the workmen's needs, but also for constructional purposes, such as for the locomotive boilers, mixing of concrete for masonry, and so forth. On the first section, every pint of drinking water had to be brought up from the base on the coast to the railhead, and as this advanced, the difficulties concerned with its transportation increased. In some instances bullock-carts were the only vehicles that could be pressed into service for its conveyance over 30 or 40 miles. Throughout the first 85 miles from Swakopmund to Usakos, not a drop could be drawn from the earth. Innumerable borings in search of the liquid were made alongside the line as it progressed, but they were rewarded with no material success. Occasionally small quantities were found, but it was too brackish and quite unfit for drinking purposes. When Usakos was gained the situation was eased somewhat by a local discovery, but the water had to be softened before it could be used by the engines, and accordingly a plant for treating the water in this manner had to be brought up country and erected. This, however, was useless for domestic purposes, and when the line was pushed on from Omaruru, special water trains had to be run for the convenience of the workmen. Huge tanks were laden on the cars and were carried from the coast to the railhead, the journey occupying several hours. The trouble and expense involved in connection with this vital requisite influenced the cost and time occupied in building the line very unfavourably, so much so indeed, that the preliminary estimates of the cost were exceeded very markedly.

This question has not been solved satisfactorily yet, and it will remain to puzzle the administration of the line until some conveniently situated subterranean water supply is tapped on the barren veldt. The load of every train has to be increased by a special tank-tender coupled behind the engine containing 2,200 gallons of water, which represents so much un-remunerative load.

The rolling stock is quite in keeping with this diminutive railway. The tiny engines have driving wheels 24 inches in diameter, while the cylinders have a diameter of 12 inches and a stroke of 17¾ inches. Yet they can haul a load of 100 tons at a speed of 25 miles an hour on the level and at 9½ miles an hour on the steepest banks of 1 in 50.

This appears to be a mere crawl in comparison with the speeds with which we are familiar on the standard railways. But when one recalls the manner in which this little 'toy' line has changed conditions of travel in a lonely corner of the African continent, and the former rate of progress possible by bullock-cart, even 9½ miles an hour appears to be an amazing speed. Before the iron horse appeared in German South-West Africa, to travel from Swakopmund to Omaruru, a mere 145 miles, was a heroic achievement, entailing a laborious slow tramp through lonely sterile wastes of boulders and scrub. A pace of 7 or 10 miles a day was considered fast travelling, and one who covered the journey in a fortnight was considered to have driven hard. Today, the same distance can be reeled off in about 12 hours.

CHAPTER 7

The Wonders of the Tyrol

Probably there is no country in Europe wherein are compressed so many and such varied marvels of engineering executed in connection with the building of the iron road as in Austria. As is well known, the country is a sea of towering rugged mountains, with steep slopes, knotted by crags and scarred by deep gullies, intersected by broad sylvan valleys.

Such topographical conditions impose a severe tax upon the skill and resources of the engineer. Consequently, this territory has been the scene of many grim grapples with Nature – some in which the odds have been overwhelmingly against the engineers, and in which success has been achieved only by dogged perseverance. Conspicuous in this direction are the wonderful tunnels.

It was the successful piercing of the Mont Cenis and St Gotthard tunnels that first spurred the Austrian engineers to work of this character. Their first attempt, the boring of the Arlberg, was such a conspicuous success that they did not hesitate afterwards to have recourse to such methods when all other means appeared impracticable. Today, the country can point to four huge Alpine tunnels which stand among the foremost achievements of their class in the world. Such ways and means for forcing the iron road from one point to another are highly expensive, but in each instance the ends have justified the means. By their provision, points only a few miles apart as the crow flies, and which with surface railways could have been connected only by wearying, devious routes, have been brought into close communication.

When the Arlberg chain was taken in hand, the preliminary surveys showed that it would approximate 7 miles in length, and that about the centre of the tunnel a solid mass of rock, 1,600 feet in thickness, would extend from the roof and track to the storm-swept mountain pass overhead.

At this time the two previous projects of this character had proved so costly, had occupied such a long time, and had entailed the grappling with technical difficulties such as never had been encountered before, that the idea of tunnelling the Arlberg was entertained with mixed feelings. But Julius Lott, the engineer-in-chief, was not to be dissuaded from his enterprise. He maintained that it could be accomplished far more quickly and cheaply than had been the Cenis or Gotthard works. True, it was not to be quite so long as either of the latter undertakings, but similar difficulties, if not others more perplexing, might lurk buried there in the heart of the crest. The engineer was urged in his decision by the perfection of a new boring implement which had been evolved during the final stages of the Gotthard tunnel. Although the circumstances there did not enable the new invention to demonstrate its possibilities to the full, yet what had been done sufficed to show that the new tool was destined to revolutionise the methods adopted in such huge boring operations.

This was the Brandt rock-drill, a wonderful appliance which in one stroke displaced incalculable manual labour. The tool is operated by water pressure, and the drill ploughs its way into the rock under a. rotary movement in much the same manner as an auger forces its way through a piece of wood. The water pressure brought to bear upon the drill is tremendous, ranging from 1,400 to 1,680 pounds per square inch, and even the hardest rock scarcely can resist its attack.

But, as may be supposed, at times the hard texture of the rock played sad havoc with the cutting edge of the drill. Occasionally three or four drills were put out of service with every yard of advance, and even then progress was painfully slow. When, however, soft rock was encountered the tool cleaved its way through very rapidly, the cutter biting ½ inch or more into the material with every revolution. Then it was found possible to speed up the rotations to as many as seven or eight per minute, with proportionate increase of life for the cutting edge.

Precisely what this Brandt drill signified to the engineers in connection with this tunnel may be gathered from the fact that from the time drilling commenced, in 1880, only four years elapsed before communication was established between Bluden on the one and Innsbruck on the other side of the range. In this short period a passage 26 feet high by 23 feet wide was cut through solid rock for a distance of 6⅜ miles at a total cost of £1,500,000, or $7,500,000. In comparison with the two previous enterprises of the same character this was a magnificent achievement! The Cenis tunnel, 7½ miles in length, occupied some thirteen years to complete, while some eight years were required to drive 9¼ miles through the St Gotthard. This was an achievement of which those engaged in the task were justly proud. Indeed, the Austrians hold a unique position in the rapidity with which they can drive these gigantic undertakings through the most formidable mountain chains.

The section of railway upon which this tunnel is situated sorely tried the ingenuity of the engineers up to the Paznaun valley. The line clings to the mountainside, which is broken up by precipitous crags, and these either had to be pierced or blasted right away to provide a path for the railway. Gushing torrents pour madly down these slopes, and had to be spanned by noble and lofty viaducts or bridges. At some places the boiling waters are deflected from their bed into an artificial channel built of concrete; at others there are massive retaining walls to prevent the waterways from breaking bounds and sweeping the embankment away. One wide gorge is bridged by a single iron span 393 feet 8 inches in length. This is the Trisanna viaduct, below which the glacial brook tumbles over the boulders at a depth of some 262 feet. Elaborate precautions also had to be adopted to protect the line from the ravages of avalanches and landslides.

Years before the Arlberg line was contemplated, however, some distinctly noteworthy achievements in engineering had been placed on record by the establishment of railway communication between Vienna and Trieste on the Adriatic Sea. Certainly the line did not follow the shortest route between these two points, but it must be borne in mind that it was undertaken in the early forties, when Great Britain, 'the home of the railway', only possessed some 840 miles of line, and railway engineering was quite in its infancy. It is little wonder, therefore, that the engineers of the project in this wild corner of Europe followed a circuitous path, to avoid fearsome obstacles as far as practicable. They resorted to sharp curves and heavy banks, and the line doubled and redoubled in the most amazing manner. Bridges and tunnels were introduced very freely, some of the viaducts spanning deep clefts on the mountain flanks being very lofty.

By the most direct route of this system, the journey from the Austrian capital to Trieste occupies 9 hours. In that journey, comparatively no longer than that entailed in speeding over the greater distance separating London from Edinburgh, one passes through four distinct expanses of scenery. Vienna nestles in a broad valley flanked on all sides by the towering snow-topped Alps. The line, upon leaving the capital, first traverses the undulating foothills, then wends its way through the mountains to gain the richly wooded, verdant and beautiful country of Styria, and finally passes over a vast stretch of wilderness to descend abruptly to the coast.

In forging this link in the railway chain the engineers had to overcome the Semmering range, which is amongst the most tumbled in the whole of the

Austrian Alps. How did they do it? By following the natural facilities open to them: a ledge here, a gallery there; passing from this slope to that by a viaduct or bridge; zigzagging up the mountain slopes; tunnelling through rocky eminences; following winding paths for miles merely to gain points only a mile or two apart in a straight line. No doubt if that line were built today it would have its length cut in half, for railway engineering has advanced by leaps and bounds since 1848, when this pioneer project was taken in hand.

In carrying their scheme to fulfilment, these early engineers unconsciously achieved one notable distinction: they built the first mountain railway. What matter if banks did assume a rise of 132 feet or so per mile, and the line did wander in apparent aimlessness among the peaks? Speed then was not the vital consideration it is today, while traffic was comparatively light, so that the haulage facilities were not taxed severely.

This mountain climb on the main line occurs between Gloggnitz and Murzzuschlag, the famous winter sporting centre in the Tyrol. The mountain crest is 4,577 feet above the sea level, but the railway does not rise to that height; its summit is at 2,940 feet in the middle of a tunnel ¾ mile in length beneath the Semmering Pass. But to gain that altitude from either side of the mountain entailed prodigious work. Pick, shovel, and gunpowder made heavy cuttings through projecting spurs, raised lofty embankments, filled gaping fissures, and cleaved galleries out of the solid rock. The two points on either side of the mountain are only 14 miles apart in a straight line; by the railway it is more than twice the distance, the outstanding features which were necessary to render the undertaking *un fait accompli* being fifteen tunnels, and a score of viaducts and bridges. To construct the 30 miles over the Semmering cost a round £2,000,000, or $10,000,000, in money, and occupied between three and four years to complete.

With the march of time, however, the traffic over this railway increased, hand in hand with the expansion of Triestfe, to such an extent that it proved inadequate. A more direct route between the capital and the port, as well as accelerated communication with the great centres of Europe, was demanded by the commercial community. This agitation became so insistent that at last the government was compelled to move, and the engineer of the Imperial Railways was commissioned to survey the country for the purpose of devising some scheme which would satisfy the public outcry.

This was no easy task. Innumerable knots of mountains break up the country between Vienna and the Adriatic, and they are compressed so tightly together that the narrow valleys between offered but slight assistance towards the solution of the problem. Then, again, those three well-known mountain ranges, the Tauern, Karawanken, and Julian Alps, stood right in the way, disputing any possibly shorter route than that already in existence.

The prospect before the surveyors was not very promising. However, they braved the elements among the inhospitable peaks, suffered extreme privations and fatigue as they toiled up and down the rugged, wild mountain slopes with their instruments, for month after month. At last they succeeded in formulating a project which was submitted to Parliament. In this it was proposed to make avail of any favourable stretches of existing railways which intersected the valleys in all directions, and to connect them together, so that in the end a tolerably direct route might be obtained. At any rate, this proposal would reduce the journey between the Adriatic and Munich by at least 11 hours. The scheme was divided into four broad sections. It was discussed thoroughly in Parliament, but in the end it was decided to carry out in the first instance the most essential parts of the project, because embarkation upon the undertakings as set forth by the engineers would have entailed the expenditure of a gigantic sum of money. Even that which was sanctioned represented a total financial commitment of about £30,000,000, or $150,000,000, for 211½ miles of line.

The accepted enterprise was memorable because it entailed the piercing of three mountain ranges by tunnels 5¼, 5, and 4 miles in length respectively. Of the total mileage, only 41¼ miles were to be level! The remaining 170 miles represented banks, with grades running as high as 132 feet to the mile.

The project as sanctioned was divided into three sections for constructional purposes. The first section is that known as the Pyrhn railway, which connects the main line between Vienna and Switzerland via the Arlberg tunnel at Linz. From this point a short branch line ran directly southwards through the Krems valley to Klaus, having been built for tourist purposes. It was decided to overhaul this spur to bring it into conformity with the conditions of a main line, and to build the new line onwards from Klaus.

From Auspoint, which is at an altitude of 1,563 feet, the line makes one continual climb, climb, to the Selzthal terminus, nearly 40 miles distant. The average rise ranges from 70 to 132 feet per mile to overcome the Pyrhn Pass, beneath which a tunnel nearly 3 miles in length was bored. This tunnel, however, is only one of many, for there are numerous short burrows through shoulders and crags. Nor are the bridges a whit less majestic. The Steyr River is crossed by a lofty single masonry arch, and again lower down by an iron suspension structure, while the Teichl is spanned by a single-span lattice steel bridge. The loftiness of these structures is an outstanding characteristic. The rivers at the points in question have cut their beds at a great depth below the banks which constitute the railway level. Swerving bends are also conspicuous, for the railway continually swings from one side of the valley to the other.

The construction of the Pyhrn railway, however, was simple in comparison with the other links of this chain of communication. At Klagenfurt, south-east of Vienna, commences the Karawanken railway, so named because it pierces the difficult mountain range of that name. The stretch is only 19 miles in length, but the country proved to be so broken that only 4 miles of level track could be introduced, and those in the vicinity of the stations! Throughout the remaining 15 miles the railway is really a gigantic switchback.

The line hugs the hillsides, and has to make the rough descent of the broken Hollenburger in order to gain the level of the Drave River, to pass between the Stattnitz on the northern and the Ivarawanken chains on the southern side of the depression. The mountainside is steep and broken in the extreme. In all directions gullies extended, where the soft earth had been washed away by the violence of the snow freshets. These had to be filled in with solid, heavy embankments, the debris for which was torn from deep cuttings through projecting humps of rock. Some of the gaps were too wide and deep to be overcome in this summary manner, and had to be bridged. The Hollenburger viaduct stands out prominently among works of this kind. From end to end it measures 262½ feet in length, and in the centre the rift is 92 feet below the level of the rails. The mountains sheer up precipitously on the one, and the beautiful valley of the Rosenbach falls away on the other, side of the track.

Gaining the river bank, the line sweeps across the waterway by a majestic lofty iron bridge 656 feet in length. Gaining the opposite bank, it plunges among the well-wooded slopes of the Karawanken belt of mountains, effecting a good climb up and down towards the Rosenbach valley, which is crossed by means of a long viaduct, consisting of four arched masonry spans each 24 feet and three steel spans of 177 feet apiece, at a height of 170 feet.

The ascent is heavy, as the objective is the northern entrance to the Karawanken tunnel, which burrows through the range for a distance of 5 miles. The piercing of this subterranean passage excited considerable attention. The Austrian engineers who had achieved such a triumph in the rapid boring of file Arlberg upheld their reputation as accomplished masters in this phase of railway building, notwithstanding the fact that the rocky mass was found to be of such unstable character that the tunnel had to be lined from end to end.

The task was taken in hand shortly after the Austrian government sanctioned these railways in 1901. Boring was carried out simultaneously from each end. The ground around each portal was quickly cleared, and when the work was in full swing 6,000 men found employment. The first step was to secure power to furnish the energy to operate the variety of mechanical appliances that were necessary to dislodge and transport the rock, as well as to dispel the Cimmerian gloom in the heart of the mountain. There was a small waterfall 6 miles from the proposed southern mouth of the tunnel, with a drop of 35 feet, and capable of furnishing some 900 horse power. This picturesque Alpine cascade was harnessed and compelled to drive turbines and dynamos to generate electricity, which was transmitted by overhead wires for 6 miles to the boring works at the tunnel entrance. Here the current was pressed into a multitude of services, not the least important of which was the driving of the huge fans, whereby a great volume of clean, pure, cool air was swept in a steady stream through the shaft to strike against the wall of rock upon which the drillers were concentrating their energies, displacing the atmosphere contaminated by the fumes of the dynamite blasting, grime and dust. Moreover, the temperature, which rapidly rose as the heart of the mountain was penetrated, was tempered pleasantly by the incoming currents, so that the fatigue of toiling in the blackness and confined space was reduced.

On the northern side of the tunnel, similar arrangements were laid down. In this instance, however, the electricity, obtained by harnessing two small waterfalls, had to operate wonderful electric drills which were used at this end for boring into the rock – on the southern side, hydraulic and pneumatic drills were employed. The working face in the tunnel was illuminated brilliantly by electric light, so that the drillers laboured under conditions vastly dissimilar to those which prevailed when the first Alpine tunnel was driven. As the top of the tunnel was cut out, the roof was shored up with heavy timbering, and hard on the tracks of the excavators came the stonemasons, cutting, trimming and setting the masonry lining into position. The work was so planned that the actual progress per day should be 13 lineal feet, and although at times the calculations were somewhat upset by something unforeseen being encountered, yet, taken on the whole, the average was well maintained. Commenced in June 1902, the mountain chain was pierced and ready for the double line of rails by November 1905, so that the work had been carried out very smartly indeed.

Emerging from the tunnel, the line once more becomes a single track, and issues into the Wurzner Save valley, the descent continuing until Assling, the terminus of the Karawanken railway, is reached, this point being 151 feet below the southern mouth of the tunnel. Here a connection is formed with the next link in the chain, this being the 'Wochenier' section, which runs to the shores of the Adriatic at Trieste.

But before the latter terminal is gained, another mountain mass has to be penetrated – the Julian Alps. It is a meandering line in very truth, for the configuration of the country prevented more than short pieces of straight track being sandwiched here and there between sweeping curves, elaborate winds, stiff ascents and descents – in fact, the longest piece of straight line is only of 6,600 feet in the first 55 miles. In running from Assling to the seaboard 28 tunnels are threaded, exclusive of the Wochenier, which is 4 miles long, 15 bridges and 30 viaducts are crossed, while the cuttings and embankments are innumerable. The railway traverses some of the most romantic and wildest scenery in the whole Alpine chain, especially as it approaches the southernmost clump of these mountains.

On this section, the engineers accomplished an unparalleled engineering feat. The narrow Isonzo gorge had to be crossed, and it was effected by throwing a single span from one bank to the other, a matter of 733 feet. This is the longest single-arch masonry bridge in the world, and the rail level is 120 feet above the level of the water. As the coast is approached the windings of the line become more tortuous, while the bridging, owing to the numerous rivers, is terrific. When at last Opcina tunnel is penetrated; the Adriatic is seen spread out in a vast panorama 1,000 feet below. To descend the mountain slopes with an easy grade for a distance of 10 miles was a stiff problem. In order to do so, the engineers had to carry the track in the form of elaborate saw-like loops. Heavy gradients could not be avoided, and this part of the line is one of the steepest and most trying to the locomotives.

Though these sections of the railway had proved difficult to carry out, it was the Tauern link in the chain that tried the energy and ingenuity of the engineers to the supreme degree, for on this stretch of railway the mighty Tauern group of mountains had to be negotiated. Surveys showed that to pierce this clump involved the boring of a tunnel for a distance of 5 miles at least. They proved the hardest 5 miles in the whole undertaking; the piercing of the Karawanken and Wochenier tunnels sank into insignificance by comparison, for this knot of the Alps was found to be formed of much sterner rock. Granite gneiss, one of the hardest substances against which it is possible to bring the edge of a drill, made progress provokingly slow. At times, when the hand drills had to be used, an advance of 2 feet in the course of 24 hours was considered excellent. The Brandt hydraulic drills, however, with the enormous energy behind them, made the task somewhat lighter, for they moved through the hardest rock at a rate of about 17 feet every day, with occasional spurts of a foot per hour.

In this undertaking, however, many misfortunes served to delay progress. The task had barely commenced, when a flood destroyed part of the works at the northern end. The river whose water had been harnessed had been deviated from its accustomed path, because it flowed over the roof of the tunnel. As the engineers had no desire to invite an inundation by tapping the bed of the river waterway, they had provided it with a new channel. Heavy snows and rains, however, so swelled the volume of the diverted river that it broke through its artificial bonds to resume its original course. The result was that, owing to the crust of earth between the old bed and the roof of the tunnel being so thin, the water crashed through, and poured into the tunnel in an immense cascade.

The men abandoned everything hurriedly, and rushed madly for their lives from the incoming avalanche of water. For days the tunnel was absolutely inaccessible. Not content with flooding the workings, the impetuous torrent completed its devastation by sweeping away many of the supports to the line conveying the water to the drills under a pressure of 1,500 pounds per square inch, leaving the slender conduit of this great force hanging in graceful festoons in mid-air. Some of these gaps were as much as 260 feet in width, and had a break in the pipe occurred, widespread damage would have been caused. But the engineers set to work, and reconstructed the temporary dam that had thus been torn roughly away and rebuilt the river's new channel. At the same time, they adopted such precautions as would preclude the possibility of the waterway again inundating the tunnel in times of the most severe floods.

Such incidents, however, are inherent to works of this character. The inundation was but one means adopted by Nature to thwart the advance of the iron road. Work had scarcely been resumed, when another disaster occurred. The drills were whirring merrily against the rock face in the tunnel, and the drillers were light-heartedly conversing with one another as they fed the boring giant in its rock-penetrating task. Suddenly there was a cry of alarm. Water was trickling rapidly from a bore-hole; it rapidly increased in volume. The drillers hurriedly withdrew their tools and backed down the cavern. There was a roar, and a limpid stream burst from the rock face. The drillers stampeded; they had tapped a subterranean spring, and it was now rushing forth with fiendish violence. The engineers hastened to the front. Such a contingency had been expected, for such incidents are inseparable from tunnelling tasks of this magnitude. The rushing stream was turned into one of the conduits at the side to carry it to the tunnel mouth, where it expended its energy harmlessly by tumbling wildly among the rocks. When pockets of water and springs are tapped in this manner, the question is to control the water so encountered in such a manner that it does not interfere with the drilling work or flood the workings. As a matter of fact, when the Simplon tunnel was in progress, these underground springs were harnessed and compelled to perform useful work; they were thrown against the rock face to keep down the internal temperature.

Work continued incessantly day and night, but it was hard and exhausting the farther the men advanced. The drills scarcely could bite into the rock, as it was so tough. At one time the question became so acute that the engineers brought up the electric drills used in the Karawanken undertaking in order to see if matters could not be expedited, but they failed to make as much headway as the hydraulic tools. Another handicapping factor was the heat, which rose very rapidly, and although it did not attain that degree experienced in the boring of the Simplon, yet it caused considerable fatigue among the workmen engaged in such a confined space. The elaborate ventilating system sufficed to keep the air as sweet and cool as possible, but it did not solve the problem completely. The workmen, cramped as they were in the confined space – the area available for manipulating the tools only measured a few feet in each direction – often betrayed painful signs of physical distress.

But at last there was a wild cheer, which echoed and re-echoed through the caverns to the tunnel's mouths. Those outside realised that something untoward had occurred, and in a few seconds the news came through the gloomy depths that the drills had pierced the last 72 inches of rock separating the two headings, and that the Tauern was conquered. That was on 21 July 1907, some five years after the first boulder was torn from the mountainside. Once this last barrier was broken down, the finishing touches were soon applied and the double track laid from end to end.

Though the Tauern tunnel constitutes the outstanding features on the section stretching from Schwarzach St Veit to Villach, there are innumerable other subsidiary works which in themselves are of importance. One of more than passing interest is a clever piece of construction in order to overcome a difference of 2,975 feet in level between the Tauern tunnel and Ober Villach by means of a huge 'S' loop 4½ miles in length.

The fulfilment of this undertaking constitutes one of the most remarkable railway engineering feats in Europe. Certainly it ranks among the most expensive enterprises that ever have been attempted west of the Urals. To the travelling and commercial community its value is incalculable, for Munich, which was formerly a tedious journey of 23 hours from Trieste, is now within 12 hours' run, while the other great centres of Europe have been brought proportionately nearer the Adriatic by this new and more direct route.

CHAPTER 8

The Reclamation of Alaska

Until a few years ago, the popular conception of Alaska was a vast country sealed against the efforts of civilisation by impenetrable barriers of snow and ice, presenting such a dismal outlook as to daunt the most intrepid spirits. But today quite a different impression prevails. Alaska is considered a coming country, although it rests on either side of the invisible line denoting the Arctic Circle. It is a vast mineral storehouse, the lofty mountains containing rich deposits of all the valuable minerals of commerce, while the dales nestling among the peaks have been found to be of wonderful fertility and capable of producing a wealth of agricultural produce. One might regard the possibility of raising wheat and hay in that northern clime as a mere fantasy, but I have seen cereals and hay cut in those valleys which compare very favourably in quality with the similar products grown in the great agricultural belts of the United States and Canada.

The fact is that the interior, far from being locked the whole year round in a temperature hovering around, or many degrees below, zero, has extremes of heat and cold. In the winter the snow envelops the ground to a depth of several feet, and the mercury descends to 40 or 50 degrees below zero, but in the summer the thermometer registers temperatures of 80 and 90 degrees. While the winter grips the country for nearly two-thirds of the year, the summer barely lasts 100 days. But what a summer it is! The sun shines from a cloudless sky the whole time, and for some 20 hours throughout the day. Consequently, it is possible to sow and to harvest the crops within eighty days.

Along the coast, extremely cold weather scarcely ever is experienced. The conditions, in fact, are very similar to those prevailing in Scandinavia. The coastline of the latter country is bathed by the warm waters of the Gulf Stream: the coastline of Alaska is swept by the warm breezes of the Japanese chinook wind blowing off the Pacific.

Yet popular fallacy resulted in the country being regarded as a closed book, and the possibility of a railway ever securing sufficient traffic to justify its existence was ridiculed to scorn twenty years ago. But the past two decades have witnessed strange developments. The railway engineer has penetrated the country, and today there is a scene of great activity to connect the remarkable discoveries of metals among the mountains with convenient points of shipment along the coast.

It was the discovery of gold, and the subsequent rush to the 'Klondike', that brought about the unlocking of Alaska, and which was responsible for bringing a country of 591,000 square miles within the purview of the railway builder. A rude collection of timber shacks and tents sprung up like mushrooms on a little indent on the seashore, and today is a healthy, prosperous town and port – Skaguay. From this point the daring spirits infected with the 'yellow fever' pushed inland over the gaunt, snow-clad mountains to the 'fields', enduring privations untold and experiences that make the blood run cold in order to gain the new Eldorado. The trail was blazed with the bleached bones of animals and pioneers eager to be first on the spot. Of roads there were none – there was not even a rough path. Those early seekers had to tread one with their own feet.

No sooner had the first reports concerning the discoveries of gold at Dawson trickled through, to be substantiated by subsequent investigations, than the possibility of building a railway from the coast to the gold fields, in order to lift the men over the most difficult and hazardous part of the journey, was discussed. Indeed, among one of the earliest bands which trailed across the Chilkoot Pass in a thick black line were one or two surveyors spying out the general characteristics of the country. Less than two years after the excitement first flared up the plans for a line 112 miles in length, extending practically through unknown country, had been prepared. One end of the line rested on the seashore at Skaguay, while the other reposed at White Horse, near Lake Lebarge, where communication was effected with the wonderful inland waterway of the country, the river Yukon. It was not a long railway in comparison with other great systems of the world, but it was a highly ambitious enterprise, for it was destined to lift man and freight over the most terrible part of the country, the coast range which had been the grave of scores of fortune hunters.

The prime mover in this undertaking was an accomplished engineer who is quite at home in such inhospitable territory. He was sanguine of its financial success, but when he approached American financiers for support he was laughed to scorn. But this man was not to be cast down so easily. Foiled in his efforts to enlist the practical sympathy of his own countrymen, he came to London and sought British assistance, for in the matter of railway pioneering the British financier is probably the greatest plunger. He required roughly £1,000,000, or $5,000,000, and what was more, he secured it. The firmness and boldness with which the capitalists of London supported what was regarded as a hare-brained scheme astonished the American financial world. The ultimate success of the enterprise, however, was even more surprising to them, and they more than regretted their refusal to support the undertaking when it was originally laid before them. One eminent authority belaboured his compatriots soundly for their lack of foresight and initiative, and aptly remarked, 'As long as the British know how to grasp the trade of the world, when and where it is most profitable, they have no immediate cause to worry about German and American competition.'

Armed with the requisite cash resources, the projector lost no time. He hurried back to Alaska and commenced his attack upon the towering mountain chain. His arrival in 'shack-town' with an efficient staff and materials signalised the transition of Skaguay from a tumbledown, disreputable collection of shanties into an important, well-built port.

The engineer realised only too well that he had a desperate task confronting him. The maps and reports of the territory he intended to traverse were found to be absolutely unreliable. He discarded the whole lot and advised his own survey expeditions to prepare their own cartographical guides. Five surveys were run, and five alternate routes for the line between the coast and White Horse were completed before selection was made definitely.

Then the rock and earth commenced to fly. There was a call for 5,000 men. Skaguay was the starting point, the first spadeful of earth being turned near the water's edge. A narrow gauge – 3 feet – was adopted as being more economical to build, while from the traffic point of view it was considered to be more than adequate. As the small gangs of men armed with pickaxes and shovels advanced up the main street of the town in embryo, defining the grade, the enthusiasm knew no bounds. It was an occasion for a frantic outburst of revelry. The conquest of the dreaded White Pass had commenced: the most northerly railway on the American continent was under way; and the time was not far distant when the miners would be able to pass from coast to gold fields with no more danger or discomfort than attends one who travels from London to Scotland or from New York to Chicago.

For the first 5 miles the going was easy, as the line was plotted through practically level country with only a slight ascent in order to strike the mountains at a convenient point. Two months after the first sod was turned down by the waterside, this section was completed and opened for traffic, an event which was not permitted to pass by without another outbreak of jubilation.

The feature that most astonished the inhabitants, however, was the vigour with which the presiding genius pushed his enterprise forward. The gold rush was at its height, and hundreds of new arrivals poured into Skaguay from every arriving boat. One and all were bound for the diggings, and they proceeded as far as possible over the railway, to continue a wearisome toil afoot from the railhead. To these men, the completion of the line meant more than one can realise from a distance. That plod over the mountain crest through a pass which is so steep that it appeared to lean back was heroic.

As the engineer penetrated the mountains his task became more exacting, perilous, and the pace of the advance eased up appreciably. There was no dearth of labour, for new arrivals, not having the wherewithal to gain the gold region, or others who, having ventured there to meet only with misfortune and ill-luck, were only too glad to seize the opportunity to earn a good day's pay on the building of the White Pass and Yukon railway, as it is called.

The engineer decided to keep his grades as easy as possible, but during the course of 15 miles through the mountains he found very quickly that this was no easy matter. He had to gain the summit of the pass, an altitude of 2,888 feet, in this distance, and it was found quite hopeless without a climb of 1 in 15. Much of the country lying in his path never had been trodden by man. Below the snow-line it was covered thickly with virgin forest, tangled undergrowth and dead-fall piled up to a tremendous height, through which the men had to axe their way at a snail's pace. Above the line where timber ceased to thrive, cliffs rose up sheer, with their faces so polished by the Arctic gales and weather as to be as slippery as ice and affording no foothold whatever. In order that the workmen might gain a purchase for the wielding of their tools, huge logs were slung down from convenient heights, held in position by massive chains attached to iron dogs driven into the rock, and on this flimsy foothold the men were compelled to prosecute their tasks as best they could.

One of the most complex difficulties was in regard to the bringing up of provisions and stores for the men, and the requisite material for the railway. The base of supplies was over 1,000 miles away, every ounce of necessities having to be brought up by water from Seattle or Vancouver. The little army was cut off entirely from the outside world, news of which could be gleaned only when a boat called at Skaguay. The absence of telegraphic communication was a deficiency which was felt the most sorely. The post, intermittent and uncertain, as there was no regular service, was the sole vehicle of communication. Consequently, extreme care had to be observed to preserve a continuous stream of the material required. The omission of this or that entailed a delay of anything from ten days upwards.

At one point, a lofty granite tooth 70 feet wide and 20 feet thick sheered up in front of the engineer to a height of 120 feet. He neither attempted to go round nor through the obstacle. He brought up a squad of expert drillers, and soon they were engaged in honeycombing the base of the cliff with deep holes. Charges of explosives were rammed home, and when detonated the whole crag, a crumbling mass of rock, rattled down into the ravine. The pedestal of this cliff was then smoothed off, and thereon the sleepers and metals were laid.

By dint of prodigious effort, continued without intermission both day and night the whole week through, without even a respite for Sundays, the engineer succeeded in carrying the railway forward for a distance of 40 miles and over the summit of the pass in a single season. Such an achievement in the face of the abnormal difficulties encountered, in such a short space of time, was indeed memorable.

Satisfied with this result, the engineer called a halt. His men were in dire need of rest, and as there was no object in exposing them unduly to the rigours of the terrible winter now that the back of the task had been broken, constructional work was suspended for a few months. But it was not a period of complete inactivity. He had planned his work for the following summer, and during the winter months he pressed the snow-covered country into service for the erection of his constructional camps, the disposition of building material, provisions and stores at convenient points over a long distance ahead.

One cannot help admiring the perspicacity of the man identified with this peculiar enterprise. When he sought financial assistance to further his scheme, he argued that directly the railway had negotiated the summit, remunerative traffic would develop. So it proved. Confident in these anticipations, the guiding hand had ordered considerable rolling stock to be hurried to Skaguay while his graders were forcing their way to the summit, and when the pass was overcome, a service was inaugurated.

Yet it is doubtful if the engineer scarcely expected the results that were experienced. The adequacy of his rolling stock over the first 40 miles was tested to breaking point. The pack trail over the pass was abandoned as quickly as a candle is extinguished by a gust of wind when the first train was announced. The miners braved the elements, pitiless cold and dazzling snow, no longer. From the railway today one can still see decaying evidences of a bygone bustle and activity attending the trek of the first prospectors and pioneers to the Klondike in the falling shacks and huts scattered along the trail, which before the advent of the iron horse were centres of life and revelry, but which today are wrapped in forlorn desolation. Scarcely a person enters or even passes their doors now.

So soon as the winter broke, the engineer brought his forces to the front once more. The line skirts Lake Bennett. White Horse, on the head waters of the Yukon, some 72 miles ahead, was the objective, and the engineer was determined to reach that inland terminus that season by hook or by crook. As the line skirts Lake Bennett, and this sheet of water is navigable, he decided to use it temporarily until White Horse was reached, the railway consequently being resumed from the head of the lake. This was a justifiable course, inasmuch as the building of the line along the waterside would have occupied considerable time owing to physical characteristics, while it was imperative that White Horse should be reached without delay.

The coming of spring saw the graders regirding themselves for another wrestle with the rock and gravel. Before they had gone very far, the edge of a lake was gained. Its banks were precipitous and did not lend themselves to a feasible track. An ingenious solution of the problem was essayed. The engineer decided to lower the level of this sheet of water by some 14 feet and to build his grade on a shelf which surveys showed there would be exposed. To this end, he cut a small outlet. But as the vent was driven through soft soil and totally inadequate to resist the pent-up force of the escaping water, the latter widened the breach into such a deep and wide channel that the lake was lowered by no less than 70 feet! This result opened up a new difficulty, escape from which was only practicable by the erection of two large bridges spanning the rift left by the receding waters. As a result, the line does not run round the lake as planned originally, but cuts directly across its bed.

When at last the metals were laid into White Horse and the Yukon River was gained, the engineer retraced his footsteps to push ahead with the last link around Lake Bennett, so that through rail connection between the coast and the Yukon River might be possible that year. This was a heavy piece of work owing to the indentation of the lake-shore and the number of crags that dropped into the water. But by blasting away the faces of the promontories to fashion a narrow gallery upon which to lay the track, and by dumping the rock shivered by the explosives into the bays to form embankments, an easy alignment was secured.

Although the railway overcomes mountains running up to a height of 7,000 feet, only one tunnel was found to be necessary. Curves are numerous and sharp, so that the line describes a sinuous route among the peaks. Although on the ascent of the mountains from a point 5 miles out of Skaguay grades of 1 in 25 were found unavoidable to gain the summit, the descent on the opposite side is much easier, for the difference in level of the White Pass summit and White Horse summit, 91 miles beyond, is only 808 feet. However, the line between these two levels is built for the most part on forced grades.

Bearing in mind the character of the country traversed, where lofty peaks and steep precipices alternate with deep gorges and wide clefts, it is obvious that such a railway as this could not be completed without recourse to heavy bridging. In all there are 11,450 lineal feet of such structures. There are seven steel bridges, one of which, just before the summit is gained, is 400 feet in length, with the centre 215 feet above the bottom of the gorge.

Taken on the whole, labour was not so difficult a problem in Alaska then as it is today, despite the remote situation of the constructional work, for reasons already explained. The enterprise found employment for about 35,000 men, and it speaks volumes for the care exercised in regard to their comfort and welfare, that only thirty-five men met their deaths through accident and disease, notwithstanding the high pressure with which work was maintained. The men for the most part were far more intelligent than those generally identified with such work.

To illustrate the extreme fascination that gold exercises over these prospector-navvies, one incident is worth relating. The men were driving the grade with great zest, quite contented with their lot, because the majority had tasted the bitterness of ill-luck at the Klondike. One day, news trickled into the camp of the discovery of a new gold-strike not far distant in British Columbia. It galvanised the labourers like electricity, awoke all slumbering ambitions and re-erected all the castles in the air which Dawson had dispelled so ruthlessly. A solid phalanx of 1,500 men threw down their tools and clamoured round the pay-office of the engineers for their wages due to them forthwith. Not having received any premonitory warning of this development, the engineer inquired what was the matter, thinking that possibly a 'strike' was being nursed. As the wages were paid, the men stampeded off to see if Fortune could be wooed any more easily at Atlin than she could be won at Klondike.

As the railway was pushed through hurriedly while the Klondike gold fever was at its height, some of the work was of a temporary character, but once the communication was established, the whole line was overhauled. Timber trestles and bridges were replaced by heavier substantial metallic structures, and the earthworks were strengthened. Today, the road compares with any to be found on the continent. The service is daily, except Sundays, and the line is patrolled regularly for boulders or avalanches which may have crashed down the mountainsides, to come to rest on the track, and which form fearsome obstructions to a train. In winter it is kept open by means of the rotary snowploughs. This is no easy task, for the blizzards among mountains of the north are ferocious in their severity. Drifting snow often fills the cuttings to a depth of 35 feet or so. Two locomotives harnessed to one of these snow-clearers generally contrive to force a clean open passage through the fleecy mass, however. It may be pointed out that this railway possesses the largest type of narrow-gauge engines in the world, the engine and tender in working order turning the scale at 106 tons. Travel from our point of view appears somewhat expensive, since it averages 1s or 25 cents per mile.

The total cost of constructing and building the railway amounted to £850,000, or $4,250,000. The most expensive section was that from Skaguay to the White Pass summit, this first 20 miles involving an expenditure of £400,000, or $2,000,000. In the first season after completion, however, its gross receipts were £800,000, or $4,000,000, 25 per cent, of which was absorbed by working expense.

One outcome of the remarkable success attending the pioneer Alaskan railway was the embarkation upon another undertaking in the same country, this time under United States auspices. This, however, was a far more ambitious scheme. It involved the building of a standard-gauge road from Seward, in Resurrection Bay, some miles north of Skaguay, to the town of Fairbanks, 463 miles inland, the idea being not only to bring the latter point into touch with the coast, but also to tap rich coal deposits and vast forests of lumber. Unfortunately, this project has not been attended with that success which marked the White Pass and Yukon line. After 54 miles were completed, its finances became so entangled as to require the offices of a receiver to straighten matters out.

However, it must be explained that several unforeseen circumstances contributed to this chequered career over which the engineers had no control. Such calamities as floods, arising from the melting snows swelling the glacial rivers, landslides and avalanches wrought widespread damage time after time. Moreover, constructional work was not quite so straightforward as on the road more to the south, for progress was arrested repeatedly by the necessity of carrying out heavier work than the surveys contemplated.

Seward is situated on a flat, and the line was driven through a convenient river valley from this point into the mountains. The absence of any roads or even trails rendered investigation of the country fringing the proposed route precarious and trying because large stretches of swamp occupied the valleys, while the mountains were torn and broken, rising up steeply on either side.

The line was to conform in every particular to a first-class trunk system, with a maximum grade of only 1 in 50, with few and easy curves. That was the idea on paper, but it proved a terrible task to attempt to reduce theory to practice. Directly the base of operations at Seward was left, the engineers found the country in its primeval condition, the ground being covered with a tall, dense, dank grass between 5 and 6 feet in height, and tangled thick forests. Clearing alone was a tedious job, and the prevalence of bog rendered movement slow and exasperating.

As a rule it is mountains which offer a deterring barrier to the engineer, but in this instance it was the valleys which presented the most searching difficulties. The practical route for the line lay through the Placer River Valley, and the negotiation of this depression in order to preserve the grade and alignment was beset with innumerable perplexities. After leaving the coast, the railway has to climb gradually until it gains and crosses the summit of the watershed at an altitude of 1,050 feet and 45 miles out of Seward. Then comes a sharp drop for 3 miles, followed by a more rapid descent for 200 feet or so. In times gone by a huge glacier filled this valley. At the head, the ravine narrows sharply and leads into a canyon, where the rocky wall rises up on either hand almost perpendicularly to a height of some 700 feet. This rift is about ¾ mile in length, and opens into another valley at the foot of a large glacier which leads to a bay on the coast known as Turnagain Arm. So sharp is the descent that in the course of 22 miles some 900 feet has to be overcome.

The drop from the summit at the forty-eighth mile-post out of Seward for a distance of 6 miles puzzled the engineers sorely. Six surveys had to be run through this short canyon, and even then a grade of less than double the 1 in 50 was found impracticable. The configuration of the rift did not permit official requirements to be carried out with economy. Even the grade twice that demanded was found unattainable without six tunnels and seven large curves.

The survey was a perilous undertaking owing to the extreme steepness of the cliff-sides and the vegetation clinging to the rocky face. The rodmen working with the survey parties had to be slung in mid-air from ropes to enable the requisite calculations to be made.

The difficulties of the survey were surpassed by those of construction. The very first tunnel brought this home with startling vividity. It is 700 feet in length, and is almost entirely on a curve of about 400 feet radius burrowing through a projecting hump of the main chain. In order to gain the tunnel, a broad sweep of the same radius as that of the tunnel curve had to be made, and the two works together form two-thirds of a circle. But one portal of the tunnel opens out on the brink of a precipice, the mountainside falling away abruptly at that point. So in order to carry the line forward a huge artificial work had to be carried out. This is a timber trestle which constitutes one of the most outstanding features of the line. From end to end it measures 1,240 feet in length, while it varies in height from 40 to 90 feet, some of the outside members being no less than 120 feet in length. Over 1,000,000 feet of timber was used in its construction.

As a matter of fact, the extent of timber trestling upon this railway cannot fail to impress the visitor. In the valleys the line is laid almost entirely upon a wooden grade, owing to the absence of stable solid ground upon which to raise embankments, while the rivers are spanned by steel bridges ranging in span from 80 to 100 feet in the clear. As the rivers rise and fall considerably according to the season, the abutments had to be set well back from the low channel, and, moreover, had to be protected heavily by piling to withstand the severe scouring that takes place when the waterways are in flood and they rush along with the speed of a cataract.

More than 50 per cent, of the work through the canyon is tunnelling, which aggregates 2,800 feet out of 4,800 feet. There was no other way of overcoming the abrupt cliff-sides, and but for the rifts and clefts in their flanks its extent would have been greater. This was the work which occupied so much time and consumed so much money, for the rock was found to be intensely hard. Steam drilling was attempted at first, but the temperature within the borings rose so high as to become intolerable. Therefore this plant had to be discarded in favour of compressed air drills. With their aid a hole 21 feet in height, by 14 and 16 feet in width, to carry a single track, was hewn and blasted out.

The installation of the power plant to operate the drills was a pretty problem. It could not be set up on the same side of the canyon as the borings were being made, so had to be rigged up at a convenient point on the opposite wall near the upper end of the gorge, the power being transmitted through piping. In order to carry the latter across the gulch a temporary suspension bridge 130 feet long was erected, and as it was also employed for the purpose of conveying materials and men from one cliff to the other, it was made heavier than otherwise.

In addition to perforating the shoulders of the mountains, deep clefts in the mountain faces had to be spanned or masses of obstructing rock had to be blown out of the way. In one instance there was a couloir which required a 90-foot span bridge to cross from one side to the other, while in another case 300 feet of solid rock, aggregating over 50,000 tons of rock, had to be torn down to enable the grade to proceed from one tunnel to the other. About thirteen months were required to carry the line through this stretch of 4,800 feet.

The struggles with the rock were equalled by the wrestles with Nature in the valleys. These are to all intents and purposes beds of rivers whose boundaries are the bases of the mountains on either side. As a result, the whole of the depression is practically a swamp, with the river cutting a tortuous path apparently through the centre. The word 'apparently' is used because what is the main channel of the river today will be semi-dry land probably next year, because in the flood season, when the rivers are fed by melting snows, to speed along with fiendish velocity, they are just as likely as not to cut out an entirely new path through the soft soil. If the railway embankment bars its passage the whole obstruction is swept away. Hundreds of feet of completed line have been demolished in this manner. If the rushing river is unable to break through the embankment it swirls around the obstruction, rapidly undermining the foundations, with the result that a bad cave-in ensues, which is in every way as bad as a clean wash-out, except that perhaps the railway metals and sleepers can be retrieved.

Even the mountainsides, solid though they appear, are not free from Nature's playful antics. When the spring sun comes round and melts heavy masses of snow on the higher levels, there is trouble looming below. The snow slips on the crest. Gathering impetus with every succeeding foot in its descent, the avalanche picks up boulders, trees and other debris, to hurl them with terrific force against the handiwork of man, wiping it completely out of existence. One slide caught the unfortunate railway in this manner, tore up 1,200 feet of permanent way, and threw it, a twisted mass of iron and splintered timber, ⅓ mile away.

Considering the overwhelming odds against which the engineer was pitted, it is not surprising that work was brought to a standstill. The situation was summed up very graphically by one of the engineers whom I met: 'If Nature would only leave us alone once we have built the line, we should not care what kind of fight she put up against us to delay our advance. But all the money which could be devoted to new construction is devoured in rebuilding track which is either washed away or buried.'

CHAPTER 9

The Holy Railway to Mecca

While the majority of railways are constructed to meet the exigencies of commerce, and occasionally from considerations of military strategy, there is one striking instance of a line being built expressly for religious purposes. This is the Hedjaz railway, which stretches it's sinuous, glittering arm of steel from Damascus for nearly 1,000 miles southwards through the inhospitable deserts of Palestine and Arabia to Mecca and Medina, the sacred cities of the Moslem faith. The railway was built entirely by Mahommedans for Mahommedans, every penny required for the scheme being subscribed by the members of this vast sect.

Every member of the Faithful cherishes one ambition in life – to make the 'Hadj', or Sacred Journey to the cradle and shrine of the Prophet. A few years ago, this was an undertaking from which all but those blinded by religious fervour shrank. The journey had to be completed afoot, by camel or caravan, according to the financial status of the pilgrim, but whatever method of transit was favoured, the self-same dangers prevailed, though obviously they were experienced most severely by those who were compelled to have recourse to Shanks' Pony.

The route extended through practically uninhabited, sterile plains, upon which the sun beat down mercilessly, and the heat overhead was only equalled by that reflected from the glaring sand, which blistered the feet and imparted a fiery, maddening thirst. Food and water had to be carried by the pilgrim, because no sustenance could be obtained by the wayside. Even the welcome oases, with their refreshing, cooling rills and pools of water beneath the shade of the palms, are few and far between.

To the dangers of hunger, thirst and physical exhaustion there had to be included those from the attacks of the marauding Bedouins, who hung on the sides of the overland route, ever on the lookout to despoil the traveller.

These brigands were most daring and ferocious in their depredations. They robbed the pilgrim of all he possessed, and if his poverty resulted in a meagre reward for their attack, they bludgeoned him mercilessly for not being better provided with this world's goods, and left him bleeding and dying in the sun.

Every year, hundreds of pilgrims paid the penalty for their zeal. They set out from Damascus on their mission of duty and faith never to return. So powerless was the Ottoman government that these relentless nomads pursued their life of brigandage and preying on the pilgrims unchecked and without fear of punishment.

The Hedjaz railway was conceived in order to remove these perils and privations. When the Sultan published the details of his idea, it was hailed with unalloyed enthusiasm by every Mahommedan throughout the world, and one and all contributed towards the furtherance of the scheme.

The fulfilment of this enterprise will always rank as a magnificent achievement in the romance of railway engineering; the methods by which the numerous obstacles were broken down as they arose contribute fascinating incidents to a thrilling story. When it is remembered that approximately 1,000 miles of metals had to be laid through some of the most sterile and difficult country on the globe; that some 4,000 bridges, viaducts and tunnels had to be built to span rushing rivers, yawning chasms, and to penetrate precipitous bluffs; that sudden drops had to be made from highlands to valleys, and equally steep ascents from depressions to plateaus, then a faint idea of the formidable character of the undertaking may be gathered.

For months, the constructional engineers were buried in the midst of the biting, scorching and driving sand, quite isolated from the outside world, the clang of the tools being the only sound breaking a silence so intense that it could be felt. Occasionally, the news filtered through that the implacable nomads roaming the sweltering plains had swooped down upon the camps and that a desperate hand-to-hand struggle had been waged. Minute details were not vouchsafed, for such incidents became so frequent as to become monotonous.

Yet the authorities scarcely anticipated that these marauders would wage such a relentless war against the advance of the railway as did eventually come to pass. Yet it was not surprising. The Bedouins realised that the completion of the railway would bring their life of pillage and murder to an end, and accordingly they challenged every foot of its advance. Sometimes they won, massacred the encampment, and destroyed the line for some distance; at others, they lost and were routed right and left. The story of the Mahdi's opposition to the British penetration of Egypt was repeated in Palestine and

Arabia, only, if anything, with more determined fury. The soldiers worked with their arms beside them, and protected by a line of guards thrown out some distance around the railhead.

The military commandant was given a free hand to keep back the savage tribes in such a manner as he considered expedient, in order to permit the engineers to lay the metals as fast as possible, and without fear of being molested. When the work was inaugurated, the Turkish government appointed a strong man to the command of the protective troops. It was a responsible and dangerous position, for the authorities recognised from bitter experience the implacable fury of these tribesmen when fully roused. Field-Marshal Kaisim Pasha was appointed to the military directorship, and he proved the right man in the right place. His reputation and grim determination to subdue lawlessness were well known to the bandits, and the government hoped that his appointment to the protection of the enterprise would strike terror into the hearts of the Bedouins. But far from it. It appeared to urge them to greater daring, and they hung on his flanks relentlessly, cutting off stragglers ruthlessly, and keeping him constantly on the alert. The Field Marshal was kept in a state of perpetual anxiety, because he never knew upon which side or where he would be attacked next. Brushes were almost of daily occurrence, and the success of one side or the other fluctuated like a barometer.

Once the nomads caught Kaisim Pasha at a heavy disadvantage. The navvies and engineers were busy at work as usual on the permanent way, with the military outpost thrown well out on all sides. Suddenly there was a savage, heart-rending yell, and the desert became alive with the swarthy, active and powerful, infuriated bandits. In an irresistible wave, they swept down upon the railhead. The outposts stood their ground, but they were overwhelmed in the rush. The Field Marshal hurriedly called one and all to arms. The navvies threw down their hammers, pickaxes, shovels, and other tools, grabbed their rifles, and supported the soldiers. But there was no stemming that savage, rushing horde. The tribesmen fanatically threw themselves upon the position, and to such advantage that the commander was compelled to retire, leaving 100 dead upon the field.

Construction was arrested completely for a time. The bandits, inspired with their initial success, hung about, and at the slightest attempt at a sally, concentrated and bore down, driving the soldiers back. The situation became so critical that Kaisim Pasha determined to teach the nomads a severe lesson once and for all. He hurriedly sent home for reinforcements, together with ten battalions of artillery, which were despatched post-haste to his assistance.

When his forces were strengthened sufficiently he issued forth, and in turn caught the nomads by surprise. The soldiers, who had been chafing under the reverse they had suffered and their prolonged inability to revenge their fallen comrades, seized the opportunity and carried home the attack with spirited energy. For a time the bandits stood their ground, offering a stubborn resistance. The artillery shelled them out of their entrenchments, and the modern machine guns and magazine rifles so swept them down when they ventured into the open, that at last they broke their ranks and fled in disorder. The Turks pursued and scattered their enemy to the four winds. The Bedouin losses were tremendous, and their ranks were cut up so completely, and their organisation was so crushed, that no further concerted action was taken to dispute the advance of the line to Mecca. Occasionally, raids were made upon stations and completed sections, but such attacks were found to be attributable to independent, irresponsible units. Comparative tranquillity prevailed until the last division connecting the sacred cities with the Red Sea was taken in hand, and then one day the tribesmen made another raid, wiping out the whole of the constructional forces.

When the line was commenced, H. Meissner Pasha, the enterprising German engineer selected to carry out the scheme, was given simply the two terminals of the line – Damascus and Mecca – roughly 1,000 miles apart, and instructed to connect them by rail as best he could. It is to Meissner Pasha, therefore, that the full credit of carrying the line to success must be extended, for upon his shoulders fell the brunt of the work. He had to plot its path, had to be at the railhead to evolve a solution for a problem as it arose, and had to force his way through, over, or around obstacles as they confronted him. In this task he displayed considerable ingenuity and resource, while he appeared to be possessed of tireless energy. The handling of huge corps of men of varying nationalities – Turks, Montenegrins, Greeks, Cretans, Bedouins, and so on – was no simple matter in itself, but he possessed the happy faculty of infusing all who worked under him with his own enthusiasm and ambition to get the line completed in the shortest possible time. In addition to these duties of an essentially technical character, he had to attend to every want of his workmen. Every drop of water, every ounce of food, of stores, provisions, fuel and so forth had to be hauled over enormous distances, and in the depths of the desert the work of maintaining these supplies became stupendous. Owing to his splendid organisation, however, his most advanced outposts never once ran short of any of the necessaries of life.

The monumental features of Meissner Pasha's constructional ingenuity, however, are illustrated in the remarkable series of tunnels, bridges, loops and windings by which the railway is carried through the Yarmuk Valley in Palestine between the Jordan and Deraa, and the negotiation of the escarpment south of Ma'an, where the line, after climbing the plateau to a height of 3,700 feet above sea level, drops suddenly into a yawning ravine.

Damascus was selected as the starting point for the railway, and the gauge of the line extending northwards from this terminus was adopted. Consequently, when the various intermediate links in the railway chain of northern Asia Minor are connected up, it will be possible to run from Constantinople to the sacred cities without change of carriage. The route selected by the engineer is practically the shortest possible between the two opposite points, and runs roughly parallel to the famous centuries-old caravan route.

It was felt, however, although Damascus should be the nominal northern terminus, that it would be more advantageous from all points of view to connect the railway with the Mediterranean Sea, so as to secure an independent outlet, and one more convenient for the handling of the constructional material than Beirut. The port selected for this purpose was Haifa, on the Bay of Acre. This sea branch runs inland broadly at right angles with the main line for a distance of about 100 miles, the junction being at Deraa. In building this section, however, many abstruse problems had to be unravelled, especially in the desolate valley of the Yarmuk. Here the line runs along narrow ledges cut in the mountainside, plunges through massive shoulders, compasses precipitous bluffs, winds from one side of the gorge to the other, and crosses deep chasms by means of heavy masonry and metal bridges. In this stretch the River Jordan is crossed by a noble stone bridge of five arches – the only railway bridge across this sacred river – some distance below its flow from the Sea of Galilee.

The substantial character of this railway is a feature that most impresses the visitor. The bridges and viaducts are permanent structures wrought in stone or steel. Ample supplies of the former material were found in the mountainsides. The steel structures are of massive and lofty proportions, and for the most part are supported upon heavy masonry piers carried deeply down into the beds of the rivers, so that the possibility of the foundations being undermined by the scouring action of the swiftly rushing waters is eliminated.

In traversing Palestine, the railway follows practically a straight line from Deraa to Ma'an, some 250 miles to the south, and runs roughly parallel to the River Jordan, which is some miles to the west, while on the east stretches the vast Stoney Plain to the valleys of the Tigris and Euphrates. Taken on the whole, these 250 miles were completed very rapidly, as there were no adverse physical difficulties to be overcome.

It was after leaving Ma'an to penetrate the wild and but little-known Hedjaz Peninsula that the engineer's bitterest struggle for mastery over Nature began. It was as if the mythical Genii of the Lamp, resenting the unlocking of the door to their kingdom, combined in their efforts to baffle the railway engineer. Owing to the rugged character of the country the changes in level are frequent and heavy, varying from 200 or 300 feet below, to nearly 4,000 feet above, the level of the Red Sea. There are few main lines in any part of the world that rise and fall so extensively and continuously.

Fortunately, in forcing the band of steel through this wild country, the engineer was able to proceed where he liked. It is simply a vast, silent waste of sand, with the rocks and mountains jutting their heads to the sky as the island eyries of the sea fowl rise from the sea. A deviation of a few hundred feet to the east or west of the air-line to avoid a saucer-like depression, with its heavy gradients, was quite immaterial. Yet even with these advantages it was not possible always to avoid sharp curves and counter curves, heavy embankments, or the blasting of deep cuttings through large clumps of rocks.

The engineer carried his line south of Ma'an steadily upwards along the longitudinal ridge of a plateau, until at last he gained an altitude of 3,700 feet. Then the bank dropped sheer into a picturesque wild chasm known as Batn-el-Ghoul, or 'the Devil's Belly'.

The line reached the brink of the precipice. From there, it had to be carried to the bed of the ravine which inclines to Tabuk, the next important point on the railway. But how was that gorge to be entered? How could the lower level be gained? A detour so as to avoid the escarpment was impossible, as the ridge stretched for miles on either hand.

Meissner Pasha hurried to the railhead. He surveyed every foot of ground in the vicinity, at one time clinging tenaciously to a crag; at another being swung over a cliff by a rope; then perched on a jagged pinnacle eagerly searching for some solution of his difficulty. He traversed the pilgrim road, which is but a mere trail dropping into the valley in a series of steep steps, time after time. The railway could not be carried parallel to the caravan road – that was perfectly obvious. The line of the overland route, which had for so long been a reliable guide, now deserted him. But the engineer refused to be daunted, and after prolonged reconnoitring he finally evolved a remarkable project, which proved a highly successful solution.

As he could not carry the line straight down into the valley, he devised a kind of spiral, in which the railway effects what may be best described as a 'corkscrew' down the cliff face. From the brink of the ravine it makes a gentle fall, the line clinging to the precipices on a gallery cut for the purpose. After descending for some distance, it suddenly describes a sharp curve and winds back again. Then comes another loop and another redouble, this meandering being continued until the bed of the ravine is gained. It is an ingenious piece of work, and will rank always as one of the most prominent wonders of the railway, as well as a monument to the engineer's ingenuity.

Its realisation, however, involved a tremendous struggle. The mountainsides are scarred and carved by the elements into most fantastic shapes, with ugly, projecting spurs. These had to be blasted away, narrow ledges or shelves in the cliff-face widened or cut to carry the metallic path, deep rifts filled in or spanned, and isolated peaks, lifting their jagged nose into the sky like gaunt sentinels, avoided.

This ravine is a striking and curious specimen of the handiwork of Nature. There is not a vestige of vegetation, and all life is extinct. The masses of rock, turned into grotesque shapes by the lathe of Nature, stand out sharply and boldly defined against the skyline, owing to the clearness of the atmosphere. They have a peculiar beauty, their weird charm being accentuated by the vivid contrasting colourings of the various geological strata standing out in distinct lines. Looking down from the brink of the gorge, in the glare of the noonday sun or the soft light of the sunrise or sunset, the floor of the valley resembles a huge Persian carpet, with its intense multitudinous hues.

There is a sudden change from this natural Oriental splendour of Nature after the ravine is left, for the railway passes over a dreary, sweltering plain until Tabuk, the half-way house between Damascus and Mecca, is gained. Then comes another steady climb through similar country until the summit level of the whole line is gained – 3,750 feet above sea level, which point also records the high water mark of the difficulties that had to be overcome.

The 587th mile-post at Medina Saleh indicates the most southerly point to which the infidel is permitted to travel over this railway. Even Meissner Pasha and his staff of engineers who were not in the ranks of the Faithful did not proceed farther towards Mecca. It was felt that Mahommedans, and Mahommedans alone, should have the glory of carrying the metals into the Sacred City. It was also feared that the presence of infidels in the vicinity of the scene of the Prophet's nativity, despite their mission, possibly might inflame religious prejudices. Consequently, Meissner Pasha handed over the reins to his first lieutenant, Muktar Bey, the accomplished Turkish engineer who had assisted him loyally in the operations up to this point. Similarly, all but Mahommedan workmen were withdrawn from the railhead. The Ottoman engineer, fired with his former chief's enthusiasm and energy, pushed forward at tip-top pressure, and the blast of the railway whistle was heard among the mosques and palms of the Sacred City for the first time early in August, 1908.

The railway is up-to-date in every respect. The carriages are of the corridor type, and the pilgrim who has suffered the rigours of the wearisome overland journey can appreciate the luxury, ease and comfort of the Pullman car. The locomotives are also powerful creations of the engine builder's craft. Owing to the difficulties attending the supply of water and fuel along the line, the engines are equipped with abnormal facilities in this direction, the largest and most powerful types carrying 4,000 gallons of water. The stations are substantial in character, being built of stone, so as to offer defiance to Arabs, who cannot stifle the desire to raid now and again. At Damascus extensive works, covering an area of 13,000 square feet, have been laid down for carrying out repairs to engines and rolling stock, the workshops being fitted with the most up-to-date time- and labour-saving machinery.

When Medina was brought into touch with Damascus, and the widespread advantages presented by the railway became appreciated, it was decided to push the line to Mecca, 300 miles distant. Muktar Bey was detailed to control these operations, and, establishing a subsidiary base at Medina, he proceeded with the extension without delay. Unfortunately, on this final division the native tribes broke into hostility once more, and resumed their brigand tactics with renewed courage. On one occasion they completely overwhelmed the constructional camp, massacred all the workmen, and delayed construction until troops could be brought up to force their withdrawal to a safe distance.

Considering the magnitude of this scheme, its completion for about £3,000,000 ($15,000,000), or approximately £3,000 ($15,000) per mile, is strikingly cheap. This low cost, however, is explicable from the fact that the Turkish military played a very important part in its construction, as many as 5,000 soldiers being concentrated on the task at one time. The masonry work, steel bridges and general earthworks were undertaken by labour recruited from all parts, only one bridge and one heavy cutting being built by the troops, who for the most part were occupied in applying the finishing touches to the permanent way and plate laying.

CHAPTER 10

The Highest Line in the World

While Europe offers the most graphic illustrations of the engineer's skill and ingenuity in overcoming rugged mountains by tunnelling through their bases, one must go to South America to discover the extraordinary methods he has adopted to negotiate similar obstructions by traversing their lofty crests. It seems somewhat strange, at first sight, that the 'land of tomorrow should have been the scene of such demonstrations of genius, but when the incalculable mineral wealth buried in the Andes is recalled, much of this surprise disappears.

The majority of the great mountain chains of the world appear puny in comparison with the mighty serrated backbone of the southern half of the American continent, which runs from the equator southwards to tumble abruptly into the sea at Cape Horn, Mont Blanc and other famous hoary European monarchs are insignificant beside Aconcagua and many other snow-clad peaks beetling to the skies in its vicinity. The Cordilleras present a compressed phalanx of pinnacles running in a fairly straight, even, and narrow line. As the equator is approached, the needle points taper to bluntly rounded and rolling heads, but the general conformation is the same. The result is that the slopes are very steep, and to carry a railway through the mass entails tortuous winding among the cones, with steep gradients and tunnels through massive obstructions of rock. The cliffs of the Andes are probably unequalled in mountain topography for steepness and height, the flanks in places dropping down plumb for several thousand feet.

There is another peculiar characteristic which severely taxes the skill of the engineer. The range thrusts itself skywards very closely to the Pacific seaboard, so that the climb commences directly the coast is left, and the maximum heights have to be gained within comparatively short distances. For instance, in the case of the Oroya line, which is the railway wonder of the world, the traveller landing at Callao, in order to reach Oroya, 138 miles inland, has to toil 15,865 feet towards the clouds in the course of 107 miles – one of the highest points at which the piston of a railway engine throbs.

This South American line is not an ordinary mountain railway: it is an audacious marvel of engineering science. Nor does it merely offer facilities for sight-seeing among the impressive Cordilleras, but acts as a traffic highway between the coast and the mines on the high inland plateau.

As might be supposed, the difficulties which the engineers had to break down were numerous and stupendous. Moreover, the work was extremely costly. In the case of the Oroya road it averaged about £60,000, or $300,000, per mile, and altogether £8,500,000 ($42,500,000) were sunk in the enterprise – more than the total cost of the St Gotthard railway, with its famous tunnel and 172 miles of track.

The first attempt to subjugate this range by the iron road was made in the sixties by a daring Philadelphia engineer, Henry Meiggs. His idea was ambitious in the extreme. He proposed to start from Callao, lift the metals over the crests of the mountains, drop down the other side on to the highlands, and to push across the plateau until he gained a point on the mighty Amazon which could be reached by steamer from the Atlantic. By this means the Pacific seaports of South America would be brought into closer touch with the markets of the Old World, avoiding the protracted and hazardous journey round Cape Horn. That the idea was never carried to success was one of the sorry tricks of Fate. Internecine strife and wars with neighbouring states sapped the financial strength of Peru to such an extent that there was not enough money to complete this grand scheme. Possibly someday the steel thread will be picked up again at Oroya and forced to its original objective.

For the first 107 miles this railway makes a continual ascent; there is not a single foot of downhill in the whole distance. Work was commenced in 1870, and was pushed forward so energetically that in the course of twelve months Meiggs had completed 20 miles of the line, and had the earthworks well advanced as far as Chosica, some 33 miles out of Callao. In order to ease his task as much as possible, the engineer decided to follow the Rimac River into the mountains. But as the innermost recesses of the Cordilleras are gained, the river narrows considerably, until it plunges merely through a slender defile, the walls of the peaks dropping down precipitously into the water. The result was that the engineer found it very difficult to find a natural lane for his metals, so he had to hew and blast galleries, to swing first from one bank to the other, in order to seize the slightest foothold.

He had plunged 47 miles into the mountains and had gained an altitude of about 1 mile, when he was brought to a dead stop. The mountain along which he had crawled laboriously broke off abruptly. Further advance was impossible. To have cut a tunnel would have been a herculean task, and as the mountain wall dropped straight down below, and towered to a dizzy height above him, he found himself in a quandary. A few feet immediately above him, however, he espied a ledge running parallel with that on which he had laid his track. He resolved to gain that upper gallery, but the crucial question was, how?

Then he hit upon a brilliant idea. It was something new and untried in railway engineering, but as he had already tested all existing methods to gain the point at which he now stood, there was no alternative but to devise new ways and means of overcoming perplexing situations as they arose, despite the apparent novelty of the solutions. He resolved to lift the track from the lower to the upper ledge by a 'V-switch'.

The embankment on the outside of the track at the point he had gained was levelled off, and a small turntable was erected. From the latter, two short lines were laid down at an angle to the track in the form of a widely opened 'V', with the turntable at the apex. The main line cuts across the top of the 'V', forming a triangle, and continues a short distance beyond. The manner in which the train is lifted from the one level to the other is as follows. The engine pulls it up the lower line on to the section crossing the top of the V, and in such a way as to be between its two angular limbs. The engine is uncoupled, and runs down one leg of the V on to the turntable, which is then swung round until the engine faces the other arm of the V, up which it passes until it gains the main line. It is now at the rear of the train which it was pulling a few minutes before. The engine is coupled up, and the train is pushed backwards until it is over the switch connecting with the upper level. It then proceeds forward in the usual manner. In reality it makes a zigzag course up the mountainside.

This ingenious means of overcoming such a difficulty was tried first at San Bartholomé, and proved so very economical and simple a solution of a grave difficulty that it was freely introduced by the inventor whenever similar conditions were encountered. True, the process of uncoupling and recoupling the engine occasions a little delay, but the switch was cheaper and quite as effective as a loop, even if the latter could have been built, for it was found possible to lay the turntable between two tiers of metals on a gradient not exceeding 1 in 25. Altogether there are twenty-two of these switches on the system. The majority of them are of the simple type as we have described above, but in some cases there is a double zigzag when the difference in level was extreme, and did not permit of the connecting bank line being raised at an easy grade. The adoption of the 'Meiggs V-switch', as it is popularly called, saved the engineer thousands of pounds.

In one case the switch is set in a very precarious situation, for the climbing line winds along a perilous ledge blasted out of the solid flank of the peak, and the traveller's heart thumps every time the train lurches as he looks down upon the curling river far, far below on the one, and the mountain wall combing some 2,000 feet above him on the other, hand. The Oroya line has been described as a railway of sensations, and it is an apt description. During the process of 'V-ing' a train, the voyager has ample opportunity to contemplate his peculiar situation at leisure.

'Highly ingenious and simple', was the verdict of the railway world when they realised Meiggs' handiwork. 'But what is going to happen if a descending train runs away at one of these switches? Will it make a bee-line for the bottom of the canyon through the air, or pile up against the dead-stop?'

Meiggs, however, did not anticipate trains running amok in this manner, but he guarded against any such contingency, because brakes sometimes will fail to act on a descending grade. Consequently, at the end of each line in a V-switch he provided a substantial bank of earth. This was a fortunate precaution. Some years ago a train, in proceeding from the upper to the lower level, did run away on the falling bank. It crashed into the solid embankment at the dead-end, and came to a stop in an ungainly, heterogeneous mass of twisted ironwork and splintered wood. Nobody was hurt, the debris was removed, and the runaway engine was recovered, overhauled, replaced in service, and is running today, little the worse for its misadventure.

Owing to the peaks of the Cordilleras being separated from one another by yawning ravines, extensive bridging became imperative. Some are short, insignificant spans; others are lofty, spidery structures, which were completed at the expenditure of many human lives from disease and accident. As a matter of fact, the railway earned an unsavoury reputation owing to the high mortality that attended its realisation.

The Verrugas Bridge was the greatest offender in this respect. It was the greatest undertaking of its type on the line. It is 575 feet in length, and cleaves the air 225 feet above the bed of the ravine. There are bigger and loftier bridges in other parts of the world, but few have been so troublesome to erect. At the time it was undertaken, it was the most remarkable structure of its kind and by the time it was completed £12,600, or $63,000, had been expended. It lies at an altitude of 5,839 feet, and was carried on three masonry piers, the centre and main support being built up from the bed of the gorge. This pier measured 50 feet square at the base, and was of solid masonry, thus forming a substantial plinth for the slender iron superstructure.

All the component parts of this bridge had to be kept within certain limits of dimension and weight, to enable them to be hauled up from the coast and set in position on the site. Large gangs of workmen were crowded upon the work, because, until this bridge was set in position, material could not be transported to the other side of the gorge for the continuation of the grade.

But the task was dogged by ill-luck. Work was in full swing, when a mysterious and malignant disease broke out. So furiously did it rage that the men were swept off like flies. There was no means of checking its ravages. It became known far and wide as the 'Verrugas fever'. It resisted diagnosis and treatment, but there was no denying its deadliness. As a result, labour gave the district a wide berth. It struck down natives and white men indiscriminately. Just how many men succumbed to the attacks of this epidemic probably never will be known. Men contracted the malady, died, and were buried all within the space of a few hours after reaching the site; indeed, it is chronicled that one man fell a victim after crossing the bridge only once.

This mysterious and terrible scourge threatened to stop the whole enterprise, though Meiggs spared no effort and money to bring about its completion. The most attractive inducements were held out to workmen to come up and risk their lives, but only the more adventurous, fascinated by the high wages, dared to face death in an uncanny form. It was mainly through the efforts of such happy-go-lucky spirits that the gorge was spanned ultimately. Meiggs himself appeared to bear a charmed life, for he haunted the fated gorge day and night. But the awful experience seriously undermined his health, his constitution was wrecked, and he was changed into an old man.

Still he clung tenaciously to his enterprise. The gorge crossed, he found himself among the wildest fastnesses of the Andes. The mountains became steeper, the intervening gulches deeper and more difficult to cross. Landslides were of such frequent occurrence that they might well have struck terror into his heart. Yet he fought his way forward. Blasting became heavier and heavier, wide sweeping curves more frequent, the ascent steeper and steeper, and tunnelling through projecting spurs more frequent.

In these upper reaches the trains play a gigantic game of hide-and-seek, darting in and out among the labyrinth of tunnels. In a distance of 50 miles he had to drive his path through no less than fifty-seven of these obstructions, while altogether there are sixty-five tunnels in the 138 miles of the railway's length. The line doubles and redoubles upon itself in the most bewildering manner in order to gain points on the mountain-sides. In the course of 11 miles between Matucana and Tamboraque, this scaling by means of the zigzag was exceedingly heavy. Standing at the latter station and looking down, one can see tier after tier of the gleaming metals, until they are lost to sight far below.

5 miles beyond Tamboraque, another remarkable achievement had to be accomplished. The line tunnels a peak, to emerge upon the brink of a drop into the river below as straight as a brick wall. On the opposite side is another towering pinnacle. To span the gulf, a heavy bridge was necessary. It is called Infiernillo Bridge, and never was a name more fittingly bestowed. Its erection by false-work or scaffolding was out of the question, as in this region not a tree exists. It had to be built out from the sides, the men being suspended in cradles and loops dangling from ropes attached to brackets driven into the solid rock above. The builders found swinging the tools from such crazy footholds to be perilous in the extreme, but there were no other means by which the bridge could be erected. It is a frail link between two dark yawning mouths in opposite towering crests, and the traveller as he rattles across scarcely can quell a shudder.

So energetically did Meiggs pursue his self-appointed task that in six years he had carried the line 88½ miles into the Andes, and had gained an altitude of 12,215½ feet. All the men that he could possibly procure were pressed into service; at one time the railway gave employment to 8,000 labourers. The amount of blasting necessary to prepare the roadbed for this single line of standard track was enormous, something like 500,000 pounds of explosives being used every month. The strain inseparable from such an enterprise told its tale at last upon the bold engineer, whose iron constitution could not withstand the anxieties and worries of the Verrugas fever, and the exposure to a rarefied atmosphere, without receiving an indelible mark. The first signs of a complete breakdown appeared as the railway was approaching Chicla, and when this point was gained in 1877 he succumbed.

The removal of the guiding spirit brought the whole undertaking to a stop. Meiggs had completed two-thirds of the undertaking, and had broken the back of the difficulties. For fourteen years not another foot of line was graded. At last the Peruvian Corporation of London, which had taken over the railway, settled a contract for its completion with William   Thorndike, who also hailed from Philadelphia.

The new engineer carried the line a further 3,450 feet above the sea, following the surveys of Meiggs, and then became confronted with his greatest obstacle – the piercing of the summit crest. Thorndike had to hew his way through the bosom of a pinnacle for over 3,855 feet at an altitude at which such work never had been attempted before. The trying character of the situation was augmented by the rarity of the atmosphere, and the fact that he had to force his way through the region of the terrible mountain sickness, with a low prevailing temperature such as is encountered in the region of eternal snow and ice. Such conditions retarded the boring of the Galera tunnel, as it is called, more than the stern resistance of the rock. The workmen invariably fell victims to the sickness, though the undertaking was not accompanied with the heavy mortality that characterised the building of the Verrugas Bridge far below. Mountain drilling, blasting, excavating and the removal of the heavy spoil proved exacting and fatiguing, and a man could work only for a few hours at a stretch. By skilful organisation and careful husbanding of his forces, however, the engineer succeeded in forcing the metal track through the mountain at record speed.

The Galera tunnel is the crowning point of a magnificent achievement. In the centre you stand on the Great Divide of the South Americas, nearly 16,000 feet above the ocean. When a bucket of water is upset, one half of the liquid runs eastward towards the Atlantic, while the other flows westward to the Pacific. Oroya is 31½ miles distant from the eastern portal of the tunnel on the great inland plateau of the continent, and only a little less than 3,500 feet below it. On this section, construction was very rapid, as there were no untoward difficulties to be overcome.

About the same time as the Oroya railway was commenced, another great line was undertaken some miles to the south. In this instance, the port of Mollendo was the Pacific terminus, the inland objective being Puno, on the shores of Lake Titicaca, that remarkable inland sea nestling among the crests of the Alps some 14,660 feet above the Pacific. The total length of this line is 332 miles, and it divides with the Antofagasta railway to the south the traffic between La Paz and the seaboard. Though it does not compare with the Oroya or Central railway of Peru as an engineering achievement, yet it possesses certain individual characteristics, the tumbled mountain country experienced farther north giving way to open expanses of bleak, dismal desert.

This line in its ascent of the Andes skirts the base of that most majestic of mountains, the smoking El Misti, whose snow-topped crater rises like a grim sentinel far above the other visible points of the mountain chain. Here the mountains are nobler and wider apart, so that one can grasp better their magnificent proportions, while their flanks are not so scarred, and there is an absence of those fearsome, yawning ravines. In making the ascent, the line describes broad sweeping curves to avoid projecting peaks, and throughout the whole distance there is a notable relief from the zigzags and switches so frequent on the sister line.

On this road, however, the moving sand threatened to be an implacable enemy. In the higher altitudes, the sand is piled up into quaint little cones ranging from 10 to 20 feet in height, and from the distance their incalculable number and regular lines present the appearance of a vast army of men grimed and covered with the dust, which illusion becomes emphasised when they are seen moving across the plains in a steady, rhythmic manner under the influence of the wind. When the railway was built, it was anticipated that elaborate precautions would be requisite to keep the track clear of this encumbrance, but it was found that the trains could plough their way through the mass with little difficulty.

In the higher levels, the sand gives way to a country of broken rock – a land absolutely void of any sign of life. This monotonous waste continues to the shores of the lake, where the dank water-grass and limpid water offer a welcome relief to the aridity experienced for so many hours. This railway was constructed with remarkable rapidity for the Land of Paradoxes, as the whole 332 miles were built in five years, and thus the isolated waters of Titicaca were linked with the Pacific by the iron road.

Not only was this railway much cheaper to construct than the Central or Oroya line, but its maintenance is not so harassing as the former system. The engineers of the Oroya road are engaged in a constant war with the elements. The landslide is the most relentless foe that has to be combated. A big slip on a slope, an avalanche of snow, huge boulders, and miscellaneous debris rattle down the mountainsides with terrific fury, blotting out the track and sweeping bridges away in their mad career.

The Verrugas Bridge was dogged by ill-fortune after its completion, for in one of these visitations the whole structure was demolished through the main central pier being knocked away. The tangled and twisted metal was left rusting in the ravine, for the bridge-builders' art had advanced considerably since the old bridge was designed, and in reconstruction it was found possible to span the gorge on the cantilever principle without the central support. All the other bridges on the railway are being rebuilt gradually on these lines, and when this task is completed the engineer will have one danger the less to fear – the collapse of the slender link of communication across the gulches.

One can enjoy a most exhilarating experience on this railway. This is the descent from Galera tunnel to Callao on a small hand-car. It is a glorious coast downhill for no less than 107 miles. One rushes down inclines, swings round curves, threads tunnels, and whisks across gorges at the exhilarating speed of 45 miles an hour. It is a unique sensation – one of the many marvels associated with this remarkable railway, which is not merely a striking evidence of civilisation, but a perpetual monument to the 7,000 lives devoted to its construction.

CHAPTER 11

Cecil Rhodes' Dream – From the Cape to Cairo (Northwards from Cape Town)

Few phrases have become so familiar to the ear as from the 'Cape to Cairo'. It is a phrase that has made history, though perhaps not so rapidly as its creator anticipated. When Cecil Rhodes first cast his eyes from north to south, and conceived the idea of binding the two extreme points of the African continent together, there is no indication that he experienced great difficulty in finding a title for his undertaking. There was Cairo in the north, and Cape Town in the south. He aspired to join the two by rail. Consequently, from the 'Cape to Cairo' was obvious. Probably the alliteration caught his fancy, and conveyed his complete thought so forcibly in three words, and in a manner that could not fail to impress the public, that it inadvertently flew through his mind.

When the materialisation of this vision commenced, the general knowledge of the interior of the continent had not been widened very appreciably since the travels of Livingstone and Stanley. It was 'Dark' in the truest sense of the word, and conquest either by the mysteries of peace or the arts of war was necessary before the steel rail could be driven either northward or southward. However, it was determined to carry the idea to fulfilment – the question of the penetration of the hostile country could be taken in hand when the railway was within measurable distance of its borders so far as Rhodes was concerned, while in the north the English government had decided to settle terms with the Mahdi.

There was one benefit accruing from the empire builder's dream – he gave the engineers of South Africa elbow-room in which to display their ability within certain limits. It might be said that he inaugurated a new railway construction policy so far as South Africa was concerned. The railway builders had an extensive territory to cover, and they appeared to cherish the belief that the best means by which this conquest could be achieved was upon the most expensive lines possible. Thus, for instance, the railway network in Natal, the Transvaal and Orange Free State cost about £15,000, or $75,000, per mile, and those of Cape Colony about £10,000, or $50,000, per mile – sums out of all proportion to the railway needs of the time, and which served to commit the countries to a heavy capital outlay and interest charges. When Cecil Rhodes outlined his project he set himself to a limit of about £5,000, or $25,000, per mile.

Such a line was a pioneer road in the fullest sense of the word, but it would suffice to meet the demands of the country for many years to come, and could be improved as circumstances demanded. The time will come, doubtless, when a standard-gauge road from the waters of the Mediterranean to the southern end of the continent will become imperative, but a few decades will have to pass before the line of 3 feet 6 inches gauge becomes inadequate.

The Cape to Cairo is remarkable in many respects: in fact, it might be described as a string of record-breaking feats in railway engineering. In the first place, it was the first trans-continental road ever to be driven longitudinally through a continent – the coast-to-coast lines in other parts of the world cut across the continent from east to west. When completed, it will be the longest continuous trunk iron road ever built. In its length are comprised both the highest and longest bridges in Africa, in its realisation the highest speed in track-laying has been recorded, and it has been driven steadily forward under conditions such as never have attended the realisation of any comparative project – war, plague and famine.

When the scheme was commenced, the railways of the southern colony had penetrated 647 miles up country from Cape Town to the diamond mines at Kimberley. Consequently, Diamondopolis was selected as the starting point for the northward advance, through the hinterland now known as Rhodesia. The first rail out of Kimberley was laid in 1889, and by October, 1894, it had gained Mafeking, 223 miles beyond.

While this part of the work was under way, the colonisation of Mashonaland had proceeded, and had progressed so favourably that the railway's advance became an urgent necessity, especially as the Matabele under Lobengula were giving signs of trouble, and it was essential that the latter should be subdued. So in 1896 the dull, grey snake resumed its tortuous crawl to the north. Further trouble was experienced at this juncture, and retarded operations to a material degree. The deadly rinderpest broke out, and swept off the settlers' cattle like flies. Transport was paralysed, and the engineers were called upon to perform a superhuman task to pour supplies and material forward. As animals were unavailable, traction engines had to be brought up-country to ply between the point where the locomotive stopped and the construction camps strung out ahead.

However, Rhodes decided that the rails must reach Buluwayo before the end of 1897. Seeing that 492 miles divided the railhead from the latter point, this was no mean order, but Messrs Pauling & Co., the contractors, promised that his wishes should be fulfilled. Large forces of natives were whipped up, and by superhuman effort the apparently impossible was achieved, the 492 miles of metals being laid in 500 working days.

As might be supposed from the low cost of the line (£4,500, or $22,500, per mile), the engineering work was not of an elaborate character. Rapidity of construction, combined with low cost, were the two governing considerations that had to be borne in mind, for the sooner railway transportation was provided, the earlier settlement would take place. The terms governing construction demanded that the line should be of such a character as 'would be capable of effectually conveying traffic at a speed of 12 miles an hour on completion, and that grades and curves were not to be sharper and heavier than generally prevailed upon a line of this gauge.' Ballasting was only to be used on such portions of the line as was necessary to ensure the safe running of the trains during the rainy season.

In laying the road very little regard was paid to formation, and wherever the surface of the ground was even it was followed, the steel sleepers being packed with the minimum of ballast to give a moderately smooth running top. The shallower streams and rivers were not bridged, but the railway was carried across over a ford. If the water rose above the track a few inches, a thrilling spectacle was offered when a train crossed. It would creep carefully down the bank and crash full tilt into the water, sending up a column of spray which entirely obliterated the front of the engine from view. Later, the line was overhauled and brought into conformity with modern requirements, bridges of steel being introduced to span all obstructions of this character. Timber was impossible, owing to the ravages of white ants, though creosoted wood was found to offer a substitute for the metal for a short period, and was adopted sparingly.

Buluwayo lies at an altitude of 4,400 feet, and from this point the line falls steadily until it gains the Gwaai River, 1,200 feet lower. Crossing this waterway, the line makes a straight cut across the flat, sandy and wooded country for 71 miles as the crow flies, to enter the Wankie coalfield.

In this district the surface run could not be continued, and consequently heavy cuttings and embankments had to be carried out over a distance of 59 miles.

Beyond the Wankie coal territory, and 282 miles north of Buluwayo, the line ran up against the first serious physical difficulty, but one of such proportions as to make amends on the part of Nature for the easiness of the grading hitherto. This was the Victoria Falls on the Zambesi River, and the location of the line compelled a crossing of this magnificent waterway just below the cataract, where the water, after tumbling over the ledge, is forced through a deep, narrow gorge 400 feet in depth.

The situation demanded the consummation of some monumental piece of work. The Niagara gorge had been bridged, but the task of spanning that chasm was mere child's play in comparison with that confronting the engineers below the Victoria Falls. The cliffs are sheer practically, for the canyon through which the water rushes for some 20 miles is but a fissure in the earth's crust.

The surveys, which were carried out with great difficulty, showed that the break would have to be bridged in a single span about 500 feet in length from brink to brink, with the rails over 420 feet above low water. For purposes of comparison, it may be mentioned that, although the structure of the same type thrown across the Niagara gorge to carry the Grand Trunk railway from Canadian to American soil has a main span 50 feet wider, while the bridge itself is almost twice as long, the rails are laid only a little more than half the height above the water – 226, as compared with 420 feet.

One early difficulty was the establishment of communication with the opposite bank, to avoid a long detour of about 10 miles in order to cross the river. First, in order to bring the camps perched on each cliff closer together, a telephone wire was thrown across the ravine. This frail connection was completed in an ingenious manner. A thin string was tied to the stick of a rocket which was fired across the gorge. The opposite party secured the stick and end of the stout twine, and by its means hauled across a thicker length of string, which in turn was followed by one still stouter, with which the telephone wire was hauled across. In this way, the opposite camps were brought as closely into touch with one another as if they were side by side on the same bank. Previously, attempts had been made to fly a string across by means of a kite, but the upward rush of eddying air from the vortex of the water caused the kite to become the sport of the wind and to play sorry pranks, without gaining the opposite bank. The complete success of the rocket caused a similar cycle of operations to be repeated, only in this case, instead of hauling a telephone wire across the gorge, a marked wire was handled, the idea being to measure accurately the width of the gap, a spring balance being introduced at one end to compute the extent of the 'sag' of the wire for the purposes of calculations.

The result of these investigations served to countercheck the surveys, which were found to be strikingly correct, and the design of the bridge was taken in hand immediately by Mr G. A. Hobson.

Actual construction was commenced without delay, the task being undertaken by the Cleveland Engineering & Bridge Building Company of Darlington, who, by the successful completion of this task, once more emphasised the predominance of the British bridge-building engineer. The main span is a graceful curve of steel springing from the cliff-face on either side, the latter being excavated for the purpose of securing the foundations. As construction was possible only on the cantilever principle from either side, facilities had to be provided for the transportation of material as it was brought up by the railway, from the south to the opposite cliff, and for this purpose an overhead cableway was slung across the gorge. This vehicle of transport was employed not only for the building of the bridge, but also for the conveyance of other necessities for the railway, as the latter was pushed ahead from the north bank while the bridge was being erected. Workmen were also slung across the gorge by this means in a little cage, and occasionally visitors who were anxious to experience a new sensation made the trip at a cost of 10s, or $2.50, per head.

One feature of the undertaking was the extreme care taken to protect the workmen from certain death in the river below if they slipped from their precarious perches in mid-air. A heavy, strong net was slung across the chasm beneath the actual working point to catch 'boys and tools should they inadvertently drop'. The two ribs of steel were pushed outwards from either bank, and finally met in the centre, where the final bolts, securing first the two sections of the bottom members together, were slipped in without any untoward incident. At the point where the maze of steel springs from the cliff-face the bridge measures 105 feet from the bottom to the top member, while at the crown of the arch the depth is 15 feet. The width at the rail level is 30 feet, while the bottom curved steel ribs, at the point where they are secured to the rock, are about 54 feet apart.

Notwithstanding the difficulties attending the erection of such a massive bridge upon such a site, construction was carried out so rapidly that the first train was enabled to cross the structure within about eighteen months of work being commenced. The celerity with which this task was completed was striking, bearing in mind that native labour was employed for the most part, under the supervision of English foremen and engineers.

At the time it was built it ranked as the loftiest bridge in the world, but it has been deposed since from that premier position by the wonderful Fades viaduct which spans the Sioule River in the French province of Puy de Dôme, where the train crosses the water at a height of 434½ feet.

By the time the Victoria Bridge was able to permit trains to pass from bank to bank, the end of steel had been hurried towards Kalomo, the capital of North-Western Rhodesia, 1,733 miles from Cape Town. On this section, another remarkable record was established. The engineer, Sir Charles Metcalfe, Bart., was in the field on one of his periodical visits, and was accompanied by an interested French engineer, who had built railways in French West Africa. The latter was greatly interested in the progress of the Cape to Cairo line, but observing the methods of the native workmen, ventured to ask how many miles of track could be laid per day.

'Well, what do you think we can lay?' asked Sir Charles Metcalfe.

'Oh, I don't think you can lay more than half-a-mile. That seems to me a fair estimate,' remarked the French railway builder.

The English engineer had a brief conversation with his lieutenant in charge of the rail-laying operations, and the latter in a few brief words galvanised the whole of the crew into electric movement. In 20 minutes the track had advanced a quarter of a mile before the astonished French engineer's eyes. He scarcely could credit what he had seen, and left the spot with a high regard for the English engineer's organisation and methods of handling the natives to be able to wrest such a spurt at a moment's notice.

This incident impressed Sir Charles Metcalfe, and, after a chat with the English overseers, foremen and engineers surveying the placing of the 33-feet lengths of steel upon the ground, it was decided to make an experiment just to see what could be accomplished under an emergency with native labour. The black men were marshalled up for a full day's work, and were urged to let themselves go, the desire of establishing a record being communicated to the more enterprising spirits. The natives love a contest, and they girdled into the work with astonishing zest. They did not seem to tire, and they spurned the heat. The result was that when the 10 hours' labour was completed for the day the steel had crept forward – no less than 5¾ miles – a world record. Yet everything proceeded so smoothly that it appeared, from the stranger's point of view, as if work were being carried out at the normal rate of a mile a day.

This result, with native labour, was remarkable. The engineers in charge of the wonderful track-layer used in America point to the speed with which the metals can be laid with its aid. Yet it comes somewhat as a shock to their pride to learn that their best performances of 3 to 4½ miles a day can be exceeded by unskilled black men, with no tools whatever.

From Kalomo, the engineers pushed north-eastwards to Broken Hill, 280 miles beyond. In this stretch, however, another obstacle had to be overcome. This was the Kafue River, which is the most important tributary to the Zambesi River, and indeed forms one leg of this great waterway. The great width of the Kafue River, 1,300 feet, called for a lengthy bridge. Although the waters are shallow during the dry season, the average depth being 9 feet, in the wet season, however, the river rises to 17 feet or so. It is a comparatively sluggish waterway, the speed of the current being about 3 miles an hour.

Mr. G. A. Hobson was responsible for the design of this bridge also, and he decided that a light structure, divided into thirteen spans each of 100 feet, would meet the case. The actual construction was carried out by Mr. A. L. Lawley as supervising engineer on behalf of the railway builders. The bridge is of the lattice girder type, the trains running through the bridge. The whole of the steelwork was prepared in England, shipped to Cape Town, and then transported 2,000 miles up country by railway to a yard improvised on the river bank, where the ribs of steel were assembled to form the spans. In addition, a pontoon, likewise of steel, was sent up in pieces in a similar manner, assembled on the bank and launched. This pontoon was utilised to float the spans into position, and also to convey material across the river to enable the grade to be pushed ahead while the waterway was being spanned. The pontoon was pulled from bank to bank by means of an endless wire cable, driven by a steam engine.

The spans are supported on masonry piers, each 18 feet wide by 8 feet thick. Mr Lawley found the riverbed to be composed of rock and gravel, which gave a first-class foundation, and favoured the expeditious erection of the piers. Consequently he concluded, if the piers were pushed forward at low water, it would be possible to set the steelwork directly the river once more gained flood-level, and arrangements to this end were carried out. Timber coffer-dams were built around the sites for the piers, and by the aid of pumps the interior was kept clear of water to permit the workmen to achieve their stone-setting task within under the most favourable conditions.

While the piers were progressing, other gangs of natives were hard at work in the improvised shipyard riveting the steelwork together. Each span measured 100 feet long, 14 feet in width, 20 feet in height, and weighed 56 tons. The pontoon itself measured 95 feet long by 45 feet wide.

Work continued so favourably that by the time the masonry work on the piers was completed the spans had been assembled, and all was ready for transhipping them from the yard to their respective positions on the piers. Novel means for transporting the weighty and bulky masses of steel were adopted. The pontoon was brought endwise against the river bank and made fast. A length of railway track was laid from end to end along the deck of the pontoon, and was brought against the ends of another short track running down the river bank, thereby making a continuous length of railway line. As the completed spans were ranged side by side in the yard at right angles to the river, they had to be hauled sideways for some distance. Rails were laid under each end of the spans at right angles to the railway and were well greased so as to become a kind of 'ways' such as are used to launch a vessel. Gangs of natives tugged at the span to haul it broadside until it rested on the railway line, which also was lubricated. Then two locomotives were brought up to the rear end of the span, and by sheer steam force pushed it down the bank railway on to the pontoon, where it rested fairly and squarely, and overhanging equally each end of the pontoon, which was 5 feet shorter than the span.

The pontoon was then released from its moorings and was hauled out into the stream by means of the endless cable, until it came centrally between the two piers on which the span was to be placed. From each pier, a hawser was passed to stanchions on either end of the pontoon. The endless cable was slackened, and the pontoon, with its novel cargo, was permitted to drift slowly downstream towards the space between the two piers, being guided in its course by manipulation of one or the other of the two hawsers. In this manner the craft was steered delicately into position and was made fast. The actual transference of the span from the pontoon to the masonry bed was carried out by hydraulic jacks, which lifted the whole mass of steel. When the jacks were released, the ends of the span rested firmly on the two piers. By hauling on to the endless cable, the pontoon now was drawn clear of the bridge to return for another load.

This novel method proved so completely successful that the thirteen spans were transferred from the bank and set in position within the short space of eight days! – half the time the engineer had computed as being requisite for the operation. The whole undertaking was accomplished in record time, bearing in mind the peculiar conditions prevailing in the heart of Africa, and the use of native labour; for, from the time the first move towards the erection of the piers was made, to the setting of the last span, only five months elapsed. The total cost of this mass of steel, weighing 728 tons and stretching in an unbroken line for 1,300 feet across the river, was £50,000, or $250,000.

When Broken Hill was gained, 2,013 miles from Cape Town, construction was brought to a stop. The mastermind had passed away some time before, and the colleague who had assisted Rhodes when other financial magnates turned a deaf ear to the project, had also joined the great majority. By the time Broken Hill was gained, £8,000,000 (or $40,000,000) had been sunk in the enterprise. For months the stack of 2,000 tons of steel for the resumption northwards remained untouched, through lack of funds, though Mr Alfred Beit had left £1,500,000 (or $7,500,000) towards the continuation of the work. Then the mineral wealth around Katanga in the Congo Free

State, which was under exploitation, demanded transportation to the coast. Accordingly, the line was pushed on to the border of the adjacent country. Rhodes' objective was Kituta, at the southern end of Lake Tanganyika, 450 miles north of Broken Hill, which point marks the limit of British sway in South Africa, a distance of about 2,700 miles by rail from Cape Town.

When Rhodes' vision presented the railway stretching in an unbroken thread from north to south, the knowledge of the country lying between the Zambesi and the Nile was somewhat scanty. As the scheme progressed it became known that Lake Tanganyika was hemmed in by precipitous mountains, where railway building would soar to an enormous figure per mile. On the other hand, the lake is a splendid sheet of water, offering excellent navigation throughout its length of 400 miles. Therefore, there should be no reason why the example of the Russian government, in regard to the use of ferry steamers on Lake Baikal, should not be emulated to transport trains intact from Kituta at the southern, to Usamburu at the northern, end of Lake Tanganyika.

90 miles north of Usamburu is Lake Kivu, and the dividing neck of land offers no great difficulties to construction beyond a gradual rise of 2,000 feet. Reaching Lake Kivu, which is also surrounded by lofty ridges, the railway would once more take to the water for some 60 miles. Continuing northwards, there is another stretch of rising country to be crossed, where the track would be lifted to its greatest height, or summit level, between Cape Town and Cairo, to gain the head of Lake Edward, which is 75 miles in length. Owing to the flat character of the country around this sheet of water lending itself to cheap railway construction, probably it would be found preferable to keep to the land, especially as the country is healthy, thickly populated, and offers great promise of becoming wealthy under commercial development.

But the line, after leaving Lake Kivu, has to pass through Belgian territory, and as this location is inevitable unless it were decided to swing somewhat to the east to pass through German East Africa, an easier route has been offered through the Congo. The railway has been taken from Broken Hill to Elizabethville. The Belgian authorities are anxious that it should be extended from that point to Bukana on the Congo River. Boats could be used between this point and Congolo, where communication by rail would extend to Kindu, to be followed by another stretch of river as far as Ponthierville. The existing railway to Stanleyville would then be pressed into service, and from the last-named point the line would debouch to the north-east to gain the Albert Nyanza, and there link up with the railway that has been driven southwards from Cairo.

CHAPTER 12

Cecil Rhodes' Dream – From the Cape to Cairo (Southwards from Cairo)

While the southern arm of the great line has been pushed on energetically northwards from Cape Town, the northern limb has descended almost as rapidly down the Valley of the Nile to the great interior, so that the heart of the continent is being eaten into spiritedly from both ends. The two branches have been built under totally different auspices. Whereas the southern section was carried out by private enterprise, the northern division is the work of government effort.

In the north, the railway has made history rapidly, and its conquest has been of a complex character. It placed a unique weapon in the hands of the government, and it wrested a vast track of Africa, aggregating 950,000 square miles, from barbarity and religious fanaticism in the form of Mahdism.

Owing to the impoverished condition of the country, the railway in Egypt has experienced a very chequered career. It commenced its pacific invasion promisingly enough, but it was found to be a highly expensive settling influence for a land whose coffers had been depleted almost to the extent of emptiness.

The early lines, when laid, were neglected, and consequently fell into a sorry condition. The majority of people who had regard for their lives and limbs preferred other vehicles of transport. Everything in connection with the iron road was conducted in a haphazard manner. Trains started without any one having the faintest idea as to where they were going or what time they would reach some destination. Lord Cromer relates that when he first went to the Land of the Pharaohs all the lines were single track. No staff or block system of any kind was in vogue, and there were no signals. A train started from a station on the off-chance that another train was not coming in the opposite direction. Needless to say, as he tersely remarks, 'he avoided those lines'.

In the Sudan matters were even worse. The Khedive embarked upon a laudable enterprise when he decided to carry the iron highway southwards from Wadi Haifa. Khartoum was the objective, but nearly half a century passed before the iron horse appeared at the latter point, for when the Khedive's railway got so far as Sarras, 33 miles south, funds became exhausted and the scheme was abandoned. Another attempt was made in 1885/6, on the occasion of the Nile Expedition, to resuscitate the scheme, and by great effort another 53 miles were tacked on from Sarras to Akasha. The life of the second section was short, for when the British forces retired, the track was pulled up by the dervishes, and Sarras reverted to its position as the southern terminus.

When Lord Kitchener was deputed to crush the Mahdi for once and for all, he found 1,200 miles of sandy desert between him in the north and the seat of the fanatic's power. The river was available for the movement of troops as in the previous campaign, but the latter had emphasised the disadvantages of that highway through hostile territory. He foresaw that only one agency would enable him to accomplish the desired end, and that was the railway. Among his officers was a Canadian engineer, Sir Percy Girouard, and he discussed the possibility of building a line across the desert to span that inhospitable gap in order to pour his troops against the Mahdi forces. The engineer realised the situation and undertook to carry the line southwards from Wadi Haifa.

The task was commenced in 1896, and railway construction was pushed forward with such spirited energy that Kerma, at the head of the cataracts, was gained in a short time. No great engineering difficulties were offered because the desert is tolerably level, and the sand provided a good foundation for the steel sleepers, or ties, with the minimum of ballasting. The greater question was to maintain the steady supply of requisite material southwards from Alexandria. Yet an average speed of 2 miles per day was maintained, the rails being laid for the most part by natives, assisted by both British and Egyptians, under the military engineers.

The objective was Abu Hamed, where the Nile describes a big elbow, and at that time this point was in the hands of the enemy. Its capture, however, by the Anglo-Egyptian troops resulted in a speeding up in constructional work on the advancing railway, and the 80 miles of line into this town were laid in about two months. Clinging to the east bank of the river, it was driven southwards to Atbara, where a halt was called, and where the headquarters were established for the Omdurman campaign. Curiously enough, although the railway has reached the capital of the Sudan, Atbara has not yet lost its importance from the railway point of view, being the administration centre for the whole Sudan government railway system.

At this place the Nile is swelled by the waters of the Atbara River, which flows in from the east. While the campaign was in progress, communication between the opposite banks was maintained by means of a wooden bridge. As the river, however, is tempestuous when in flood, during which period it rises to a high level, a more permanent structure was demanded for the iron horse. The width of the waterway called for the erection of over 1,000 feet of steel bridging. When the advance of the railhead was determined, it was decided to rush the railway across the river before it once more rose in flood. Tenders were invited, only to be received with dismay, because it was found that the structure required was of such an elaborate character that no English firm would undertake to complete it within two years.

This upset official calculations severely, and accordingly fresh tenders for a simpler type of bridge were called. The task was thrown open to the world, and celerity of construction was the primordial condition. The British firms re-tendered, but to their disgust they were beaten hopelessly both in regard to the cost of the structure and the time in which it could be erected by the American engineers. The result was that the contract went to a Philadelphia firm. Five weeks after the receipt of the order, the steelwork left New York, and within a further few weeks communication across the river was provided by seven spans of steel, each 147 feet long, resting on cast-iron cylinders.

The most remarkable feature about this contract was the public outcry that ensued. British methods were held up in comparison with American hustle, much to the disparity of the former. British builders were assailed as lethargic, wedded to obsolete methods, and consequently had suffered the penalty of such conservatism by being beaten in a most hollow manner. The same critics, however, failed to shriek so loudly in acclamation a year later in appreciation of a British firm which accomplished a feat which even startled the Americans. This was in connection with a bridge of five spans, each 105 feet long, which was turned out of a Midland shop to replace the structure which had been destroyed by the Boers across the Tugela River in Natal. Both British and American engineers were invited to tender, and the American firms, despite their wonderful organisation, hustling methods, and their remarkable facilities for accomplishing quick work, were dismayed to find that they had been beaten by their British rivals as hollow as the latter had been vanquished some months before. The successful firm rolled 100 tons of steel, had it inspected, tested and passed by the Natal Government engineer in 8 hours. It had undertaken to deliver the first span within six weeks of the receipt of the order – as a matter of fact, it was completed within nineteen days. The Americans themselves admitted that the British performance was wonderful, and that complete revenge had been taken for the Atbara contract.

As the railway pushed its way towards Khartoum, the ranks of the labourers were swelled by large numbers of dervishes, who had grown disheartened at the result of their resistance to the British advance on the northern borders of the Mahdi's stronghold, had realised the impotency of their efforts, and consequently had decided to throw in their lot on the railway. The increased labour enabled the work to be prosecuted even more energetically, though a certain amount of time was lost in drilling this raw material into the mysteries of wielding the white man's tools.

When the dervishes first saw the locomotive they marvelled. Steam was beyond their comprehension. They believed stoutly that the engine's boiler was packed with animals, and when the driver blew his whistle many fled in complete terror. To them, the agonising shriek of the animal on wheels was more terrifying than the hail of lead from a Maxim gun. Indeed, it is reported that one chief, when he saw a locomotive puffing along slowly and laboriously with its load of cars, went so far as to assail the British officers for their callous cruelty in making so small a beast pull such a heavy, long load!

The Atbara Bridge, after fulfilling all requirements for eleven years, had to be reconstructed. It was not found strong enough to withstand the heavy loads of today, for on the Sudan railway weights, lengths and speeds of trains have increased strikingly during a decade. When overhaul became imperative, an English firm secured the commission to rebuild the American structure, and today there is nothing left of the bridge which provoked such acrimonious discussion at the time of its erection. Owing to the elaborate nature of the building operations, a temporary bridge had to be thrown across the river to carry the railway traffic.

When Khartoum was gained another pause was unavoidable owing to the necessity to cross the Blue Nile in order to continue southwards to Sennar. This arm of the great Egyptian river is fickle, for in times of flood it rushes along at some 11 miles an hour. The contract for carrying the railway to the opposite bank was secured by the firm entrusted with the overhauling of the Atbara Bridge, and it is a noble work of its class. The river being navigable, facilities had to be provided to permit vessels to pass up and down. This end was met by introducing an electrically operated rolling lift span working like a drawbridge. To enable railway construction to be carried on while the river was being negotiated, a temporary timber bridge was thrown across the waterway. While this was in progress, the power of the waters rushing through this tributary when in flood was emphasised in no uncertain manner. A considerable quantity of scaffolding intended for the support of the steel bridge during erection was torn up and hurried downstream.

When Sennar was gained, a deviation directly eastward was made in order to gain El Obeid, which is the centre of the gum trade, one of the most prosperous and expanding industries of the Upper Sudan. Owing to its more convenient situation on the main river, Omdurman always has been the market for this article, the supplies being conveyed across country by camel caravan. It is generally considered that now El Obeid has been gained by the railway that the decadence of Omdurman is certain, but though this may be inevitable up to a point, the town is always bound to command a certain position of importance inasmuch as it is the centre of a considerable pilgrim traffic.

On the advance to El Obeid, the bridging of the White Nile had to be carried out, and here again British engineering triumphed, for the contract was awarded to the builders of the Khartoum Bridge. This firm, with these two Nile bridges and the Victoria Bridge across the Zambesi, may be said to have imprinted their name indelibly in Africa in connection with bridge engineering. The point of crossing is Goz Abu Guma, and owing to the erratic character of the White Nile its design occupied considerable deliberation. This river is sluggish both in time of flood and in the dry season. Indeed, it might be described as a huge ditch. When low, the water occupies a channel about 1,500 feet in width, but in the wet season it sprawls across the country for a matter of 3 miles or so.

It was decided, however, that the bridging of the normal channel would suffice, the line being carried over the part subject to periodical inundation upon well-built embankments. The over-water structure comprises nine steel spans each 146 feet in length, and one swing-bridge span 245½ feet in length to permit navigation up- and down-river, because the Sudan Development & Exploration Company maintain a steamship service between Khartoum and Gondoroko, the head of navigation on the Nile, 1,081 miles from Gordon's city. The spans are 6 feet above the level of High Nile, and are supported on masonry piers sunk in steel caissons, or cylinders, under the agency of compressed air, to a depth ranging between 30 and 50 feet below low water.

Although the iron link has stretched beyond Khartoum to the south, Alexandria and Cairo are not in through railway communication with the capital of Sudan, 1,480 miles away. The Egyptian railways have their most southerly outpost at Shellal, just below Assuan, which is about 24 hours' journey from the Mediterranean seaboard by the White de Luxe express. The terminal of the Sudan system is at Haifa, just south of the border between the two countries. The river Nile constitutes the artery of communication between these two railway points, the steamer occupying about 40 hours. This break in the iron chain possesses distinct drawbacks, the most serious of which is transhipment between steamer and railway. The expense and inconvenience of this route, with its breaking bulk, reacted severely upon the Upper Sudan and accordingly the latter government decided to secure an independent outlet to the coast. There was only one means of accomplishing this end, and that was to strike eastwards across country to gain the Red Sea.

This was not a simple enterprise, especially under conditions which did not lend themselves to the expenditure of a large sum of money. An easy graded line was imperative, and the surveyors had to search diligently for such a route, because a range of hills breaks away from the northern edge of the Abyssinian plateau, to run parallel with the coastline of the Red Sea to the Gulf of Suez. Investigations along the coast resulted in Suakin, 305 miles distant from Atbara, being selected as the sea terminus, and the surveyors succeeded in securing a location giving no banks heavier than 1 per cent, and with no curves of a sharper radius than 1,155 feet.

As the constructional engineers were confronted with some heavy work shortly after leaving Suakin, in order to overcome the coast range, building was commenced from both ends of the line simultaneously. This procedure, however, did not prove entirely satisfactory, owing to the cost and delay in bringing material down from Alexandria to Atbara, so when the engineers at the Suakin end had subjugated their obstacle and the material could be landed easily from vessels and hurried to the railhead, operations were suspended from Atbara. The remoteness of Suakin, however, produced individual handicaps, the greatest of which was in regard to labour. The scattered natives were given employment, but as they were unfamiliar with the tools and methods they did not prove successful, and large numbers of Egyptians who had toiled on the other lines were shipped to the Red Sea terminus. They were housed in military tents, and a stranger happening suddenly upon a railway camp might have been pardoned for labouring under the impression that he had alighted upon an invading army under canvas, because the tents were pitched in such regular rows as to indicate military occupation.

The mountains occasioned some little anxiety owing to the damage that was caused by washouts due to the heavy rain, but these were soon mastered. This abundance of water later on gave place to extreme scarcity, for when the constructional forces had penetrated the heart of the desert, this commodity was found only with great difficulty and by infinite labour.

Above: Views of the St Gotthard Railway, Switzerland, taken between *c.* 1890 and 1900. (LoC)

Previous page: View of Göschenen and the Damma Glacier, St Gotthard Railway, Switzerland, *c.* 1890–1900. (LoC)

Göschenen, general view of the St Gotthard Railway, Switzerland, taken between *c.* 1890 and 1900. (LoC)

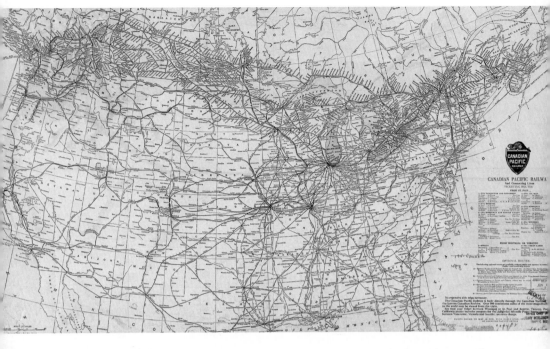

Map of the Canadian Pacific Railway and connecting lines by Canadian Pacific Railway Company, 1912. (LoC)

The first safety switch on the Canadian Pacific Railway, Wapta Canyon, British Columbia. (LoC)

EXECUTED BY THE AMERICAN OLEOGRAPH CO. 83, 85 & 87 FIFTH AVE. CHICAGO.

Undated postcard of the Canadian Southern Railway. (LoC)

Opposite above: Great tubular bridge, Grand Trunk Railway, Montreal, Canada, 1856. (LoC)

Opposite below: Map covering the south-western states extending from Chicago to the Pacific coast, showing the new transcontinental route of the Atlantic & Pacific Railroad and its connections. (LoC)

GREAT TUBULAR BRIDGE, GRAND TRUNK RAILWAY, MONTREAL, CANADA.

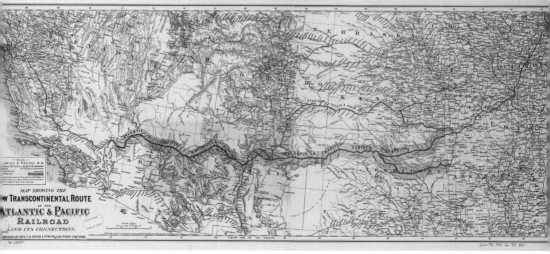

MAP SHOWING THE
W TRANSCONTINENTAL ROUTE
OF THE
ATLANTIC & PACIFIC
RAILROAD
AND ITS CONNECTIONS.

Central Pacific Transcontinental Railroad, Tunnel No. 25, Applegate, California, a segment of the western half of the transcontinental railway. (LoC)

Promontory route railroad trestles, trestle 790C, 11 miles west of Corrine, Box Elder County, Utah. (LoC)

Two women and a man viewed sitting on the front of the engine of a logging train that is loaded with huge logs crossing a trestle in the Cascade Mountains, Ore, *c.* 1906. (LoC)

Scenes on the line of the Denver and Rio Grande Railway, 'Garden of the Gods' in Colorado Springs, *c.* 1870–1886. (LoC)

18591—President Driving the Last Spike on Alaskan Railway at Tanana River.

Keystone View Company
Manufacturers COPYRIGHTED MADE IN U.S.A. Publishers

Meadville, Pa., New York, N.Y., Portland, Oregon, London, Eng., Sydney, Aus.

18575—President Harding's Special on Alaskan Railway, the President in Engine Cab.

Cape to Cairo railway bridge over the gorge of the Zambesi River, Africa, *c.* 1880 and 1930. (LoC)

Opposite above: President Warren Harding driving the last spike on Alaskan Railway at Tanana River, 19 September 1923. (LoC)

Opposite below: A front view of President Harding's Special on the Alaskan Railway, with the President in the engine cab, *c.* 1923. (LoC)

Photograph of construction work on the Eastern Siberian Railway near Khabarovsk, taken by William Henry Jackson (1843–1942), *c.* 1895. (LoC)

Opposite above: View of Cairo railway station, *c.* 1900–1920. (LoC)

Opposite below: Ariel view of Peking railway station, 1912. (LoC)

Photograph of a Chinese railway station, taken by William Henry Jackson (1843–1942) in 1895. (LoC)

Despite these drawbacks, however, the 305 miles of line were laid and opened for traffic within the short space of fourteen months, which testifies to the high standard of the constructional organisation and the energy with which the undertaking was pushed forward. The significance of this branch from the Nile to the sea was revealed instantly, but unfortunately it was realised that the terminal point on the coast left much to be desired. Further investigation revealed a better site for a harbour 50 miles north of Suakin, and this point, now known as Port Sudan, is the terminus of the line, the harbour being equipped with modern facilities for handling traffic between ship and railway. The new port is connected by rail with Suakin, however, which is being retained as an outlet.

The railway will creep gradually southwards along the bank of the White Nile in all probability, but in the meantime the river will constitute the artery of communication. The waterway abounds with sand bars and other obstructions to navigation which provide very little depth of water in some places, but the Sudan Development & Exploration Company have met this situation by the utilisation of steamers which draw extremely little water and are able to pass through the shallows in perfect safety. The Sudan government also maintains a steamship connection between Khartoum and Gondoroko. This water link is about 1,000 miles in length, and the round trip occupies about twenty-three days. A few years ago, the possibility of being able to proceed so far up the river under steam was feared to be impracticable, owing to the dense masses of floating tangled masses of vegetation, or 'sudd', which blocked the river. But this has been broken up and a clear fairway is maintained. As a result, Uganda now has an outlet to the Mediterranean which can be developed considerably as the northern extremities of that country are opened up.

Unfortunately, beyond Gondoroko the river cannot be used, because for about 100 miles – from Rejaf to Dufile – there is a continuous chain of rapids. These two points therefore will be connected by railway probably. When Dufile is gained, the river can be used once more so far as Lake Albert Nyanza, where the line from Cape Town would be met, although there is a belief that the Sudan government intends to push the railway to a far more southern point.

It will be seen that although Rhodes' great scheme was for a continuous steel road from north to south, this idea has had to be modified in order to meet unexpected conditions, which at the time of the railway's inception were not apparent. In reality, one will travel from the 'Cape to Cairo' over a combined rail and water route longitudinally through the continent. At the present moment one can cover the whole journey by rail and water, except for a distance of about 600 miles, and this gap is being closed rapidly. As the settlement of the country along the line of communication becomes effected, and the heavy drawbacks incidental to transhipment become more and more emphasised, there is no doubt but that the water route will be superseded gradually by the railway, so that in time the original idea will be consummated, and trains will pass right through from the Cape to Cairo over a continuous path of steel some 6,000 miles in length.

CHAPTER 13

Gridironing the Rocky Mountains

If one consults a map of the North American continent, it will be observed that the rolling plains, stretching westwards from the shores of the Great Lakes, are fringed on their western edge by a massive, tumbled and lofty wall – the Rocky Mountains. This is the backbone of the New World, stretching from Mexico in the south to far-away Alaska in the north, on the slopes of which rise the mighty rivers to flow east and west to swell the waters of the Atlantic and the Pacific. Their successful conquest by the iron horse on its way from coast to coast contributes some of the most thrilling incidents to railway history.

If the map is consulted closely, it will be seen that this range assumes its most broken character in the State of Colorado. Here Nature became unduly playful in her process of moulding, and left her handiwork in a badly finished condition. Beetling peaks crowned with eternal snow are separated by yawning ravines – mere cracks in the earth's crust – where the walls are ½ mile or more in height, and through which rivers foam and tear along tumultuously. Yet the dishevelled mass of rock is intersected by steel threads which comprise the respective systems of the famous Denver and Rio Grande, and the Chicago and North-Western railways, the latter being known popularly as the 'Moffatt' road, after its originator.

To grasp some idea of the exceptionally mountainous character of Colorado, a comparison with Switzerland may not be amiss. This state is so vast that the playground of Europe might be stowed within its borders six times over, and then there would be several hundred square miles to spare. Among the Alps, the number of peaks which jut their pinnacles over 13,000 feet towards the clouds may be counted on the fingers of the hands; on the other hand, in Colorado there are no less than 120 such monarchs, thirty-five of which rise to an altitude of more than 14,000 feet. In other words, there are compressed about ten times as many lofty summits in the 193,925 square miles comprising this state as are to be found scattered throughout the whole of Europe.

The village having the loftiest situation in Europe is Avers Platz in Switzerland, which nestles among the Swiss Alps at an altitude of 7,500 feet above the sea, while the highest inhabited point is the Hospice of St Bernard, at 8,200 feet. Contrast either of these with the flourishing town of Leadville, whose 15,000 inhabitants move, live and have their being at an elevation of 10,200 feet above the ocean. Yet this does not mark the uppermost limit of civilisation among these rocky fastnesses, because there are several prosperous mining camps at 13,000 feet or more.

The highest artery of traffic in Europe is the wonderful Stelvio road, which enables the Tyrol to be crossed at an altitude of 9,042 feet. This is a zigzagging highway for vehicular and pedestrian traffic. In Colorado, the Denver and Rio Grande railway crosses the backbone of the continent through three passes, each over 10,000 feet above the sea, while at Ibex the station platform is at an altitude of 11,522 feet. On the Moffatt road, in order to overcome the range, the metals are lifted still higher at the Rollins Pass – to 11,600 feet, or nearly 2¼ miles above the Atlantic.

Incalculable mineral wealth lies, buried in the hearts of these peaks, and it was the discovery of this rich storehouse of Nature that led to the opening up of the country by the iron road. There was a gold rush in 1859, followed by a silver strike, and Leadville was one of the first towns to spring into existence in the wild scramble for sudden wealth. Though this locality nestles in the range some 70 miles distant, the pioneer miners braved perils and privations untold to gain this hub, and the town sprang up as if by magic. But the isolation of the situation, and the lack of transportation facilities soon became manifest to an acute degree. Every ounce of material had to be carried to and fro from the outside world by wagon, mule-pack, or manual effort, involving an exhausting, slow and expensive journey through deep gulches and over broken mountain trails.

The cry for a railway was raised, but it was difficult to find pockets sufficiently deep or capitalists so plucky as to finance such an undertaking. However, constant agitation maintained for years bore its fruit. A small company was formed, and the Pueblo and Arkansas railway was commenced. The promoters shrank somewhat from the project, fearing that construction would run into such a prohibitive figure as to bring ruination in its wake, so they resolved to spend the minimum amount of money on the scheme. To this end, they decided to follow the easiest route available, and suggested the course of the Arkansas River from Pueblo into the mountains, and then at a convenient point to strike into the range to make the ascent to Leadville. Yet those half-hearted financiers had visionary dreams, and were spurred on by a certain amount of ambition. They did not intend to come to a dead-end at Leadville, but once they had gained the higher level, to push right across the Continental Divide to Salt Lake City, and thence to the Pacific Coast. Some thirty years passed by, however, before the latter part of the project was completed.

Though the course along the Arkansas River was selected as the cheapest and easiest route, the preliminary surveys sufficed to demonstrate that even that location would offer difficulties out of the ordinary. The 9½-mile run through the Royal Gorge, one of the natural wonders of North America, promised a heavy struggle. This defile at places is 2,700 feet deep, and the walls rise up so perpendicularly as to defy the slightest foothold to a chamois, let alone a railway. The bottom of the gulch was found to be occupied by the turbulent waters of the river, which in times of flood lapped the base of the mountain wall on either side, though at normal level a narrow shelf was exposed at the foot of one cliff.

The engineer responsible for the building of the line, Mr. A. A. Robinson, decided to seize that shelf. It could be made just wide enough to carry the line and no more, while it could be raised sufficiently to escape the ravages of high water. The river was kept within bounds by a wall of rough, heavy masonry carried to a point well above the highest watermark, and on this the track was laid upon a bed of rock ballast hewn from the mountain slopes.

However, when the eastern portal of the ravine was gained, a serious obstacle loomed up. The ledge which the engineer had pressed into service up to this point disappeared abruptly into the water, and did not reappear for some distance beyond. The two sides of the canyon, towering up to nearly 3,000 feet, come closer together, leaving only a narrow vent barely 30 feet wide. As a result, the river channel is constricted, and the water thunders over the boulders through the wedge-shaped defile with the velocity of a cataract.

The engineer was brought to a full stop. How was he to span that gap? The character of the torrent absolutely prevented any possibility of sinking piers in the waterway to carry a bridge across the breach in the ledge. Nor could a path be carved out of the mountainside to carry the line around the obstacle, because the maximum gradient had been attained already on either approach to the gap.

As Mr Robinson related, the first solution that occurred to his mind was to tunnel the shoulder, and thus to avoid the difficulty completely. But the bogey of expense stood in his way. There were scarcely sufficient funds available to build a surface line, and, under these circumstances, tunnelling was quite out of the question. Moreover, it would have required considerable time, and the public was clamouring wildly for the completion of the line.

He haunted the gorge for days, and spent much midnight oil in the hope of discovering some simple, quick and cheap means of solving the problem. But the quest seemed hopeless. Then suddenly it occurred to him that, as he could not hope for assistance from the riverbed, why not force the walls of the ravine to his aid? In short, why not sling a bridge from the cliff faces on either hand?

Thereupon he evolved a plan to throw heavy iron girders in the manner of rafters across the gulch, to anchor their ends to the solid rock, and then to suspend the bridge carrying the metals from this structure in such a way that one side abutted against the wall. The more he pondered, the more convinced he became of its practicability, despite the fact that it was something entirely new to railway engineering.

Being intimately acquainted with the late Mr C. Shaler Smith, who at that time was one of the foremost consulting bridge engineers in the country, he communicated his plans to him. The consulting engineer was interested, and arranged to accompany the designer to the site to judge the feasibility of the scheme at first hand, and after acquainting himself with the prevailing conditions. As a result of this investigation, Mr Smith concurred in the method of spanning the gap, and there and then the arrangements for carrying out the work were commenced.

It was realised that the task was somewhat delicate, and Mr Robinson accordingly entrusted the preliminary operations to Mr J. O. Osgood, who was appointed Division Engineer on this section of the railway. Mr Osgood carried out the whole of the surveys for his chief personally to facilitate the accurate design and details of the whole structure.

The surveyor related to me that when he first entered the canyon no one had ever traversed the gorge at that point, except on the ice, for the simple reason that it was impassable. Nor could one get across by clambering along the rock face where the line was to go, as it was too steep. The situation was first reconnoitred from all practicable points of vantage. Then, in order to complete the essential preliminary work, he caused a narrow pathway – nothing more than a ledge, from 12 to 18 inches in width – to be hewn in the cliff above the site, from which he made his final surveys.

The cutting of this path in itself was a tedious task, and gave some idea of the labour that would have been involved in tunnelling the rock. This narrow shelf, however, proved of inestimable value in handling the heavy overhead members of metal and setting them into position. The dimensions and weight of the latter had to be kept as low as possible to facilitate handling under the peculiarly cramped conditions. Actual erection was exciting and hazardous. The men had to be lowered by ropes and had to ply their tools while swinging in mid-air or when clinging to precarious footholds. However, the cumbrous overhead pieces were successfully set in position, the ends were bolted to brackets sunk deeply into the cliff faces, and from these girders the track floor was suspended, the ends resting on the solid edges of the rocky ledge, while one side was bedded against the wall.

Such is the story, as communicated to me by the engineers, of the origin and erection of what ranks as an unparalleled novelty in engineering. The 'Hanging Bridge' was built in the Royal Gorge nearly thirty years ago, and although the first structure has been replaced by one of larger and heavier dimensions to accommodate weightier trains, the fundamental principle is precisely the same as conceived by Mr Robinson.

Yet the 'Hanging Bridge' is but one of many engineering wonders to be found on this railway. Go where one will over its 1,800 miles of track among the Rockies, and some striking and daring work confronts one at every turn. Here the railway threads its way through a winding abyss, there it passes over the crown of a towering peak, or toils laboriously up the side of a sheering cliff. No two miles are alike. In all it traverses five yawning canyons, each possessing a strange individuality, and crosses the mountain backbone by which the continent is split in twain by three different passes. Level sections are practically unknown. It is one continuous up-hill pull up the one, with a long coast down-hill with steam shut off, on the other, side – a switchback upon a stupendous scale.

Let us take the route over the Marshall Pass. At Poncha, on the Atlantic side, the line is at an altitude of 7,480 feet. The summit is 6 miles away by the iron road, but in that distance the train has to climb steadily at 211 feet to the mile over an extremely meandering route. The mountains become wilder and more broken as the summit is approached. The engineer took advantage of every natural facility that opened up to him. In turn, the rail crawls along ledges cut in the mountain flanks, over lofty embankments, spidery trestles, doubling and redoubling upon itself in the most amazing manner. The occasional presence of snow-sheds draws attention to the fact that the metals are above the snow-line, and the many terrible dangers to which the track is exposed from avalanches and landslides.

Two huge engines are required to negotiate the heavy ascent, and at last, when the top is attained, the train is 276 feet in excess of 2 miles above the

Atlantic on the eastern, and the Pacific on the western side, respectively. The tortuous path of the iron road is revealed below in a graphic manner. It may be seen in no less than four separate terraces, rising in steps one above the other, the lowest being almost invisible, connected by huge loops, until it finally winds away and is lost in the dim haze of the horizon. The descent is a replica of the ascent – the same gradient prevailing, *viz.* 211 feet to the mile. No steam power whatever is needed to drive the train. It is travel by mere gravitation alone, held in check by the powerful air-brakes.

Yet the railway is crossing the Divide at another point some miles to the north rises twice to an altitude exceeding 10,000 feet. This is on the extension of the original line from Pueblo to Leadville, where, after leaving the mining town, there is a tedious climb to Fremont Pass, where the track is laid 11,330 feet above the sea. A few miles to one side the line attains its maximum altitude, with 11,522 feet, at Ibex station, on a short branch road. After negotiating the Pass there is a sharp descent to Leadville junction, where another locomotive has to be hitched on to haul the train up a bank, rising 211 feet to the mile, to the summit of Tennessee Pass, lying at 10,240 feet, the highest point being gained in a tunnel, 1 mile in length, bored through the mountain peak.

On the southern section of the system, the line passes through some of the wildest and most impressive country it is possible to conceive, and time after time the constructional engineer was puzzled sorely as to the best route for the road. It overcomes the Divide through the Cumbres Pass. On the uphill pull the railway skirts a towering mountain spur, making a detour of 4 miles to circumvent the obstacle, and then bursts suddenly into a strange country. Strange monoliths rear up on all sides their fantastically wind- and weather-carved sides, glistening weirdly in the sunlight. The line swings round these grotesque evidences of Nature's handiwork in a sharp bend known appropriately as 'Phantom Curve', and then disappears into the depths of the Toltec tunnel, which is carved through solid granitic rock for some 600 feet. The peculiarity of this work is that it is carried through the crest, and not the base of the peak, for the opposite portal of the tunnel stands on the brink of a precipice which drops plumb ¼ mile into the valley.

This gulf is spanned by a solid masonry bridge almost as wonderful as the Hanging Bridge. It recalls a swallow's nest built under the eaves of a roof, for it is thrown across the gap to the opposite mountain ledge in the form of a balcony. Sudden emergence from the inky blackness of the mountain's heart to this frail-looking link with the frowning wall opposite, and the depth of the fissure is decidedly startling. If the Eiffel Tower were planted in this gorge, it would be dwarfed into insignificance, for its topmost platform would be over 500 feet below the railway track. To throw the bridge across this rift, the men had to be slung out from derricks, manipulating their trowels from an unsteady platform – the snap of a rope, a missed footing, and certain death on the splintering crags below awaited the unlucky.

It is upon this same section that one traverses the wonderful Ophir Loop, by means of which the Divide at Dallas is negotiated. The towering Ophir Mountain stands directly in the path of the line. A detour was impossible; the mountain had to be ascended, but in so doing, the engineer imposed a fearful task upon the locomotives.

The rise is 4 per cent. In other words, for every 25 feet the train advances, it has to rise 12 inches. The line skirts the base of the mountain, describes a sharp semi-circular curve, and then runs directly backwards, the track being parallel with that a few feet below. The Stelvio road over the Alps is a wonderful zigzag climb, but it does not double and redouble more than this ascent up Ophir Mountain. Terrace after terrace of track is left below, extending through cutting, over embankment and high trestles, until the top is gained.

Though the ascent and descent of the passes are impressive, they are equalled in their daring by the winding through the rugged canyons bathed in everlasting shadows cast by the mountains. The Royal Gorge is only one out of five that are threaded. The others are equally awe-inspiring, but each has a totally different aspect. There is Animas canyon. The name of the gorge is musical – 'Rio de las animas perdidas', and trips readily off the tongue, but the Spaniards were adept in christening Nature's wonders. 'The River of Lost Souls' is melancholy, but how strikingly suitable! The whole bed of the canyon is occupied by the river. There was no convenient shelf by the water's side to carry the track. The walls rise vertically on either side, and the foam of the water as it tumbles through the gulch is scattered high on either wall. The engineer, deprived of a natural pathway, cut one for himself. And it does not cling to the river's side. It is high up on one wall, and was blasted foot by foot out of the solid rock. At one point it is 1,000 feet above the water, and the grade is necessarily steep as the riverbed rises very abruptly towards its upper end, where the line emerges but a few feet above the water.

When the pioneer engineers laid this remarkable railway, the exigencies of the present were their sole concern. As years rolled by the narrow gauge proved a handicap, so it was converted to the 4 feet 8½ inches gauge. But as there was still a considerable amount of narrow-gauge traffic, the line is adapted for both classes of working, there being three rails laid, so that it is as easily available for the narrow as the standard-gauge vehicles. Then the necessity arose for doubling the track to give an up-and-down main line through Eagle River canyon. The surveys soon convinced the engineer that it was absolutely impracticable to parallel the original line, as the earthworks along the tortuous river could not be widened to carry the second pair of metals. Consequently, they had to be laid on the opposite side of the water, at a cost of £20,000, or $100,000, per mile for 5 miles. The result is that now the river has a canal appearance, its limits being bounded on either side by solid masonry.

A few years ago, a well-known banker and prominent citizen of the city of Denver, the late David H. M. Moffatt, the Silver King, created a sensation by suggesting that the time was opportune to give the important trade centre in which he resided more direct communication with the Pacific coast. He pointed out that before setting directly westwards, one had either to travel 107 miles to the north to join the Union Pacific, or 110 miles south-east to Pueblo. Why should not this mileage be saved and the journey accelerated by following the bird's course towards Salt Lake City?

Notwithstanding the severely broken character of the Rockies, he decided to drive his railway almost in an airline. The surveyors pointed out that approximately 75 per cent, of the track could be laid along river banks threading the mountains where grades and curves could be kept tolerably easy. The greatest and costliest features of the scheme was the double toil over the Great Divide.

The mountain ramparts practically lock Denver in upon its western side, and the railway makes a direct plunge into the mass. The South Boulder canyon affords the causeway for the railway through the first clump. Certainly the gorge is well named, for its sides are ragged in the extreme, precipitous, and strewn with ugly, projecting masses of rock.

Being unhampered financially, the engineers were enjoined to carry their work out upon the most solid lines. Timber trestling across clefts on the hillside was to be avoided; the line was to be carried well above the river, and in such a manner that easy alignment was secured. This involved keeping well into the side of the mountains, only to meet obstacles in the form of massive humps of rock projecting from the slopes. They could not be blasted away – the only solution was tunnelling. Consequently, the train plays a game of hide-and-seek as it darts in and out a chain of tunnels. In the course of 13 miles there are no less than thirty tunnels through these spurs, ranging from 73 to 1,720 feet in length, and aggregating 16,000 feet in all. It was the constant recurrence of these tunnels that provoked a querulous traveller to ask why the engineers did not 'tunnel the range the same as they do in the Alps and have done with it?'

In order to fulfil the demand of the 'Silver King', heavy excavation was inevitable. The rock thus removed was put to useful account to fill crevices and rifts to avoid trestling. It was expensive construction, but at the same time it ensured an excellent permanent way – permanent in the fullest sense of the word.

When Boulder River canyon was threaded, the rise to the Continental Divide commenced. The precise point at which this should be effected demanded repeated surveying, and some time passed before the engineers found the shortest and easiest path through the range. This was by means of a tunnel through the summit. A heavy piece of work was advocated – 2½ miles in length – but as considerable time would be required for its completion, it was decided to take the metals right over the crests, with a temporary line of 28 miles, in order to proceed with the grade and to open up the country beyond, leaving the boring of the tunnel till a later date. Consequently, the track was carried through Rollins Pass, 11,600 feet above the level of the sea, through a world of perpetual snow.

To lift the line over that summit proved a tremendous task: it involved the laying out of tremendous curves and wide, sweeping loops. When built, it was quite as difficult to keep open during the winter months, when the Rockies are swept with terrific blizzards, which bury the steel highway deeply beneath hills of snow. Yet arrangements were completed to meet this emergency. A rotary snowplough, the biggest and most powerful of its type that ever had been designed, was acquired. With this huge machine the snow gangs were out from morning to night, but they kept that narrow channel of communication clear, though it was almost a hopeless task at times.

While the railway was being pushed on from the western side of the range, the boring of the tunnel was taken in hand. It was urgent, for it reduced the summit, 2,200 feet below Rollins Pass, the portals of the tunnel being 9,930 feet above the sea on either side, rising therefrom at 1 in 400 to the tunnel's centre line.

Although the tunnel takes the bulk of the traffic both summer and winter, the route over Rollins Pass has not been abandoned entirely. The excursion traffic mounts to the 11,600 feet, for from that tremendous altitude the panorama of glistening snow and glacier caps is magnificent. What such a summit means may be grasped better, perhaps, by comparison with the maximum altitudes attained on British railways. The Scottish Highlands railway rises to 1,484 feet above sea level between Dalwhinnie and Dalnaspidal, while the Great

Western climbs to 1,373 feet at Princeton, Dartmoor. Such altitudes are trivial beside the dizzy summits attained on the American continent. Yet the tunnel under the Rollins Pass brought its own benefits. By its provision, the town of Vasquez on the western slopes of the Divide was brought 25 miles nearer Denver, the distance being 81 miles by the temporary line over the Pass, and only 56 miles via the tunnel. Such reductions of distances, with easing of grades, count materially in questions of traffic nowadays.

CHAPTER 14

The Iron Horse in Australasia (I)

Probably owing to its somewhat remote geographical situation in relation to the busy centres of the northern hemisphere but a hazy, conception prevails of the great activity that has been, and still is being, maintained in regard to railway conquests in the far southern continent. Although large expanses of its territory still rank as terra incognita, the iron horse is tearing the veil from the unknown with amazing rapidity; it is fulfilling the dual role of exploring and colonising force simultaneously. Several imposing feats of engineering have been consummated in the task of wresting the interior stretches of the country from oblivion.

As is well known, the island continent is divided into five states, and each has worked out its own salvation by means of an independent railway system, though the practice has been the same in each instance. The early lines were laid through the fringe of settled territory along the coast, and some time passed before the rails ventured inland. As the agricultural, forest and mineralogical wealth of the country became known, however, and attracted large flocks of settlers, the map was rolled back by the railway in the various states. Up to the year 1870, railway expansion developed very leisurely. Then there came a sudden awakening. Railway development went forward with a tremendous rush, and this feverish expansion has been maintained steadily ever since.

The fact, however, that there was no general plan of campaign has in a certain measure produced confusion. Each state had to consider its individual purse and to calculate carefully how much it could afford in the work of railway colonisation. The result is that there is a sad lack of uniformity among the gauges. Indeed, Australia is worse in this respect today than was the United States thirty years ago. In the latter country, three gauges struggled hard for supremacy, viz. the narrow 3 feet 6 inches gauge, the standard gauge of 4 feet 8½ inches, and the wide gauge of 5 feet 6 inches. In Australia, the gauges vary from 2 feet 6 inches to 5 feet 3 inches. For instance, New South Wales is threaded entirely by the standard gauge of the world – 4 feet 8½ inches – for some 4,000 miles. Its neighbour to the south, Victoria, favours both the gauge of 5 feet 3 inches and that of 2 feet 6 inches; its western neighbour, Western Australia, has the wide gauge and the intermediate gauge of 3 feet 6 inches; Queensland adopted this gauge also. With such a variegated system, each state becomes isolated so far as through railway communication is concerned; change of carriage at the borders is inevitable. This disadvantage is experienced emphatically when it comes to the transportation of merchandise.

The locomotive made its debut in Australia in 1885, in which year the first length of railway from Sydney to Paramatta in the oldest colony was opened. From that small beginning, extension did not proceed very rapidly, for while the population of New South Wales remained small and scattered, the outlook from the financial point of view was not promising. Consequently, the network only extended over 473 miles twenty years later. Since 1875, however, the iron tentacles have grown with tremendous speed, no less than 2,995 miles of track having been laid in the course of thirty-two years.

In the early days, while money was scarce, the cost of construction had to be kept down very severely. The coast of New South Wales is hemmed in by a high mountain range, set from 20 to 70 miles back from the water's edge. This barrier forms the rim of a tableland some 200 miles in width, extending from the extreme northern to the southern border of the State, and runs roughly parallel to the shore. Consequently, it was obvious that whatever direction the railways might take to tap inland territory, the mountains had to be crossed. The state railway system is divided into three divisions, the main northern, southern and western lines respectively, and the range accordingly is crossed at three points.

The first subjugation of this rugged, frowning barrier was brought about by the urgent necessity to connect Bathurst with the coast at Sydney. Years before gold had been discovered on the highlands, a flourishing little community had sprung up and had founded a promising town. But the inhabitants felt their isolation keenly, and they petitioned the government relentlessly for railway communication. At that time, the line had gained a point known as Penrith, about 22 miles from Sydney, lying at the foot of the mountains, and heavy expensive work confronted the engineers anxious to proceed farther inland. Moreover, owing to the steepness with which the edge of the plateau rim dropped into the valley, it was realised that the metals would have to be lifted quickly to a great height. As the engineer was handicapped by financial stringency, he was compelled to resort to heroic measures.

He set to work and succeeded in reducing the costliness of the earthwork by adopting grades of 1 in 33, introducing what is known as a 'zigzag'. The track, instead of climbing the bank continuously in terraces, with curves connecting the successive tiers, makes a diagonal cut up the cliff face to a dead-end. From this joint another stretch of line cuts similarly up the flank, to terminate in another dead-end, to lead to another diagonal rise, and so on until the upper desired level is gained. Meiggs introduced a similar system when he built the Oroya railway to overcome the Andes, and in the days the 'zigzag' was carried out it was considered the only means of solving the situation with the minimum of expense. The grades on the 'zigzag' were as heavy as 1 in 30, but their introduction served to lift the track to the summit of the tableland 3,500 feet above sea level at a distance of 28 miles from the capital.

Some twenty years ago this 'Small Zigzag', as it was called to distinguish it from the similar and more imposing work of the same class on the opposite side of the range, was cut out. A direct descent was provided by driving a tunnel through the spur which the zigzag followed, and the curves were eased. The realignment cost about £50,000, or $250,000, but the interest on this capital expenditure is less than the saving in the expense of working the trains over this section.

Gaining the top of the spur, the railway continues a gentle ascent until it notches an altitude of 3,658 feet, when the descent of the western slope commences. The Lithgow valley is the objective, and the precipice tumbles down suddenly for 600 feet. To carry the line down the mountainside appeared impossible, and when the engineer-in-chief, the late Mr John Whitton, surveyed the scene, to say that he was perturbed fails to express his thoughts adequately. He could overcome the descent fairly easily if he were permitted to carry out tunnelling operations, whereby he would secure both easy grades and curves. But he was overruled. Tunnelling was considered too expensive and could not be countenanced; in fact, the whole conquest of the mountains provoked a long-drawn-out and bitter controversy.

The general attitude towards railways, and the slight knowledge concerning their construction and operation in those early days, is afforded from the engineer-in-chief's struggle with the Governor-General for permission to follow his own inclinations, which, as he pointed out, might entail heavy initial expenditure, but would pay in the long run. When the scheme was unfolded and the engineer admitted that the work, however accomplished, must prove costly, the Governor-General pointed out that a high road had been built over the mountains for pedestrian and wagon traffic. Consequently, he suggested that this channel should be used, that the lines should be laid in the middle of the road, and that the trains should be hauled by horses! The engineer had considerable difficulty, and had to resort to prolonged communications and lengthy explanations, to impress upon the official mind that the locomotive was the best means of hauling trains. He became so insistent, and persecuted his demands so relentlessly that the Governor-General, probably sick at heart over the whole thing, gave way at last to the engineer's importunities, but stipulated that the constructional cost should not exceed £20,000, or $100,000, per mile.

By imposing this financial drag, the official possibly thought that he had discomfited the engineer. But this was by no means the case. Certainly, it ruled tunnelling out of consideration as a means of overcoming difficulty, but it only served to stimulate the engineer-in-chief to something more startling. As he could not make his way from the summit to the lower level by the direct route, he decided to saw his way down the precipice. The rocky wall rose up for about 470 feet so steeply as to defy a mountain goat to secure a foothold. The surveyors had to be lowered from the top by means of ropes and chains to carry out their tasks with the transit and level to plot the path for the line. Here and there were wide, deep V-shaped rifts breaking the profile of the precipice. Massive arches in masonry were thrown across these obstructions, and a path was cut in the side of the cliff to carry the track.

The line struck along the face for about a mile, descending steadily 1 in 42 feet. It then came to a dead-end. Another mile of track with the same falling grade wound backward to terminate in a second dead-end, and lower down came another mile of descent in the reverse direction to gain the valley. It required 3 miles of line to carry the track downwards 600 feet. When one stood at the top of the 'Great Zigzag', one saw the three tiers of track sawing the slope, to disappear finally in the depths of the valley. The engine in the descent pulled the train down the top side of the serrated road to the dead-end, pushed it backwards along the second gallery to the second dead-end, and finally hauled it to enter the depression.

The 'Great Zigzag' for years stood as a striking monument to the ingenuity responsible for the work, for it is even more daring than Meiggs' famous V-switches. As time passed and the railway traffic of the state increased, the heaviness of the grades, the sharpness of the curves and the time occupied in negotiating the zigzag, reacted more and more adversely upon the economical operation of the line. Moreover, it constituted a serious menace to safety, although fortunately it never was the scene of an accident. Still, a proposal for its abolition was advanced so far back as 1885, although it was realised that heavy and costly reconstruction was the only alternative.

The proposed deviation was discussed more or less for several years, but was deferred from motives of expense. But when the traffic had gained the respectable proportions of some 2,585,000 tons in 1908, it was recognised that the inevitable could be postponed no longer. It was pointed out that if there were no zigzag, the number of goods trains using this part of the line could be cut down by over 30 per cent, since a single locomotive would be able to handle a heavier load and longer train than was possible at that time, while so far as passenger traffic was concerned, no less than 686 hours could be saved every year, and operating expenses could be reduced 50 per cent, upon this division.

Accordingly the deviation was commenced. The surveys for the new line had been prepared by Mr Henry Deane, M.INST.C.E., while engineer-in-chief for railway construction. He proposed a series of tunnels built on a gradient of 1 in 90 running through a number of spurs projecting from the main range, and although these were intercepted by gulches, the latter could be filled with the rock excavated from the tunnel borings. The line in many places hugs steep precipices where the land falls away vertically for a distance of 1,000 feet or so into the Kinambla Valley.

The task was commenced in July 1908 under the guidance of Mr James Fraser, M.INST.C.E., the engineer-in-chief for existing lines, to whom I am indebted for this information, and in a short time 1,000 men were engaged in boring the tunnels and making the deep, heavy cuts through the sandstone rock. All tunnels were attacked simultaneously, and the blasting assumed heavy proportions. In one case, a shaft was sunk practically to formation level. When completed, it was charged with about 10,000 pounds of blasting powder and 125 pounds of gelignite. It was fired electrically, and the splitting force of the explosives dislodged 35,000 tons of rock. In another case, 1,000 pounds of blasting powder were tamped home in the face of a cliff, and 10,000 tons of rock were shivered to be used for embanking purposes.

In order to rush the work through at tip-top speed, special arrangements were made to facilitate the handling of the necessary supplies and men, as well as the operation of the tools. As the new line passed 350 feet below the old line, connection between the two at this crossing was effected by means of a funicular railway with a grade of 1 in 1.87. The material was brought by rail to the upper end of this temporary line, and from a special siding was dispatched direct on to the works. A small electric generating station was set up, and wires for the transmission of current for power and lighting were strung along the route from end to end to compress the air to drive the rock drills, for the motors actuating the ventilating fans and also the water pumps.

The scheme as originally planned provided for the building of 6 miles 858 yards of new double track, which represented a saving of 22 yards upon the line that was being displaced, though the curves and grades were easier. It was estimated that the earthworks would involve the handling of 466,000 cubic yards apart from the tunnel borings. Eleven tunnels were planned, representing a total length of 2,991 yards, but during the work it was decided to cut out one tunnel as the rock was found to be shattered. Consequently, it was converted into an open cutting, the sides of which are 132 feet high. Some idea of the speed with which the task was pushed forward may be gauged from the fact that in 11 months 410,000 cubic yards of excavation were completed, miles of permanent way were laid with a single line, and 1,430 yards of the tunnelling were completed. The total cost of the work was estimated at £256,000, or $1,280,000. Its recent completion, although it relegates an imposing engineering achievement to the limbo of things that were, has resulted in the creation of another achievement equally as notable.

In building the north coast line which connects Sydney with the Queensland border, a feat of a totally different character from the zigzag was completed. This is the massive bridge, 3,000 feet in length, which carries the track across the Hawkesbury River, 36 miles distant from the capital. It is divided into seven spans, each of which measures 416 feet in length, supported on substantial masonry piers.

The erection of this structure, which still ranks as the largest work of its type in Australia, occasioned considerable difficulty, both in regard to the piers and the setting of the steelwork into position. Indeed, it is doubtful as to which section of the work provoked the greater anxiety. The difficulty with the piers was the great depth to which the engineers had to descend to secure a foundation, because in mid-stream the 40 feet of water flows over a bed of mud ranging up to 120 feet in thickness.

The only practicable means by which this essential subaqueous work could be carried out was by sinking a huge steel cylinder filled with concrete. The bottom section of this huge tub, or caisson, as it is called, was closed, and after it was completed on shore, it was towed out to the site where the pier was to be erected and sunk by the introduction of the concrete. The underside of the caisson was fitted with a knife-edge, by means of which it could cut its way through the soft soil, the driving force for this purpose being the weight of the superimposed concrete. The mud over the area representing the superficies of the cylinder bottom was removed from the inside to enable the mass to settle down. The steel shell was built up continually from the water level in rings, until a solid foundation was gained. When this was reached and deemed satisfactory, the spaces through which the spoil from below had been withdrawn were likewise filled with concrete, so that the contents of the cylinder really form a huge pillar of concrete homogeneous from end to end.

The conditions prevailing also compelled each span to be completed near the bank upon a pontoon, the steelwork being supported upon a heavy scaffolding. The pontoon was somewhat shorter than the span of steel which projected an equal distance over either end of the former. When all was ready, and when the tide was approaching its highest point, the pontoon, with its ungainly load, was towed and was warped gently between two adjacent piers, in such a way that the ends of the span were brought into their relative positions upon the masonry. The pontoon was then made fast, and the actual settling of the steelwork was left to the movement of the tide. As the river fell, carrying the pontoon with it, the span descended until in due course the ends rested on the masonry. The water still falling, the scaffolding presently dropped below the steelwork, leaving the latter clear in position. Finally, when the tide had fallen still more, the pontoon was cast off and drawn away, leaving the two piers connected by the steel.

Such methods demand extreme care, unerring judgement, and a readiness to meet any emergency on the part of the engineers. The American bridge builders who carried out this undertaking had several exciting incidents. The most thrilling and anxious was when one of the pontoons got out of control with its precious freight and became stranded on the bank, where it had to remain in a dangerous listing condition until the tide rose again, to enable it to be floated off and towed to its destination.

In comparison with the New South Wales railways, the lines of the other states lack outstanding features, yet their work has been attended with peculiar difficulties. In South Australia, where settlement has not proceeded so rapidly as in the adjacent state, the policy is to build the lines with the minimum of cost to meet the demands for cheap railways to connect communities scattered over a large area. That this is a remunerative practice is borne out by results. Although the wide gauge of 5 feet 3 inches is adopted on what may be called the trunk lines extending from Adelaide to the eastern border, to effect junction with the Victorian railways, thereby securing through railway communication between Adelaide and Melbourne without change of carriage, the greater part of the railway system is the narrow gauge of 3½ feet.

The railway thus acts as a pioneering campaigner in the fullest sense of the word, and in this way it has been possible to push the iron road towards the heart of the rich inland country so far as Oodnadatta. Queensland is practising the same principle, three lines having been forced slowly towards the eastern boundary of that state in three roughly parallel lines from three different points on the coast – though the latter in turn are connected. In due course the inland ends of these lines will be joined up, and there will be a complete circle from which spurs can be driven to meet development.

Railway construction in South Australia is noticeable because of the cheapness with which it is carried out in the first place, with an accompanying economy in maintenance. The whole of the work is effected for the most part by the government department, small contracts for construction only being let on rare occasions. This policy, combined with the application of every modern appliance which can establish reason for its utilisation, has been eminently satisfactory from every point of view.

At the present time the tendency is to anticipate the settler, and thus, by the provision of transportation facilities, to attract the farmer into the district. The reverse is generally the method adopted – the farmer establishes himself on the land, and then when there is an agitation for transport the railway is advanced. In this state, however, the railway creates the situation, and in this manner a large area of good agricultural land has been opened up for cultivation. This is the policy which Mr James J. Hill followed in the western United States, and its soundness in the course of time is demonstrated conclusively from the enormous traffic which flows over his systems.

In order that this pioneering may not saddle the South Australian government with an unremunerative heavy debt, the line in the first instance is of the lightest possible description. As the country traversed develops and more traffic accrues to the road, rendering improvement advisable, the track is overhauled and relaid with heavier metals, the lighter rails being shipped to another point to enable the pioneering process to be continued.

This is an elastic system eminently adapted to such a country as South Australia, which is still in its infancy, and where the demand for railway communication is confined almost entirely to agricultural requirements and to the transportation of farming produce, especially in the more remote up-country districts.

CHAPTER 15

The Iron Horse in Australasia (II)

Whereas the Southern Australian and Queensland railways are called upon to meet the demands of agriculture, the roads of Western Australia, on the other hand, have been laid out to satisfy the extensive mining movements along the western shore of the island continent. The engineers, however, have not been called upon to face particularly stern grapples with Nature, owing to the country traversed being, for the most part, of a give-and-take character, and to there being an entire absence of high mountains and wide, rushing rivers. There is only one chain of hills of any magnitude that has to be crossed by the lines. This is the Darling Range, which runs parallel to the coast from near Geraldton to the southern extremity of the country.

In order to gain the gold fields around Coolgardie, as well as the eastern and southern stretches of the state, the difficulties confronting the engineer in connection with this low ridge were not so great as those prevailing in New South Wales. For instance, only one tunnel, 1,096 feet in length, has had to be bored. Indeed, the engineer seized the opportunity to build the line cheaply to such an extent that the lowest watermark in this respect, bearing in mind the configuration of the country, may be said to have been attained. True, the grades and curvature are heavy, the former running up to as high as 1 in 50 (2 per cent), while the curves are of 266 feet radius. Some of the most difficult spurs in this range are traversed by the line which taps the extensive coal-fields in the Collie district – the bulk of the coal used in the state is obtained here – where sharp curves of 176 feet radius, and banks rising 1 in 40, have been introduced.

The first railway built in Western Australia was a short line from the coast to Northampton. This was completed in 1879. In those early days, the finances of the country were at a very low ebb, and the engineer was forced to carry his track through the hilly country with the minimum of earthwork. The result was that curves so sharp as 88 feet radius were adopted.

The Upper Darling Range railway also deserves more than passing notice. It leaves Midland junction at the foot of the hills, and 10 miles from Perth. The precipitous character of the spurs so puzzled the engineer that he was driven to imitate the method of extrication from a difficulty of this description practised in New South Wales. He had to "zigzag" the line up the face of the bluff. Another feature of interest is on the spur from the eastern railway, known as the Smith's Mill branch. A deep cut had to be driven through a hill, which the excavators, when they set to work, found to be a solid mass of pipe clay!

Though the engineering trials on the railways in this state may not compare in calibre with those in other countries, there is one other difficulty which is far more significant from the railway's point of view. I refer to the question of water supply. On the coast, where the rainfall varies between 15 and 40 inches per annum, this does not occasion any apprehension, but rain becomes scarcer and scarcer as the great interior deserts are approached. This condition prevails along a belt 150 miles or so wide, extending from Albany to Geraldton. When the discovery of gold at Coolgardie, some twenty years ago, sent a wave of excitement round the world, the miners and others who rushed to the El Dorado suffered terribly from the dearth of this indispensable commodity, and when the mines were set to work it hampered operations to a very pronounced degree. In the gold country the rainfall does not exceed 6 inches per annum, and consequently water had to be husbanded carefully.

The mining activity, however, brought about a remarkable expansion in the iron road, which pushed inland for nearly 600 miles. Then the water question became one of vital importance, because the locomotives required copious and frequent drinks to slake their tremendous thirsts. To bring this article up from the coast was costly. The scanty rainfall was collected so far as possible by impounding, but the water thus secured was found to be useless for the railway's purposes. It became so heavily charged with deleterious substances, as it flowed over a salt-impregnated soil, that it set up heavy incrustation in the boilers.

This was a serious drawback, because it reduced the life of the engine's internal organs very materially, and militated against the iron horse's efficiency. To remedy this state of affairs, the earthen dams constructed at various points along the route, which formed small reservoirs, were supplemented by condensing plants. The most notable installation of this description was completed at Coolgardie. This plant was designed primarily to utilise the salt water from the adjacent mines. The Coolgardie condenser was capable of supplying about 60,000 gallons of fresh water per day, at a cost of 37*s* 6*d*, or say $9 per 1,000 gallons, and to furnish this requirement entailed an expenditure of £15,000, or $75,000, on the apparatus. A large distilling apparatus was set up also at Geraldton to supply the Northern railway running into the Murchison gold fields, where the water question was also a serious factor.

While this palliative met the situation up to a certain point, it was far from satisfactory. Consequently, a few years ago a huge project was evolved to supply the Coolgardie gold fields with unlimited quantities of excellent water. A large dam was thrown across a rift on the western slope of the Darling range about 20 miles from Perth, whereby 4,600,000,000 gallons of water are banked up. The water is dispatched from this reservoir to the goldfields 350 miles away through a pipe 30 inches in diameter, which is sufficient to ensure the inhabitants in the gold country receiving a steady and continuous supply of 5,000,000 gallons per day. At intervals along the line large intermediate tanks are provided, together with pumping plants. As the pipeline runs alongside, and the pumping stations are situate beside the railway, the latter can now secure ample supplies of pure water, so that the Eastern gold fields railway is concerned no longer with troubles in this direction.

Great activity is being displayed now in opening up the country in suitable districts alongside the main line, where fruit growing can be practised with distinct success. These agricultural roads are built lightly in the first instance to reduce capital outlay, the average cost being about £1,200, or $6,000, per mile, but these lines will be replaced by heavier metals as the land becomes settled.

The Western Australian railways now extend for about 2,500 miles through the state, and, in addition, private enterprise is represented by the Midland Railway Company, which runs from a point 10 miles out of Perth northwards for 276 miles to Walkaway, whence Geraldton is reached by a government line. In addition, there are numerous short roads belonging to companies working the resources of the country, especially of timber, but one and all have adopted the narrow 3½ feet gauge so as to secure uniformity and intercommunication. Bearing in mind the undulating and easy nature of the country, railway constructional costs have not been heavy. On the trunk lines outside the Darling Range, the cost has varied from £3,000 to £4,000 – $15,000 to $20,000 – per mile, according to the distance from the coast. The heaviest expenditure was incurred in traversing the Darling Mountains, where the expenditure ranged between £4,000 and £7,500 – $20,000 and $37,500 – per mile.

During the past few years, the question of building an Australian trans-continental railway has been brought to the fore, the idea being to link up the railways on the eastern, with those on the western, sides of the continent. Such a railway would be of far-reaching strategical importance, and Lord Kitchener, during his visit to the Antipodes, urged its necessity. The proposal comprises the connection of Kalgoorlie in the Coolgardie district with Fort Augusta in the neighbouring State of South Australia, whence Adelaide, Melbourne, Sydney and Rockhampton on the Queensland coast could be reached by rail from Perth. To complete such a scheme would entail the crossing of the edge of the Victoria desert, but as the physical character of the country does not offer any great difficulties, it is estimated that the 1,070 miles of line could be built for £5,000,000, or $25,000,000.

When the states were federated, Western Australia, feeling that it was cut off from its sister states, concluded that if it cooperated to form a homogeneous commonwealth, the construction of a trans-continental highway would follow as a matter of course. This anticipation caused the western state to throw in its lot with the other territories. Western Australia for a long time previous had cherished the idea of connecting itself physically with the east by means of the iron road, but it was not financially in the position to undertake the project unaided. Still it authorised one of its engineers, Mr John Muir, to run through the country it was intended to traverse, and to report generally upon the feasibility of the scheme.

The journey undertaken by this engineer gives an interesting sidelight as to the task of surveying a new road in Australia, especially in the lesser-known hinterland. M. Muir organised a small party, with camels as the vehicles of transport. The beasts numbered twelve in all, five being utilised for riding purposes and the remainder as pack-animals, carrying the restricted requirements for the little party. They set out from the most easterly point to which the Western Australian railways had penetrated in the requisite direction. Leaving the gold-field country, they entered the Great Victoria Desert. Water was the one difficulty they apprehended, for they knew from the experiences of various explorers in this arid belt that this commodity could be found only here and there. The camels, consequently, were restricted to short rations – one drink every five days, the party carrying sufficient of the liquid to meet its own needs during the intervals. The animals evidently did not appreciate these strict regulations, because the party, whenever they left a water-hole, had the greatest difficulty in persuading the camels to continue the journey, and even when they did resume the trail, the beasts frequently stopped to turn their heads longingly in the direction of the last water station.

This small party covered 1,000 miles, collecting valuable data, which, upon return, was investigated searchingly and compared with the information that other travellers had gathered when piercing the country at different times. As a result, a comprehensive scheme was drawn up, and the possibilities of such through communication were revealed in no uncertain manner.

Some years later, the Commonwealth sanctioned the completion of a more exhaustive survey, Mr H. Deane, M.INST.C.E., formerly engineer-in-chief to the New South Wales railways, being placed in charge of the whole undertaking. The enterprise was divided into two sections, the Federal government undertaking to complete the task from Coolgardie to the eastern frontier of Western Australia, while South Australia decided to complete the work so far as it affected its own territory. Mr John Muir, who had been through the country previously for the Western Australian government, was selected by the chief engineer as first lieutenant on the former division, and he enrolled four other surveyors.

For this task no less than ninety-one camels were acquired. Of this total, thirty-six animals were deputed to haul three team-wagons, a like number were subdivided into three strings of pack animals, three carried stakes for locating the line, while the others were used for various purposes. An important task was the distribution of stores to the extent of 18 tons along the route for the survey party, together with ample supplies of water for both man and beast, the water stations being spaced at intervals of 7 miles.

To plot the route the chief surveyor set out ahead of the main party. He ran the line by the aid of a compass, and checked his work by means of stellar observations. The last camel in his train was required to haul a heavy bullock-chain, the free extremity of which was knotted, and as this dragged over the ground it left a trail which could be picked up and followed easily by the main party following in the rear. The latter measured the distance by chains and took levels at frequent points, and these were checked constantly. This survey party moved forward at the rate of 6 miles per day, and it covered the Western Australian section of 455 miles in eighty-nine days.

The South Australian government engineers experienced greater difficulty in completing their part of the work, for on their section, extending over 608 miles, the scarcity of water was felt acutely. They were caught by the intensely hot summer, which dried up all available founts of supply speedily, and consequently the men and the eighty camels could not advance very rapidly, their daily movement averaging about 3 miles. In due course they gained the inter-state boundary and picked up the last stake indicating the route left by the party, which had advanced westwards from Kalgoorlie.

A sum of £20,000, or $100,000, was expended upon this preliminary work. In addition to location, other valuable details were secured, the most important of which was in regard to the economic possibilities of the territory traversed. Far from much of the country being sterile, as previous reports had indicated, it was ascertained that, under proper scientific farming, it could be brought to a high standard of fertility and productiveness. There is one long doubtful stretch of 107 miles through a waterless plain, but if it were possible to adopt irrigation, there are great hopes that this country might be found excellent for grazing purposes.

The standard gauge was advocated for the trans-continental highway, and it was pointed out that if this connection were forged, not only would the line prove of distinct military value, but that it would possess great commercial attractions as well. For instance, there is a considerable and increasing trade between the Coolgardie goldfields country and the eastern states, which has to be carried out by steamer at present, involving a long, tedious journey, whereas by rail the two centres would be brought within direct and accelerated connection of one another. Another feature was emphasised also, and that was the great saving in time possible by dispatching the European mails and passenger traffic overland from east to west, instead of by sea as at present.

The Commonwealth appears resolved to carry the scheme to fulfilment, especially in view of Lord Kitchener's strong advocacy of the project, and when this is accomplished, passengers landing at Fremantle will be able to travel by rail so far as Rockhampton in Queensland, a distance of 3,800 miles. Owing to the varying gauges in Australia, such a journey would involve no less than five changes of carriages at least, and this is the one great disadvantage connected with the scheme.

In order to observe railway engineering in its most spectacular form in the Antipodes, one must cross the Tasman Sea into New Zealand. The England of the south is provided with a backbone of lofty and extremely broken ridges. Indeed, the advance of the railway builder through this country has been beset with abnormal obstacles which recall the conquests of the Rocky and Cascade mountains in North America. The most outstanding feature on the whole network of railways operated by the government is the amazing number of bridges, the cost of which must represent a huge sum. In the early days, chasms and gorges which the railway was forced to cross were spanned by wooden structures, but these have since been replaced by substantial and often lofty steel structures. Whenever the engineer has essayed to leave the coast on either side of the island, the mountains have reared up to dispute his advance, and it has been only by dint of great effort that the metals have been carried over these great barriers.

At the present time, the country has one gigantic project in hand which is without a parallel south of the Equator. This is the Otira tunnel, which is being driven for 5½ miles under the gorge of the same name. This great work occurs on the line which is destined to connect Christchurch on the east, with Greymouth on the west, coast of the South Island. The two points are separated by the Southern Alps, many peaks of which jut 12,000 feet into the clouds. This undertaking was commenced by private enterprise, but when 35 miles of the line had been completed, the physical difficulties to be overcome were found to be so great that the company shrank from attempting the apparently impossible, and accordingly the ambitious idea was abandoned.

The result was that the government took the railway over and determined to penetrate the mountain chain at all hazards. The Otira tunnel, though the most notable feature, is but one of many notable works, for the bridges and smaller tunnels compel just as much attention. To give some idea of their frequency and character it may be mentioned that, in a short length of 9 miles, there are four high steel viaducts, one of which carries the rails 236 feet above the floor of the gorge, and no less than seventeen short tunnels, the longest of which is about 2,000 feet, while there is scarcely a mile of level line! The grades on this railway in some cases are very severe, that through the Otira tunnel itself being 2 per cent, or 1 in 50.

From the earliest days one dream had occupied the attention of all concerned in New Zealand's welfare and progress. This was a trunk railway from Wellington to Auckland. The fact that only some 450 miles separated the two cities by a feasible route was hammered home vehemently by enthusiasts, but it was some time before the requisite courage and determination to effect the connection could be summed up. Pessimists pointed out the great mountains and deep, wide gorges that would have to be conquered, and the enormous expenditure their subjugation by the steel highway would entail. Today, however, the North Island Trunk railway connects the two points, but it proved a prodigious undertaking, calling for the display of remarkable ingenuity.

The early surveyors pointed out that Mount Ruapehu would demand much hard and heavy thinking on the part of the engineers. So it proved. The railway skirts the base of this peak, but has to make a stiff ascent in a short distance. The engineer did not resort to a zigzag to overcome the difficulty, but profited from the example of Hellwag on the St Gotthard, who had to extricate that line from a similar tight corner. Recourse was made to a spiral. The result is that the railway emerges from a tunnel burrowed through a crest, and shortly after sweeps round in a graceful curve to cross the tunnel through the same obstruction; the railway overcomes the steep ascent by means of a stretch of corkscrew track.

Near the base of the same mountain there is a deep gorge over which the line was forced to pass. From the point at which the track gained the brink it was about 800 feet to the opposite cliff edge, and the precipice delved down to nearly 300 feet. This is the famous Makatote Gorge, and the engineer decided to spring across the gap.

The contract was secured by Messrs J. & A. Anderson of Christchurch, and they lost no time in attacking the task. When they appeared on the scene there was no road to the site of the viaduct, and the railway was still 20 miles distant, so the prospect was not inviting. The sides of the mountain were covered with dense primeval jungle-like bush, which had to be hacked back to permit of investigations of the situation, and six months passed before the wagon road for the purposes of the railway was driven through the district. This constituted the only channel over which the requisite steel material could be transported.

The constructional engineers concluded that the best means of meeting the situation was to erect a workshop on the spot where the necessary steelwork could be prepared. Electricity was generated to operate the various tools demanded. The rainfall averaged about 96 inches per year, and at times the insignificant stream flowing through the V-shaped fissure was nothing but a foaming torrent, sweeping everything away in its mad rush.

The constructional engineers were faced with the erection of one tower springing from the bank of the waterway beneath to a height of 270 feet, while other towers of 249, 208, 175 and 110 feet in height respectively were demanded. The spans were of equal length, *viz.* 100 feet, flanked on either side by approaches, and the undertaking called for the use of about 1,000 tons of steel.

The foundations comprise concrete pedestals which were sunk into the ground, and these carry steel towers somewhat after the American pattern, giving lightness, with rigidity and strength. Every piece of steel was riveted to its neighbour by means of pneumatic tools, which not only expedited the task of securing the sections together, but eliminated the possibility of accidents arising from the swinging of sledge-hammers, especially at the greatest heights. The spans of steel connecting each tower with its neighbour were erected from the rail level, without recourse to false-work. Owing to the many and careful precautionary methods adopted, the erecting work was carried through without the slightest hitch or the loss of a single life. When the task was completed, the strength of the constructional engineers' handiwork was tested thoroughly by a train of the heaviest locomotives used upon the New Zealand railway being run across the bridge at varying speeds, until the maximum attained in practice was reached. The Makatote Viaduct stands as one of the finest pieces of its work of this type that ever has been completed in the Antipodes.

Another striking engineering achievement was the building of the Central Otago railway which runs from Dunedin to the interior of Otago. The line not only threads knots of mountains, but also spans numerous rifts. Indeed, so much bridging became necessary that the railway has become known as 'The Bridge Line'. In completing this road, nearly every type of structure known to the engineer was adopted. The largest structure is the Wingatui Viaduct, where the rail is carried about 146 feet above the floor of a broken, winding gorge on a creation of steel comprising three spans, each measuring 196 feet in length, and five smaller spans, each of 66 feet, supported on pyramidal steel towers. Another work of a similar character is the Flat Creek Viaduct, where the fail runs across the rift about 100 feet above its deepest part in six spans of 66 feet each. These mountain creeks, it may be pointed out, are simply masses of rocky boulders in the dry season, but when they are called upon to carry away the accumulation of water, they are nothing but torrents tearing along with fiendish turbulence, and bearing down considerable quantities of heavy stones, against the batterings of which the erections of the engineer would be futile were they not carried out upon the most substantial lines. In contrast to the permanent metallic structures is the Waian timber trestle on the South Island main trunk line, which measures no less than 613 feet from end to end. Verily, New Zealand may be described as the land of the bridge builder *in excelsis*, owing to such varied opportunities to demonstrate his skill.

CHAPTER 16

Across Siberia by Rail

The success with which San Francisco was brought within two or three weeks of Europe by means of the Union and Central Pacific railways prompted far-seeing individuals to aspire for a similar acceleration of travel around the other half of the northern hemisphere. This could be done by driving the iron road straight across Europe and Asia, and it was pointed out, in support of the scheme, that the industrial and commercial centres of western Europe would be brought within about a fortnight's journey of China.

The construction of a railway across Siberia was discussed for over half a century. In 1851, Count Mouraviev-Amoursky, the Governor-General of Eastern Siberia, suggested that he should be brought into more immediate touch with the heart of the Russian Empire. He suggested that first a high road should be built across the continent, upon which the iron rails should be laid later, thus converting the channel of vehicular and pedestrian traffic into a railway.

It was a brilliant idea, but like many other great schemes suffered from being premature. However, as Siberia developed, the building of independent railway lines in various parts of the country, to be connected together by short links, thereby forming a chain of railways stretching from the Baltic to the Pacific Ocean, was mooted frequently. The government viewed the recommendations sympathetically, but nothing definite was arranged.

In 1869, the administrative authorities scattered throughout Asiatic Russia became so energetic in their demands for improved communication with western Europe that the government entertained seriously, the bonding of the empire. The question arose, however, as to the most advantageous location. What direction should it follow in order to serve the most promising interests from an economic point of view? This was a problem that demanded searching investigation, but meanwhile the railway commenced to move eastwards, the existing system of Russia in Europe being driven more and more towards the Ural Mountains. By 1888, the railhead was within easy reach of the eastern frontier of Europe, having gained Zlatoost.

A halt was called at this juncture. The outposts of steel were three in number, Orenburg, Tioumen on the Asiatic side of the Urals and connected with Ekaterinburg, and Zlatoost. A decision was necessary to determine which of these three railheads should be the jumping- off point for the long toil through Siberia. Three surveys were made, and as a result of prolonged consideration of the advantages and disadvantages of the respective routes from every point of view, among the most important of which was the question of cost, Zlatoost was selected as the most favourable starting point. From that point, the location was by way of Tcheliabinsk–Kourgan–Petro–Pavlovsk–Omsk–Tomsk–Krasnoiarsk to Nijneoudinsk, as this offered the shortest length of line, traversed the most densely populated and most fertile country, and at the same time could be built far cheaper than either of the alternative routes.

It was recognised that the line would entail the expenditure of a huge sum of money, no matter how cheaply it was constructed, and that there could be no hope of any return upon the investment for many years to come owing to the unsettled character of the country. Accordingly, it was decided to avoid all pretentious engineering exploits – in fact, to build the line upon pioneer principles. A 5-foot gauge was adopted to harmonise with European Russia, and in order to cut the cost of construction down to the lowest possible figure the lightest material was employed, the rails, for instance, only weighing 54 pounds per yard. It was realised that the paramount condition was to open up the land and its resources without delay, and to overhaul the line as traffic increased, thereby bringing it gradually into conformity with the generally accepted standards of a modern railway.

As the project was of such far-reaching significance to the Russian Empire, it was resolved that it should be carried out as a national undertaking. Every ounce of material required was to be fashioned in Russian workshops – there was only one important departure from this decision, and that was the construction of the huge icebreaking ferries on Lake Baikal, which, being beyond the capacity of the Russian builders, were designed and constructed at the Elswick works of Sir W. G. Armstrong, Whitworth & Company, Limited – and that it should be built by Russian labour under Russian engineers with Russian money. It was an Imperial enterprise from end to end.

To govern the work of construction a national committee was established, composed of interested ministers, under the presidency of the Grand Duke

Heritier, the present Tsar, who upon his ascent to the throne retained his seat upon this commission. Indeed, the Emperor has displayed the greatest interest in this undertaking from its inception, and, in fact, inaugurated the work by laying the stone commemorating the turning of the first sod at Vladivostok on May 18, 1891, during his visit to the East.

Owing to the gigantic character of the work, it was divided into several distinct sections comprised as follows –

	Miles
1. The Western Siberian Railway from Tcheliabinsk to Obi	885.14
2. The Central Siberian Railway from Obi to Irkutsk, subdivided into two parts, the first from Obi to Krasnoiarsk, and the second from Krasnoiarsk to Irkutsk.	1143.75
3. The Baikal Railway from Irkutsk to Myssovaia	192
4. The Trans-Baikal Railway from Myssovaia to Stretensk	690.4
5. The Amur Railway from Stretensk to Khabarovsk	1383.75
6. The Ossouri Railway from Khabarovsk to Vladivostok	476.8

This was the manner in which the 4,771 miles of line constituting the link between the Urals and the eastern seaboard of the Pacific was split up. The difficulties that were likely to be encountered were realised only too well. Though great engineering achievements were not to be permitted from lack of funds, it was recognised that in certain places heavy initial expenditure could not be avoided. The rivers which flow northwards to the Arctic sea, and thus cut across the direction of the railway at right angles, were to be feared the most, owing to their great widths, velocity, and the ice-packs with which they were obstructed during the early spring. Here metal only could be employed, and as the waterways to be crossed were numerous, it was seen that the expenditure under this heading would have to be enormous. There was another factor which had to be taken into consideration. These waterways during the summer season are the great high roads of communication through the country, and consequently it was imperative that the rails should be carried at a sufficient height above the waterways as to offer no obstruction to steamboat navigation.

As a matter of fact, it may be conceded that the huge bridges across such rivers as the Irtych, Obi and Yenisei constitute the outstanding features of the work. They were built massively, and although their erection in many cases taxed the skill of the engineers to a superlative degree, owing to the difficult conditions prevailing, their successful completion is a striking tribute to the men responsible for their consummation. The fact that these waterways were frozen during the winter, harassed the engineers in one, while it was a distinct boon in another, direction. Rails could be laid upon the ice, over which the construction trains could proceed from bank to bank, hauling the requisite supplies and provisions for the workmen, whereas in the summer such work had to be effected by ferries and boats demanding transhipment at the banks, whereby considerable time was lost, as well as incurring the liability of damage to the material handled.

Work was commenced on the various sections as soon as it was possible to gather the requisite material and men on the spot. Owing to the extreme difficulty attending access to the middle parts of the country, these sections were not taken in hand until some two or three years after the earth and rock had commenced to fly at the extreme ends. As already mentioned, construction actually commenced first at Vladivostok, but some months later, on 7 July 1892, the engineers commenced to drive the steel highway eastwards from the European terminus at Tcheliabinsk, to which point the line had been carried forward from Zlatoost.

The country entered after the Urals were left behind was the fringe of a vast steppe covered with tall bush, which continues until the Obi is gained. Then the character of the country changes with startling suddenness, desert giving way to dense forests, where heavy clearing was necessary to secure the right of way. The timber, however, was of slight use for building purposes, and this deficiency, together with that of stone, proved a serious drawback. Timber had to be hauled from long distances and pressed into service for spanning the smaller waterways, creeks and streams, there being over 260 temporary structures of this type upon this division. Difficulty was also experienced in securing material for ballasting the line, and in some instances it was necessary to haul the material for this purpose 20 miles across country.

Four large steel bridges had to be erected in order to carry the railway across the Tobol, Ichime, Irtych and Obi rivers, all of which are navigable. The last two waterways demanded the heaviest pieces of work of this character, the Irtych Bridge being about 2,130 feet in length, divided into six spans, each of about 354J feet. That over the Obi measures some 2,650 feet from end to end, built up of seven spans, three of which are of 594½ feet, and four of 291½ feet respectively.

The rigours of the climate were felt severely. The summer is short and hot, while the winter is long and intensely cold, the temperature ranging between -5 and -13 degrees, while at times the mercury was found to descend to -40 degrees. Moreover, the steppe is swept by terrific winds, and the conditions told heavily upon the labourers working in such an exposed situation. In summer, after making allowances for wet and fete days, only about 120 days were left for operations, and consequently it was essential to continue work during the winter as far as practicable. The sparsely populated character of the country militated against the engineers, and the labour for the most part had to be brought from Europe, for the peasants were unaccustomed to navvy work. The scarcity of water was another adverse factor that found in the more sterile reaches being brackish and unfit for consumption. To meet this contingency, water had to be brought over long distances for the workmen, while in places artesian wells were sunk which relieved the situation slightly. Under these conditions, the completion of the 885 miles of line comprised in this section within four years was an excellent piece of work.

The Central Siberian railway, as it ran through two diametrically different stretches of country – plain and mountainous respectively – was subdivided into two divisions. The first section, stretching from the banks of the Obi, where it connected with the Western Siberian railway, was taken in hand in May 1893, and the work was pushed forward so vigorously that it was completed in advance of the scheduled time. Trains from St Petersburg could not run over this section, however, until two years later, as the struggles of the engineers upon the mountains, in the second moiety, demanded the utilisation of the first section for the handling of their supplies and material. The broken country proved to be exceedingly troublesome. Moreover, a large number of wide waterways had to be crossed, such as the Yenisei, where a magnificent bridge 2,856 feet in length had to be erected. It is a massive structure, and at present constitutes the largest and heaviest work of its description in Siberia.

The traveller as he rolls over the iron road cannot resist contrasting the solidity and permanent appearance of these noble bridges with the temporary character of the line in other places. The difference is so great as to be incongruous. Yet it was in accordance with the original plans. The earthworks and permanent way can be replaced at leisure, but the bridges, and the reputation of the rivers they span, led the authorities to decide that in these instances first cost should be last cost. When the whole railway is brought up to the standard of the bridgework, it will be comparable in solidity and travelling comfort with the leading lines of other countries.

Rapidity in laying the track on the first section was due to the fact that the line traversed an undulating plain where heavy works were not demanded. The climate for the most part was found to be analogous with that prevailing in Western Siberia, the mean temperature in summer hovering about 70 degrees, to fall to about -7.6 degrees in winter. In order that the workmen during the latter season might not be interrupted in their tasks of fashioning the stonework for the bridges, special workshops were provided, heated with steam and stoves, and similar shelters were built over the sites of erection on the ice, where the workmen were enabled to lay the masonry in comfort. At the same time, these measures permitted the cement to dry slowly instead of being frozen, only to fall to pieces with the approach of spring.

As the engineers pushed farther and farther away from the European frontier, the country was found to be more and more thinly settled. Along the line of the Central Siberian railway the average population was one person per square mile, and the majority of these people were colonists who had emigrated from European Russia to practise agriculture in the East, and they were settled for the most part along the postal road to Tomsk.

Under such conditions, labour had to be brought from several hundreds of miles to the rear. Huge depots had to be established to house provisions and large camps formed for the employees. Furthermore, thousands of horses and hundreds of wagons were required in addition to sleighs. Roads had to be cut for the passage of these vehicles, and at various points stores of provisions and other necessaries had to be stored in deep pits dug in the ground, and covered with heavy tree-trunks to secure protection against bears and other marauders.

The penetration of the dark and matted primeval forests was terrible. The ground was swampy, and in order to facilitate the advance of vehicles the soft soil had to be rendered firmer by tree-trunks laid down to form a kind of timber road. The men engaged in this essential undertaking suffered extreme privations, not only bodily, but mentally as well. The terrible solitude preyed upon their minds, while the rainfall and entire absence of the rudiments of comfort told upon their constitutions.

In order to facilitate the transportation of the provisions and material from European Russia to the main depots along the line, the great waterways were utilised to the fullest extent. Boats of all descriptions took on these stores at convenient points near the Urals, such as Tioumen, and by traversing the various tributaries of the mighty Obi were able to gain numerous points along the location, where they discharged their cargoes. Thence the goods were dispatched to the scattered depots and camps by road.

When Irkutsk was gained, the first serious troubles arising from the mountains confronted the engineers. The survey showed that the line here would have to describe a huge detour to round the southern extremity of Lake Baikal, a sheet of water as large as England. The country was broken up to an extreme degree, and among other works of a heavy nature involved was a tunnel nearly 12,500 feet long through the Zyrkousounsk mountain chain, which towers to a height of 12,000 feet above sea level. But the tunnel was only one obstacle which would have to be overcome, for heavy cuttings through rock and big fills to cross depressions were indicated on all sides. Some idea of the outlook was afforded from the estimated cost of this 182 miles of line which was ciphered at £2,700,000, or $13,500,000. As, after compassing the lake, the line swung sharply north-eastwards to gain Myssovaia, practically opposite the point on the west bank, a bold temporary expedient was suggested. This was the installation of a large vessel combining the features of an ice-breaker and ferry, which should carry the trains intact across the lake, a distance of about 45 miles. By this means construction from the eastern bank could be hastened, leaving the line around the end of the sheet of water to be built at leisure at a subsequent date.

The construction of this vessel was entrusted to Sir W. G. Armstrong, Whitworth & Co., Limited, who had undertaken the ice-breaker Ermak which had proved such a unique success in the Baltic Sea. It measures 280 feet in length and has a displacement of 4,200 tons. It is propelled by twin screws driven by triple expansion engines developing 3,750 horsepower. A third screw is placed in the front, which not only serves to assist propulsion, but also to crush the ice, the vessel, as it were, cutting its own channel.

Rails are laid upon the deck of this steamer so that the train, when it comes to the water's edge on one bank, proceeds under its own power on to the steamer, and upon reaching the opposite bank of the lake runs on to dryland. In addition, there is accommodation for a large number of passengers.

The vessel was built on the Tyne and then dismantled, every part being numbered to show its relative position. It was shipped to St Petersburg, and from that point dispatched to Krasnoiarsk. Here on the shores of Lake Baikal the parts were reassembled and the vessel was launched. This ship-building operation was no mean feat in itself, bearing in mind the remote situation of the lake and the complete absence of those thousand-and-one facilities which are to be found in a shipyard on the Tyne.

The vessel proved a complete success, and the authorities were so gratified at this solution of a difficult problem that they secured a second ice-breaker, together with a floating dock where these craft could be repaired and overhauled as occasion demanded, together with sufficient equipment for such work. The total expenditure upon this trans-Baikal marine work alone amounted to £684,190, or $3,420,950.

The line around the shore of the lake, however, has been completed, providing through continuous railway communication across Siberia. Passengers can still enjoy the lake trip if they desire or are in a hurry, as the steamers are still in service, not only for this special purpose, but also to serve various other points along the shores of Lake Baikal, thereby bringing a great territory within easy reach of the railway.

The forging of the link around the lake, however, proved the most difficult part of the whole undertaking. Bridges across yawning deep gulches had to be introduced freely and projecting spurs had to be tunnelled. Heavy gradients and sharp curves could not be avoided owing to the configuration of the country, and at many places the work is extremely daring. Despite the difficulties with which the engineer had to grapple, this trying section was completed two years before the anticipated date, a result in the main due to the energy and initiative of one man – Prince Khilkoff.

This scion of one of the oldest and most noble families in Russia was an extraordinary man, and probably the most famous railway engineer that Russia has produced. His career was as extraordinary as his character. When a young man, he determined to see things for himself. For several months, he worked at a bench in Liverpool in order to become familiar with the trade of a mechanic. Then, when one of the early trans-continental railways was being driven across the United States, he proceeded to that country and joined the navvying gangs at the railhead, becoming acquainted in turn with the difficulties of penetrating the mountains, railway building and a thousand-and-one other details pertaining to such operations in a new country of a diversified character. In this way he gained valuable first-hand knowledge from practical experience. Afterwards he turned his attention to the operating side, serving first as stoker and then as driver. Still climbing the ladder, he became traction manager and was responsible for the running of the line. Few men ever have gained such an all-round knowledge of the intricate art of controlling a railway as did Prince Michael Ivanovitch Khilkoff, and one of his most treasured possessions was an old certificate of character that was given to him by his superior when he severed his connection with an American railway, in order to facilitate his securing another post.

The knowledge he thus acquired stood him in valuable stead when he returned to Russia, where the development of various means of communication throughout the empire was in a state of transition. On account of his wide and varied experience, he was appointed to the directorship and control of various railways, and soon brought them to a high state of efficiency. He achieved the topmost rung of the ladder when he was appointed minister of all the roads, canals, rivers and railways of the empire.

The Trans-Siberian road thus came under his control, and he set to work energetically upon the completion of this tremendous enterprise. His influence was demonstrated on every hand. Lackadaisical methods made way for strict business routine, and in a short time the whole organisation was running with the precision of a clock. His subordinates when in a quandary never hesitated from seeking his advice and assistance, which were granted always with sympathetic interest; and when the obstacle assumed more than normal proportions he did not attempt its negotiation from an arm-chair thousands of miles away, but hurried to the spot to study it at first hand, and to recommend and assist himself in the breaking down of the difficulty. He had become so saturated with American railway methods that he travelled up and down the line continuously; no detail, no matter how slight, missed his eye. At the time the Circum-Baikal line was in progress he scarcely ever left the railhead, as it was just one of those complex and exasperating fights with Nature in which he revelled. At seventy-five, he was as active and as keen as ever, and it was a distinct misfortune for Russia that he was struck down by a paralytic stroke from which he never recovered. Still, he left a host of recommendations for the improvement of the Trans-Siberian and other railways, including the double tracking of the great transcontinental steel way, which are now being fulfilled.

When Lake Baikal was crossed, the engineers experienced a grim struggle for supremacy through every foot of the way. There is an uphill pull from the shore of the lake over the Yablonovoi range, where the railway attains its highest point on the continent, *viz.* 3,412 feet above sea level, and then makes a descent to gain the valley of the Amur. The country traversed is of a varied character, and was found to be tightly in the grip of frost, for the winter is terribly severe. The land, in fact, may be described as eternally frozen, for in summer, although the temperature rises to about 62 degrees, it does not thaw the ground to a depth of more than 7 feet below the surface. In the forested parts where the branches shut out the genial rays of the sun, ice is found at about 20 inches below the surface in midsummer.

Under these circumstances advance was trying. The top soil was as hard as rock, and could not be displace except by dynamite, so that in the deep cuttings in midsummer it was just as arduous to cut a way through the frozen loam as through the solid rock. The rivers, although they flow with a fierce velocity, freeze up quickly, and the ice assumes a great depth – a train can cross on the congealed surface with perfect safety.

In this country, strange to say, it was found to be easier to work during the winter, notwithstanding the extreme cold, than during the summer, for a higher rate of advance could be maintained when the country was frost-bound. There is an almost total absence of snow, but, on the other hand, during the summer the rainfall is tremendous. The wet season lasts continuously for nearly two months – from the middle of June to the middle of August. The downpour is so terrific that floods are precipitated on every hand, and the resultant situation, as may be surmised, is of the most miserable character. In 1897 the effect of this deluge was experienced to an abnormal degree, for several villages were overwhelmed, and widespread misery was inflicted among the peasants. The railway did not escape, for large stretches of line were washed away and large quantities of material were lost.

The scarcity of labour was felt very severely. Sufficient men could not be recruited locally, and to import navvies from Europe was hopeless. To meet this contingency, the Administration authorities sanctioned the employment of exiles, while criminals were requisitioned to build the grade under a military guard. Though recourse to prison labour has been often advocated for railway construction, this is one of the rare instances where it has been brought into actual application through absolute force of circumstances. Assistance was rendered by Chinese labourers, and though at first they proved indifferent in the manipulation of tools, their assistance ultimately proved invaluable, as the majority developed into expert workmen.

As in other parts of the country, the inhabitants were favoured so far as possible in regard to the acquisition of horses, which were necessary for teaming and haulage work generally, in a district where steam traction engines were quite out of the question. The camps were provided also, so far as practicable, with local produce. In this territory, however, a serious situation was precipitated. The harvest failed, and the peasants were faced with starvation. Then the dreaded disease known locally as 'Siberia' ravaged the country. It is a plague analogous to the rinderpest of South Africa, and has wrought tremendous havoc throughout the eastern corner of the Russian Empire, its effects being experienced along the shores of the Pacific. In 1898, this calamity assumed such proportions that work had to be brought to a standstill for lack of transportation facilities. The government attempted to alleviate the situation by organising a special veterinary service to study the plague on the spot, with a view to elaborating some palliative measures. In order to meet the local deficiency the engineers were compelled to dispatch emissaries into Mongolia to purchase the hardy beasts of burden peculiar to that country. Large herds were acquired in this manner and were driven several hundred miles to the grade.

By means of this section the railway was carried so far east as Stretensk, from which point the line was to be continued to Khabarovsk. A modification in the arrangements, however, took place. Under the original scheme the line was to traverse Russian territory entirely, although Manchuria thrust its border so far to the north as to demand a wide detour in order to gain Vladivostok. At last, however, it became possible to carry the railway into Manchuria, and as a link was being built across this country, affording a shortcut to the seaboard, the Amur railway was abandoned, a short length being built to the Chinese frontier to connect with the Eastern Chinese railways instead.

The result is that the extreme eastern end of the line comes to a dead-end at Khabarovsk, and in itself is far from being remunerative. At the time the engineers appeared on the scene, the territory had not been explored, signs of settlement were very few and far between, there were no roads, and the population was composed mostly of exiles and prisoners deported from Europe. Construction had to be carried out almost exclusively by convicts, assisted by the military, Chinese and Korean labour. The climate being extremely humid in summer, the work during that period proved terribly exacting, and the difficulties were enhanced by the ravages of the cattle plague. All material, being manufactured in European Russia, had to be brought to the extreme eastern end by water, either via the Suez Canal or the Cape of Good Hope, and consequently delays were frequent and often serious for both grade and men.

The primeval forest was terrible to penetrate owing to the huge trees, which, although they provided ample material for constructional purposes, demanded considerable effort and time for their removal from the right of way. As the conquest of Manchuria commenced while this work was in progress, and a shorter cut to Vladivostok was being provided, a spur was driven westwards from Nikolsk to the Chinese frontier to meet the Manchurian railway.

Owing to the rearrangement of the railway chessboard in the East in consequence of the Russo–Japanese war, it is quite possible that the Trans-Siberian railway will be completed as originally planned – that is, through Russian territory entirely, by the completion of the Amur railway from Stretensk to Khabarovsk.

The total cost of the through main line as now in operation was approximately £33,000,000, or $165,000,000. When the various other works incidental to the scheme, such as the connections with the Chinese frontier, are included, the total approaches the enormous figure of £40,000,000, or $200,000,000. This merely represents the building of the track itself between Kotlass in European Russia – now considered a part of the scheme – and Vladivostok, without a single railway car, wagon or engine. As originally designed, the capacity of the line was fixed at three trains each way per day, but the lightness of the construction did not permit this being maintained when the railway was subjected to great pressure, such as attended the transport of troops to the East.

The overhaul of the line was commenced immediately, and the question of doubling the track taken into serious consideration. This latter work is now in progress, and it is estimated that this task alone will represent a prodigious expenditure.

The effect of the railway upon the movement of traffic around the northern hemisphere became manifested immediately. There were two ways in which China and the east generally could be gained from Europe. One route was by steamer all the way via the Suez Canal, the second was by way of the Atlantic, across America by rail, and by steamship across the Pacific. But the Trans-Siberian route was far and away the shortest and quickest, and as the campaign of overhaul is proceeding, acceleration is taking place. Now it is possible to reach Shanghai from London within sixteen days, and one can encircle the northern half of the world in less than forty days.

The extreme precautions observed to preserve communication on the line are noteworthy. The whole railway is divided into sections, each measuring 1,174 yards in length. Each station is provided with a cottage housing the stationmaster, his family and the employees. Some 4,000 of these officials are scattered along the route between the Ural Mountains and the city of Tomsk. The men have a common uniform, which is rather of a military appearance, and it is no uncommon experience to hear passengers unfamiliar with this feature remark that the line is guarded from end to end by soldiers. As a matter of fact, it is just the same as if the various employees of our railways, such as porters, signalmen, guards, ticket collectors, and so forth, were attired in khaki.

CHAPTER 17

The Leopoldina Railway

South America has constituted a happy hunting ground for the railway engineer determined to carry out his conquest with steam and steel in the face of all opposition on the part of Nature. The famous Oroya line is described in another part of this volume, but on the eastern side of the continent is another railway which is equally as remarkable, and which constitutes one of the most interesting engineering achievements in this particular field of endeavour south of the Equator. Indeed, in many respects it ranks as one of the most interesting lines in the world.

This is the Leopoldina railway, which, with its hub resting on the Atlantic seaboard, has its tentacles spreading through the provinces of Rio, Minaes and Espirito Santo to the extent of some 1,500 or more miles. In reality it is a combination of many units. In the sixties of the nineteenth century, Brazil resolved to criss-cross its territory with steel, and short lengths of line were laid on all sides. But the finances of the country became so strained from internal troubles and the decline in the price of coffee that money could not be spared to build or to operate railways successfully. An English company was organised, therefore, to take over a number of these individual roads, and they were combined into a homogeneous whole to form the Leopoldina system.

When the Englishmen entered into possession, they found a sorry state of things. The finances were in a hopelessly involved tangle, and months elapsed before they were straightened out. The tracks likewise were in a pitiable condition of decay. They had been built cheaply, and had suffered severely from the innumerable enemies to railways in a tropical country. Lack of funds had militated against repairs being carried out upon a comprehensive or thorough scale, with the result that the whole system presented a patched and dilapidated appearance.

However, no time was lost in placing the undertaking upon a firm footing. Within two months of the acquisition of the railways, a large staff of men for both the administration and engineering sides of the enterprise were dispatched to South America, with Mr F. W. Barrow as general manager and Mr Norman B. Dickson, M.INST.C.E., as engineer-in-chief. The engineer was commanded to overhaul the whole network, to reconstruct it if necessary, so that the lines might be capable of meeting the exigencies of the traffic awaiting creation from the development of the country.

At that time, Rio de Janeiro was an insalubrious city – in fact, it was almost a graveyard for Englishmen. Mr Dickson found this out in a very short space of time. The company lost three accountants and a number of British assistants under the malignant scourge that prevailed – yellow fever. Since those days, Rio de Janeiro has made great strides and has undergone extensive improvement. The city has been rebuilt, and has been provided with a complete sanitation system, to bring it into line with the other great ports of the world. But in those days it was absolutely untenantable from the white man's point of view, and the railway authorities were compelled to provide accommodation for their imported staff in a healthy spot outside the city, where the men underwent what might be described as a process of acclimatisation lasting over eighteen months.

The first few years were strenuous to the engineer-in-chief. He was confronted with a formidable task on all sides. The line is of metre, or 39.3 inches, gauge throughout, and had been built in a somewhat flimsy and haphazard manner. The majority of the bridges and culverts had been erected of timber, the greater part of which either had reached, or were approaching closely, the span of life.

These had to be replaced by permanent structures in masonry or steel. The track, too, had to be overhauled from end to end, reballasted, provided with new sleepers and rails, and at frequent points where it was in an exposed position, and liable to suffer from the peculiar visitations which wreak such widespread destruction in that country, had to be strengthened and protected by heavy retaining walls and revetments of masonry.

Yet the Brazilian engineers had attempted a daring engineering work in the first instance. The configuration of Brazil is somewhat peculiar. A few miles from the coast, and running roughly parallel to the water line, is a rugged range of mountains dividing the low-lying stretch of shore from the fertile highlands in the interior. The mountain ridge is not regular, but is badly broken up, forming, as it were, a succession of walls placed one behind the other. In order to gain the interior, and owing to the abrupt nature of the ascent, the line has to climb sharply, at the same time winding in and out among the clumps of mountains in a bewildering manner. In fact, the differences in level are so sudden that the track could be lifted only by means of resort to the rack rail, and other devices such as are adopted in Switzerland to ascend the steep mountain slopes.

For instance, after leaving the coast, the first ridge is met within 30 miles, and in the course of 5 miles the line has to rise some 3,000 feet. This involved the use of grades varying from 15 to 18 per cent – from 1 in 6⅔ to 1 in ⅝ – and when first laid down the line was worked upon the Riggenbach system.

It is worthwhile to recall that it was on the low-level part of this section to Petropolis that the iron horse made its first appearance in South America. The short length of line, representing about 13 or 14 miles, between Maua and Raiz da Serra was the first stretch of railway to be laid and used on the continent south of the Equator.

On another part of the system – the line running inland from Nictheroy, on the eastern side of the bay of Rio de Janeiro – the Brazilian engineers were compelled to overcome one of the most searching problems in railway engineering in the world. After traversing 40 miles of the level country, the mountain ridge barred their way. They realised that it could be surmounted only by some exceptional system, and the local authorities seized a unique opportunity. The Mont Cenis tunnel, connecting Italy and France, had been bored successfully, and this new steel highway through the heart of the range displaced the construction railway operating on the Fell system which had been laid over the crest of the Cenis range. The Brazilian engineers thereupon approached the Swiss authorities for the purchase of this abandoned stretch of mountain line, and their offer was accepted. Thereupon the Mont Cenis 'Fell' railway was torn up, transported to South America, and pressed into service to help the Brazilian engineers over the obstacle that confronted them.

The solution proved completely successful, and the engines fulfilled their task upon the 8 per cent, grades with perfect satisfaction for several years. Then the Baldwin Company, of Philadelphia, undertook to eliminate the special locomotives required on the 'Fell' system, and to convert the railway to adhesion working. Recalling the fact that for every 12½ feet of advance one makes a vertical rise of 12 inches, such a conversion appears remarkably daring, but the experiment justified the transformation, for the adhesion locomotives, notwithstanding the extreme severity of the gradient and the sharpness of the curves, which have a minimum radius of 75 feet, have accomplished the work formerly completed by the 'Fell' locomotives with equal success. The result is that this represents the steepest length of line upon a trunk railway to be worked by adhesion traction in the world.

The locomotives weigh 40 tons, and they are capable of hauling a train weighing 45 tons on the drawbar up this bank. In comparison with such climbs, the 'Big Hill', which worried the Canadian Pacific railway engineers for so many years, appears insignificant. The disadvantage of the grade on the latter system was the frequency with which trains ran away down the declivity to enter one or other of the switches or catch points, which deflected the train or locomotive from the main track and piled it against a bank of earth. Such accidents on the 'Big Hill' were nothing to what have occurred on the Leopoldina line. The great difficulty is not in regard to ascending the grade with a load, although there is a possibility of the engine failing to take the hill, and to let its driving wheels spin round idly on the metals without forging a foot ahead. The traffic destined for the interior is comparatively light. The heaviest loads are brought from the highlands to the coast, and consequently the question is to hold the train in check as it descends. Ordinary braking is useless, as, although the wheels may be locked, the whole train is liable to toboggan down the metal slide almost as furiously as if the wheels were running freely. The situation has been met by firstly reversing the engines and letting a small amount of steam into the cylinders sufficient to act as a break, and by retaining the centre rail of the Fell system and to grip it by means of a strong scissors brake. Inasmuch as the engineers are extremely careful when descending the hill, runaways are few and far between.

Now and again, however, a train gets out of control, especially when the rails are wet and slippery. To meet this condition of affairs the driver, of course, makes liberal use of sand, but here again the fates are against him, for owing to the sharp curves it is no easy matter to induce the sand falling from the engine's sandboxes to drop on the face of, and not between or outside, the rails. When a train does get out of hand on the descent, the driver has to trust to luck to gain the bottom of the bank in safety, or to regain control of his charge. Sometimes he succeeds and sometimes he fails. In the latter case derailment generally ensues, with more or less disastrous results. Mr Dickson had a narrow escape from this danger himself one day. He was carrying out his periodical inspection of the line from his special carriage coupled to a locomotive. In coming down the bank something went wrong, and the train got away. The engineer-in-chief admits that he had an uncomfortably anxious few minutes. He felt the train gather speed, and suffered violent oscillation as the train swung round the bends. Just as he was wondering what would be the end, there was a jump and a crash. The engine had left the track, rolled over, and his car was astride the overturned locomotive. He crawled out of the wreck, badly shaken and bruised, but otherwise little the worse for his adventure, though the unfortunate driver was killed.

In order to negotiate the third mountain range, another solution of the difficulty was adopted. The precipice was so steep that the engineers could not introduce the loops requisite to carry the line continuously from one level to the other. So they had recourse to the switch-back, wherein the line runs downhill for a short distance to a dead-end. This brings the engine of the descending train to the rear, and by giving the latter a slight push it is sent down another similar switch-back to another dead-end, where the engine is brought once more to the front of the train. In this manner, alternately pulling and pushing, the train gains the bottom or top of the level of the line, according to the direction in which it is travelling. In reality it is a zigzag, similar in character to that which was used for so many years upon the New South Wales railways, as described elsewhere.

Although on the eastern side of the continent the engineer is spared the ravages of snow and avalanches, he suffers from other disturbing elements which perhaps are more to be dreaded. These are floods, washouts and landslides. The rainfall in this territory averages between 90 and 100 inches during the year, and when the rainstorms break, the downfall is tremendous. The rivers are converted into roaring cataracts, huge cavities are torn in the flanks of the mountains, and enormous quantities of debris are released. Should the line be in the way of such a visitation it suffers severely. It is no uncommon circumstance for a huge gap to be cut in the railway, showing where the tearing water or descending mass of earth has crashed through the track, sweeping everything before it. Nothing can withstand the force of these onslaughts, and although heavy retaining walls of masonry may serve to check their fury, they are not completely successful. The result is that when the rains are expending their violence, the engineer-in-chief is prepared for some heavy repairing work, for possibly 100,000 tons or more of earthen embankment may be demolished.

Then the engineer hurriedly completes a new survey, and replaces the track around the scene of the accident, because reconstruction, as a rule, is more economical and quicker than attempting to repair the injury inflicted.

This, at times, and in a cramped valley, is no easy task, for the curvature has to be borne in mind. Consequently, the destruction often precipitates a pretty engineering problem, extrication from which depends upon the engineer's resources and ingenious ability entirely. There is no doubt that the control of a South American railway, where such conditions as these prevail, imposes a supreme task upon a man's capacity. Washouts and landslips will find the engineer out more quickly than any other emergency, because he is called upon to keep the track going at all hazards, and when a breach does occur, his own enterprise and initiative alone determine the length of the period of interruption to traffic. On such a line as the Leopoldina railway this is a serious factor, because there is a constant heavy volume of produce, especially coffee, maize, tobacco and sugar, pouring towards the coast. During a recent year floods, washouts and landslides cost the railway no less than £24,500, or $122,500. This was a year of abnormal disaster in this direction, but the item generally approximates between £12,000 and £14,000, or $60,000 and $70,000, in the course of the twelve months.

The replacement of the decrepit bridges occasioned Mr. Dickson no little perplexity, but this work became all the more urgent, as the original structures could not withstand the heavier locomotives and trains that were introduced by the British company. One of the most difficult undertakings of this character was the erection of a massive masonry arch bridge in three spans upon the rack system of the Petropolis branch. Each span is of 50 feet, and the work was complicated by being on a curve of 80 metres, or about 266 feet radius. It had to replace a trestle bridge, and reconstruction had to progress without interfering with traffic. Another notable piece of work which he completed successfully was the erection of a single steel girder bridge of 160 feet span across the Parahybuna River. Owing to the velocity of the current and the great depth of water, false-work was quite out of the question, so the steelwork had to be erected on shore, rolled out, and launched into position, being held in check by cables, which proved a trying ordeal owing to the current. When brought into position between the abutments, the steelwork was lifted by means of jacks, the temporary nose was dismantled, and the span lowered until it rested in the desired position upon its supports.

Occasionally the advance of the railway has been resented by the inhabitants. For instance, when it was decided to carry the railway across the Parahybuna River at Campos, the populace of the latter town considered it an unwarranted intrusion. They were urged that the railway bridge would cause their trade on the waterway to shrink to infinitesimal proportions. Thereupon the inhabitants raided the railway, and zealously set to work to destroy everything destined for the bridge. The situation looked ugly, but the authorities took stern measures and quelled the riot, though not before damage to the extent of £40,000, or $200,000, had been wrought.

This bridge is one of the most important upon the whole system. From end to end it measures 1,113½ feet, divided into six through truss spans supported upon five pairs of piers in the waterway.

This outbreak of hostility, however, was quite exceptional. In the interior the natives have welcomed the railway rather than attempted to arrest its progress. This feeling has taken an unusual turn at places where the communities have presented the land for the right-of-way, and in other cases have built stations at their own expense. Since the railway has been under British control the expansion of the country has proceeded rapidly, and the exploitation of the soil has proved highly profitable. The railway maintains an active progressive policy, throwing out spur lines wherever the local conditions promise an equitable return, to encourage development. These branches are not built upon pioneer principles, but are equal in every respect to the trunk roads.

The amount of earthwork incurred in the construction is enormous. 90 per cent of the mileage of the line is carried out upon the sides of the hills, necessitating cuttings sufficiently deep and wide to carry the track. The location for the most part is along the banks of the rivers, inasmuch as these offer the easiest channels to penetrate the mountain ridges. As these waterways describe extremely meandering courses, the railway is a maze of twists and turns. In fact, the line might be described, after it leaves the flats along the coast, as a continuous succession of curves and reverse curves, more often than not, without an intervening stretch of tangent, or straight, length of track. As a result, fantastic 'S' windings, horseshoe bends, and figure-eight loops abound, though the minimum curve is of 266 feet radius.

Despite its remarkable serpentine character, however, the Brazilian engineers displayed marked ability in the original location, bearing in mind the state of railway engineering at the date these lines were undertaken. When Mr Dickson appeared on the scene to straighten out the railway, the natives constituted his sole labour, and he found that the Brazilian engineers were adapted eminently to the work of surveying and locating, being possessed of a specially good eye for a railway line through difficult country. The labour, too, in general, was found to be of a high standard. The Chinaman is generally regarded as the best navvy, but according to this engineer who has had experience in railway construction in all parts of the world, his preference is overwhelmingly in favour of the Brazilian Portugese. He takes a pride in his work, is conscientious, and performs his task thoroughly. These traits stood the engineer-in-chief in good stead in his work of overhaul, for it enabled him to produce a line which, from the point of excellence and solidity, would be difficult to rival in more advanced countries. In the upkeep of the line the same characteristics are observable. The men are tidy, keep the track in excellent condition, and leave little cause for complaint in regard to the maintenance of the railway buildings, taking pride in their individual sections. They have proved first-class engine drivers, displaying every care, for on a railway of this character, bristling with sharp curves and steep banks, accidents are liable to be caused from the slightest miscalculation. When disasters have occurred, it has been found that the causes have been quite beyond the men's control.

Under British management, the railway has been rescued completely from its former moribund condition, greater stretches of fertile country have been brought under cultivation, and a general air of prosperity has been imparted to the territory which it serves. From the financial point of view the investment has proved a complete success, with the result that the Leopoldina railway today offers a most powerful example of the beneficial influences of English management among the railways of South America.

CHAPTER 18

The First Canadian Trans-Continental Railway

As the railway expansion of Canada developed by leaps and bounds, ambitious spirits contemplated larger and larger conquests, culminating in a desire to build a link of steel right across the country from coast to coast. This feeling was natural. On the Atlantic seaboard, settlement advanced at a rapid rate in the Lower Provinces and forced its way steadily inland. On the Pacific side, civilisation firmly planted in British Columbia spread towards the Rocky Mountains. These two colonising forces, working in the same country, were as wide apart as if at the Poles, for the intervening plains stretching from the Great Lakes to the Rockies were considered useless.

British Columbia felt this isolation keenly. All traffic had to be carried round the southern extremity of the American continent. To travel from London to Vancouver in the fifties was a heroic undertaking, involving a journey more than halfway round the globe. Some of the trade, however, was maintained overland. For instance, the provisions for the Hudson's Bay post at Vancouver were dispatched from Montreal over a trail some 3,000 miles in length. But it was a tremendous task, occupying several weeks. The pack train left Montreal in May, and the water route was followed so far as practicable to Fort Garry, where Winnipeg now stands. Here the rivers were abandoned in favour of horses, mules and wagons which trekked slowly across the prairies – the voyageurs living on the buffalo which roamed the plains in their thousands – threaded the terrible mountain rifts, and dropped down to the coast, reaching Vancouver about the end of September. The trail was ill-defined and the journey bristled with exciting incidents and adventures.

The disadvantages of this means of communication between the opposite sides of the continent were realised only too fully, so when the railway had become established in Eastern Canada and had demonstrated its tremendous possibilities, an iron link across the Dominion was advocated strenuously. But the vastness of the undertaking was deemed to be beyond the possibilities of the country; the cost was contemplated to be so huge that capitalists would not venture to commit themselves to the fulfilment of such a project. One of the advocates of the enterprise suggested that it should be built by convict labour in order to reduce the expense of construction, and curiously enough he suggested that the line should be carried through the Kicking Horse Pass, through which the Canadian Pacific makes its way to the Pacific today.

It was in 1851 that the idea of a trans-continental railway first crystallised into a tangible project; but as it eclipsed in conception anything attempted in railway building up to that time, there was considerable timidity in launching out upon a line some 3,000 miles in length. So matters drifted until the first trans-continental railway was thrown across the United States, and San Francisco was brought within a few days' travel of New York. The agitation then broke out anew for a Trans-Canadian line, and Sir Hugh Allan approached the government with a definite scheme. However, he failed to enlist the practical assistance of financiers, and so the theme ranked as a perennial topic of discussion until the ratification of a project supported by the government in 1881.

It is doubtful in the history of British North America whether any project of avowed benefit to the community has experienced such vicissitudes as the first Trans-Canadian railway. It wrecked ministries, brought about the political extinction of more than one promising Member of Parliament, provoked heated agitation, and involved the abortive expenditure of large sums of money.

The government, however, decided to help private initiative sufficiently daring to attempt the undertaking in a liberal manner. In the first place a subsidy of £5,000,000, or $25,000,000, was granted to aid construction; the government undertook to build 713 miles with its own resources, and made a free gift of 25,000,000 acres of land fringing its route. At that time the land was worthless, so its bestowal was not of immediate value, but today it represents an asset of incalculable value, and gives the company a sheet anchor of tremendous strength.

In the end, the government went very much farther. It made a free gift of the line it had constructed, which was worth at the very least £7,000,000, or $35,000,000. While construction was in progress, there was urgent need for further money. Financiers refused to provide funds, and as a result the government stepped in and advanced a loan of £6,000,000 – $30,000,000 – which action was so bitterly criticised at the time that the Ministry was urged to wipe off the debt once and for all by making it a gift, for all the prospect there was of it ever being repaid. But the loan was redeemed, partly by an issue of stock, and partly by the government buying back some 7,000,000 of the 25,000,000 acres which it had given to the company in the first place at 6 shillings per acre, representing to all intents and purposes a further gift of some £2,000,000, or $10,000,000. Probably no railway undertaking has ever been treated with such prodigal liberality in the history of the iron horse; but at the time it was warranted fully, bearing in mind the magnitude of the scheme and the tremendous difficulties which confronted the company at every turn.

When construction commenced in grim earnest, the builders found that the critics had not erred on the side of under-estimation in regard to the character of the difficulties to be overcome. The thin band of steel was driven through country of which practically nothing was known; where every succeeding mile revealed something unexpected. For instance, in following the shore of Lake Superior it was one desperate grapple with Nature for every yard. Mountains dropped sheer into the lake, and their humps were divided by stretches of wicked muskeg, the Indian name for swamp, where in many cases the bottom defied being discovered, and where thousands of tons of rock were swallowed up without showing any gratifying result.

Today it is possible, from wider knowledge, to criticise the company upon their selection of this route, but at the time it was taken in hand there was no alternative. For a solid 100 miles along the shores of Lake Superior the work assumed a spectacular aspect. The high rocky cliffs either had to be tunnelled, blasted right out of the way, or deep long cuts had to be driven through the solid obstruction.

In those days the camps did not enjoy the comforts that are possible now. The food was of the coarsest description – in fact, often it was nauseous. Yet it was the best that could be secured under the circumstances. I met one of the men who had helped to drive the grade along the shore of Lake Superior, and he described the interest and curiosity that was provoked by the arrival of the first tin of condensed milk. To them, milk was a luxury indeed, and they as much anticipated its association with their tea or coffee as they would have entertained the possibility of receiving a glass of champagne. The tin of milk was produced, and when the first recipient had read the story of the label it was handed round to every man in turn. They scarcely could conceive the possibility of being able to preserve such a perishable product in a tin, and they refrained from investigating the contents. At last, one of the more daring spirits took out his ponderous pocket- or jack-knife and plunged it into the lid. Tipping the vessel slightly, he watched the contents exude in a thin viscous stream on to his finger. Hesitatingly he tasted it, and the intense satisfaction with which he smacked his lips showed that it was a tasty article at all events, although it might be rank poison for aught they knew. All in turn submitted the commodity to this preliminary test, and there was a unanimous exclamation as to its palatable qualities. Very little of that tin of condensed milk was employed for its avowed purpose: the majority of the men preferred to enjoy it in its raw condition, as it was something entirely new to their frontier table. As a result, the greater part of the coffee and tea was drunk that morning in its black state, relieved with sugar only, as the contents of the tin disappeared in a far from orthodox manner.

The resistance which the rock offered was heart-rending. The men, by superhuman effort, could make their way forward only a few feet per day. Under these circumstances, the task swallowed money as remorselessly as the muskeg absorbed dumped rock. Results proved that the construction of the line along this shore for about 100 miles was as expensive as threading the mountains, and in one instance the price mounted to as high as £140,000, or $700,000, per mile, rendering it easily one of the most costly stretches of road ever constructed.

But though the fight offered by the rock was stern, that presented by the muskeg was every whit as bad, though it was of a different character. The great danger against which the company had to contend was the creeping of the rails. The spongy nature of the soil over which the track was laid caused a movement of the metals under the weight of a passing train. It was just as if the rails had been laid on a mass of resilient India rubber. The lines would move to one side or the other and often widen out sufficiently to permit a train to drop between them. It was observed that as a train passed the elastic soil rose and fell in a series of little waves, often attaining a height of 6 inches, while the engineers could see the rails moving under the passing of the train. It was quite out of the question to spike the rails firmly to the sleepers, since the movement was so great that the metals would have forced themselves from their foundation. As it was, the gangers had to overhaul the stretch of track crossing the muskeg once every week. The engineer strove valiantly to overcome the eccentric movement of the rails, and only succeeded by dint of great effort in rendering it perfectly safe. But in this work he had to use sleepers measuring 12 feet in length, instead of those of standard dimensions of 8 feet.

Then trouble arose with the contractors in regard to the cost of excavation. Naturally, the expenditure under this heading varied according to the character of the material encountered, for obviously gravel, clay and loam were far easier and cheaper to remove than rock, and this latter varied in its workability according to its geological formation. In one case this dispute became a bitter bone of contention between the company and the contractors. Upon the completion of the work, the former came to the conclusion that it had been charged an excessive sum for the work, and upon consideration of the returns of the earth removed were convinced that an erroneous return had been made. Amicable adjustment of the difference proving fruitless, recourse had to be made to the courts, and the authorities ordered the cutting to be re-measured so as to determine the quantity of soil removed. In one instance the contractors were forced to return a sum of about £60,000, or $300,000, and many other firms of constructional engineers had to make repayments. It was not a question of fraud, but purely misinterpretation of the character of the soil handled; yet it served to promote inharmonious working between the company and its contractors.

On the prairie, constructional effort was not taxed to a supreme degree except in regard to water. This was found to be scarce in many parts, and is even so today. The country threaded is a continuation of the arid stretches of North Dakota and Montana, and where the land can only be brought to a state of remunerative productivity by recourse to irrigation. Science, however, has discounted the deficiency of nature, and today this dry belt is as generously supplied with water as those more favoured with ample natural resources farther north, though of course the settler is compelled to pay his quota to the expense of irrigation in the form of a higher price for the land.

It was when the mountains were met, however, that the real troubles of the company commenced. The battle against the rocky bluffs round Lake Superior was as mere child's play to what was encountered when the mountain barrier was entered. The government had surveyed a route through the mountains, and its choice had fallen upon the Yellowhead Pass, the lowest summit in the range, which is only 3,723 feet above the level of the ocean. It was the obvious portal through the mountains to the coast, but the company decided to thread the chain farther to the south. This decision aroused considerable criticism, and the government only relented by stipulating that if the Rockies were penetrated at any other point, it should be at least 100 miles north of the International Boundary. When the project was consummated it was stipulated that grades should not exceed 1 in 52.8 feet, and the Yellowhead fulfilled this requirement strictly to the letter.

However, the government's requirements being fulfilled, the line was forced through the range by way of the Kicking Horse Pass, a high road used by the *couriers du bois* for some years previously. But it proved a trying piece of work. The river is a boiling stream and difficult of approach. The mountains rear up on all sides, and in order to force their way forward, the engineers had to resort to herculean efforts, spanning tumultuous streams and carving narrow winding ledges on the sides of the mountains. Moreover, it is a heavy uphill pull for mile after mile, until at last the summit is gained at an altitude of 5,329 feet. To gain this point, the line winds in a bewildering manner, but the vistas of mountain scenery that are unfolded are difficult to parallel out of Switzerland.

When this part of the work was taken in hand, the original arrangements comprised tunnelling beneath a glacier and through the hump of Mount Stephen, but as there was loud clamouring for the completion of the line, this undertaking, which would have involved a great length of time, and which would have proved exceedingly costly, was abandoned for the time being in favour of a 'temporary line'. That deviation, however, fulfilled its temporary requirements for a prolonged period – a matter of some thirty years to be precise – and only recently has been improved.

In making the deviation, serious delays were experienced. A rocky obstacle stood in the way and tunnelling was commenced, but this work had to be abandoned owing to the collapse of the burrow, and a sharp curve and heavy bank introduced. The result was that it was found impossible to comply with the government's requirements concerning the maximum gradient, because in order to descend from Hector to Field, a distance of about 10 miles, a difference of 1,143 feet had to be overcome. This introduced a grade adverse to eastbound traffic of 237 feet to the mile, and it proved a heavy stumbling block against the economical operation of the line for many years, and one which increased in severity with every succeeding year.

Yet the conquest of the Rockies was a marvellous piece of engineering, especially on 3 miles of this bank, which was so steep as to earn the name of the 'Big Hill', for it rose 12 inches in every 22 feet, and was one of the stiffest pieces of road to be worked by adhesion that ever had been laid down on a railway. It was so steep as to be dangerous, a fact testified by the number of safety switches, or 'catch points', that were introduced. The man in charge of one of these points, observing an engine coming downhill, did not know whether it had run away or not until the engine driver whistled a signal which conveyed the information that he desired the switch to be set to the main line, for normally it was left open and a runaway at that point would have been turned into the bank, to end its mad career in a wreck. Now and again engines did run away, and the 'Big Hill' has witnessed many exciting escapes among the engine drivers and train gangs. To grasp the significance of this engine 'pull', one required to see the 'Limited' steaming from the Pacific to the Atlantic. It got to the bottom of the hill; and there three other engines were attached to the train to push it up the ever-dropping metals for over 3 miles, while the clouds of smoke and live cinders belched into the air, and the terrible roar of the engines straining at the load testified to the tremendous effort that was required to get a speed of 5 miles an hour on the train. It was this feature that led a humourist to remark that the Canadian Pacific railway never had any occasion to ballast the track on the 'Big Hill'. The engines performed this operation spontaneously and automatically in their labour, and to far better effect than would have been possible by ordinary means.

Considerable excitement was experienced in its construction. According to some of the men whom I met, and who had been connected with the grading through the Kicking Horse Pass, the ballast trains failed time after time to secure a grip on the metals, and with their driving wheels spinning round madly in the forward direction they skidded backwards downhill. Now and again, there would be a nasty smash, in which engine and the ballast cars were mixed up in an inextricable heap. It is reported even that on one occasion, while the snowplough was out clearing the drift on the 'Hill', the driver of the locomotive lost the plough, and did not discover the fact until he had gained the top, although he was pushing the snow-clearing apparatus! It was so difficult to keep the wheel gripping the rails that he did not notice the difference in the resistance when the snowplough went over one side.

From the government's strict point of view, the Canadian Pacific was not completed until about two years ago, although trains have been running between the Atlantic and Pacific for some thirty years. The authorities pointed out that the grade was an essential part of the contract, and yet, in order to pass through the Kicking Horse Pass, the company had exceeded that grade to a very considerable extent. Consequently, 8 miles of line was non-existent so far as the government was concerned, and it declined to contribute any subsidy to that short length of the railway. Two years ago compliance was made with the government's agreement. The route through the Kicking Horse Pass was realigned. This piece of work was carried out by the late J. E. Schwitzer, and from its daring nature it will always stand as a monument to his engineering ability. He cut out the 'Big Hill' entirely. Where previously a bank rising 1 in 22½ existed for 4.1 miles, he provided a stretch of line double the length and of one-half the gradient, so that the engines only have to overcome a climb of 1 in 45½.

In order to ease the grade, the line swings from one side of the narrow valley to the other. Travelling westwards, it disappears into the flank of Cathedral

Mountain, describing a curve in the tunnel to emerge into the valley about 40 feet below the point where it enters the mountain side. It then strikes across the valley to enter the slopes of Wapata Mountain, where another tunnel on a curve like a corkscrew lowers the level of the line for another 40 feet. Once more it crosses the valley, the meanderings being so bewildering as to form a perfect maze. It recalls the wonderful spiral tunnel work on the St Gotthard railway where a similar difficulty had to be overcome, and, indeed, the conquest of the Kicking Horse Pass in this manner was based evidently upon the great work in Switzerland. Still, it marks the first application of this ingenious solution of a trying problem to the American continent.

To bring the Kicking Horse Pass section of the line within the recognition of the government, however, entailed the expenditure of some £300,000, or $1,500,000, and found employment for about 1,000 men for twenty months. Train-load after train-load of dynamite was brought up in order to enable the path to be hewn through the mountain flanks, and by the time the task was completed over 1,500,000 pounds of explosives had been used – something like £50,000, or $250,000, had vanished literally in smoke to tear down the rock. But the outlay will be recouped well. Where four engines were required formerly, two now suffice to handle a 700-ton train, and they can rattle through the Pass at a steady 25 miles an hour, whereas previously a bare 6 miles could be notched.

Emerging from the Rockies, the engineers were confronted by another towering obstacle – the Selkirks. This range was to be dreaded more than the barrier just left behind, for there was a trail through the Rockies to guide the engineers, whereas the Selkirks had never been threaded. The Indians and Hudson's Bay voyageurs, after emerging from the Rockies, turned sharply south to follow the Columbia River.

The first task, therefore, was to discover a rift through the Selkirks through which the metals might be carried. It was shorter to go through the mountains than to go round them if any pass could be found to exist. Major Albert B. Rogers, an American engineer, accordingly saddled his horse and with a supply of provisions set off to search for a 'Pass'. He wandered up and down the range without success for week after week, and then, just as he was despairing of success, his eye alighted on a narrow breach between two serried lines of snow-clad peaks. He spurred forward, traversing territory on which the feet of neither white nor red man had been planted, climbing and toiling arduously among the crags, until at last he gained an altitude of 4,351 feet, from which the opposite sides of the range sloped down once more to the Columbia River Valley.

Rogers' Pass, as this defile through the Selkirks was named in honour of the discoverer, was followed. It did not offer any great difficulties from the grading point of view. The greatest enemy was snow and avalanche. The snowfall among these mountains is the heaviest along the line, while the avalanches are of terrible frequency. Consequently, the absorbing question was how to keep the line intact after once it had been laid. It was impossible to avoid the defined paths of the snow movements entirely, and in these cases huge sheds had to be erected to carry the avalanche harmlessly over the track to expend its violence in the gulch below. The extent of snow-shedding through the Selkirks is amazing, and it has proved terribly costly.

When the engineers attacked this country, as the laying of the track was the paramount requirement it was pushed forward with all speed during the short summer, and parties of men equipped with meteorological instruments, and vehicles for movement during winter, and supplies of stores, were left at different points to study the snow question, so as to collect data for the situation of the snow sheds. There was no difficulty in determining this latter point, for the avalanches appeared to rain down upon the track from all sides. The question was not so much where to introduce the sheds, but where they could be omitted. It appeared as if the line would have to be carried almost continuously through a wooden tunnel to ensure its safety.

That the snow-fiend is no mean enemy was brought home forcibly some three years ago. While a snow train was climbing up the western slope, clearing away the accumulated mass of snow and debris deposited by a slide upon the track, another avalanche swept down upon the little band working so desperately to cut a path for the mail. Over 100 men were on the train when the terror of the mountains struck them and swept the whole into the gulch below, the locomotives and plough weighing over 50 tons being bowled over and over like an India rubber ball as they were hurtled down the steep slopes. Over fifty lives were lost in that catastrophe, and it was but one of many which have happened since the Selkirks were first gridironed by the railway.

But snow shedding, while securing the safety of the line, has its drawbacks. If a structure is made too lengthy, it becomes filled with suffocating smoke which obscures all signals, and deadens all sounds. In summer, another danger exists. The district threaded is one ravaged heavily by forest fires, and the danger from this enemy was only too vividly apparent. At this juncture Mr W. C. Van Horne came to the rescue of the engineers, as he had done on many previous occasions, to extricate them from their difficulty. He suggested that the maximum length of a single shed should be 3,000 feet, and where the conditions demanded a long continuous length of this protection, that it should be broken up into units with wide, clear intervals of open line between.

To prevent these 'breaks' becoming filled with debris, he resorted to an ingenious expedient. Up on the mountainside he built what is known as a 'split fence'. This is a triangular erection, with the apex pointing towards the mountain top, of heavy massive construction and filled and banked with masonry. The descending slide strikes this obstruction, becomes split in twain, one half is deflected so as to roll over the roof of the snow shed on one side, and the other half caused to glance off in a similar manner on the other side. If one of these constructions did not secure the desired end, then another was planted above it higher up the mountain side. The success of this system has been remarkable, and it has enabled the company to reduce the lengths of the sheds very appreciably.

Shortly after the line was opened, the protective handiwork of the engineers was subjected to trying tests. The winter of 1886/7 was one of excessive severity even for the Selkirks. In less than a week 8½ feet of snow fell, and the blizzard raged continuously for three weeks. Slides were of daily occurrence, the silence of the mountains being broken by the continuous roar of the avalanche. The snowfall on the summits exceeded 35 feet, and the white mantle was piled upon the roofs of the sheds to a depth of 50 feet. The slides were of terrific fury, some rattling down the slopes with such force and speed as to rebound 300 feet or so up the opposite mountain side. Thousands of tons of rock, some pieces as large as a small villa, were caught up in their frantic rushes, while tall, thick trees were snapped off like matches and tossed about like straws.

Yet with one exception the sheds withstood the terrible bombardments to which they were subjected. The solitary case had the roof torn off completely to be thrown well above the track on the mountainside.

Mudslides were another visitation which had to be respected, for time after time a cutting had to be cleared of a viscous mass which had slipped into the excavation. These movements are produced by a kind of sand, which, when it becomes saturated with water, slips and slides in all directions in an amazing manner, carrying everything with it. In winter, when under the grip of frost, the soil looks perfectly safe and stable, but when the weather breaks innumerable springs come to life, and in a short time the whole mass commences to move like a lava stream.

In addition to resorting to extreme protective measures against the avalanche where these could not be avoided, some magnificent pieces of bridge work were carried out at other points to avoid them. In the first instance several were erected in wood to save time, to be replaced by permanent metal structures at a later date. In many cases, however, iron, and in others masonry, had to be adopted in the first instance.

There was one gully which perplexed the engineers sorely. It was just a cleft in the perpendicular mountain cliff. The engineers called it the 'Jaws of Death', and the name was appropriate. They had to cross this couloir, and a temporary timber bridge was built by dint of tremendous effort. The engineers congratulated themselves upon their success, but their gratification was short-lived. A constructional train ventured to cross and the structure collapsed under its weight. Here was a dilemma. Work was brought to a standstill and there was grave deliberation. Mr Van Horne heard of the accident, and hurried to the front. He surveyed the gully, and there and then decided to throw an arched masonry bridge across the breach. It was built, and what was more to the point, it stood; the constructional gangs could get forward.

At Stoney Creek there was another trouble of a like nature. The V-shaped ravine was deep and wide, and it was recognised that something different from what had been done in bridge-building up to this point was imperative. Two wooden towers were built on either side to a height of 200 feet, and these supported a single span of 172 feet over the gulch, which was carried out in wood also. From end to end the bridge measured 490 feet, and for years it ranked as the highest wooden bridge on the continent. The timber structure, however, has long since made way for a noble arched steel bridge springing from the rocky sides of the gulch, and it constitutes one of the most graceful bridges on the whole of the system.

The descent from the Selkirk summit involved the execution of some startling pieces of engineering to gain the banks of the Illecillewaet River. The line makes its way down the mountainside in a series of steps or terraces connected at the ends by sharp loops, doubling and redoubling on itself to overcome a difference of 600 feet in altitude in the most extraordinary manner. The train is first running eastwards, disappears round the corner and then is making its way in the opposite direction a few feet below, to round another curve and once more steams eastwards, this alternate running backwards and forwards continuing until the valley of the Illecillewaet River is gained, by which time the train has travelled over 6 miles of metals to make an actual advance of only 2 miles.

Issuing from the Selkirks, another barrier, the Gold Range, had to be traversed, but this was a comparatively easy matter, as the Eagle Pass is a natural causeway among the peaks for the iron road, although its discovery taxed Walter Moberly to an extreme degree, as is narrated in another chapter. In this pass the engineers, driving the line from the east, met the forces advancing from the west. They shook hands at a point known as Craigellachie, where the connection between the two arms was made – where the 'golden spike' was driven home – and the Pacific seaboard was brought into touch with the Atlantic through Canadian territory.

The Pacific end of the line was taken in hand by the government, and it must be conceded that they had most difficult work to accomplish, for they had to force their way through the Fraser and Thompson River canyons, producing the heaviest 300 continuous miles of engineering on the whole line. They had to fight for every inch of the way through these ravines, as the bottom is entirely occupied by the water. The line is laid on a gallery carved in the cliff-face 200 feet above the waters boiling beneath, in a succession of cuts and tunnels, with some fine examples of bridging, of which the cantilever structure across the Fraser River of 300 feet span was the second of its character to be built on the American continent. This link cost about £2,000,000, or $10,000,000, to build, representing about £16,000, or $80,000, per mile purely for the formation of the grade ready to receive the metals.

Considering the magnitude of this undertaking and the fact that the railway extended through extremely diversified country from level plain to tumbled lofty mountains, construction at the rate of some 500 miles per annum was a magnificent achievement. For the greater part of the distance it traversed country where the white man was not in occupation, and where several years were certain to pass before it yielded any economic value capable of producing traffic to the railway. The enterprise was jeopardised seriously by the financial panic in the United States, and the Northern Pacific railway crisis, which misfortunes did not augur well for the success of another trans-continental railway. When it was finished, the inquiry as to why it had been built through an absolute wilderness from end to end was raised on all sides. The present day supplies the answer to that criticism to a complete degree. From the day of its completion, the Dominion went forward with a rush, and it cannot be denied that the province of British Columbia played an important part in the development of the country when it insisted, as a return for its entrance into the federation of the provinces, that a railway should be built across the continent to link the east with the west within ten years.

CHAPTER 19

A Railway Over the Sea

The Florida express was speeding southwards over the railway which skirts the coast of Florida for mile after mile. Among the passengers was Mr Henry Flagler, one of America's captains of industry and finance. He was gazing out idly to sea. On the horizon were streams of vessels steaming northwards and southwards in two long flung-out lines. They were units in the great coastal service of steamships which ply incessantly up and down this long stretch of coast between New York, the West Indies and the ports dotted along the shore line of the Gulf of Mexico.

At that time the island of Cuba was undergoing a wonderful change. Its vast resources were being exploited by men of initiative and energy from the two sides of the Atlantic, and the steamship traffic between the island and the mainland was advancing by leaps and bounds.

The financier was cogitating deeply. His thoughts had strayed to the subject of this development, and the fresh impetus it would receive when the Isthmus of Panama was at last pierced and vessels could float through the neck of the continent from the Atlantic to the Pacific. He was the controlling force of the railway over which he was then travelling, and he was weighing the question as to whether new sources of revenue could not be tapped for this system. The southernmost point reached by the Florida East Coast Railway was Miami, and though it was a rising town, he saw that its future was limited, because it formed, as it were, a dead-end to the line.

As a result of his ruminations, he decided to make a bold bid for the Cuban trade – to deflect traffic from the decks and holds of the passing steamers. A hundred miles or so south of Miami was one of the most strategical commercial ports of the country – the outpost of the United States – where more than 50 per cent, of the vessels trading up and down the coast make a call. Moreover, it was the point nearest to the island of Cuba, Havana being scarcely 60 miles away. Yet Key West was completely isolated; there was not a single stretch of steel binding it to the intricate railway network of the country.

The magnate decided to forge this missing link in the railway chain; to bring Key West into direct touch with New York, Chicago, San Francisco, or any other town on the continent. From his point of view he could see no obstacle to the realisation of such a scheme beyond the capital cost of the undertaking.

When he returned to New York he summoned his surveyor, to whom he unfolded his idea, and to seek his opinion concerning the technical aspect of the proposition. Mr Flagler's proposal was to carry the line southwards from Miami to the extremity of the country lying at the outermost end of a chain of coral reefs, and from that point to transport trains intact on the deck of large ferry boats to Havana, where they could be pushed on to the tracks of the Cuban system. Transhipment of passengers and the breaking bulk of freight between the great centres of the United States and the island would be obviated, while the time that would be saved on the passage was considerable, and, indeed, sufficiently attractive to tempt one to embark upon the enterprise.

The engineer admitted that the scheme was alluring, but pointed out that for some 30 miles south of Miami the line would have to be pushed through one of the worst stretches of country in the United States, 'The Everglades', emerging from which heavy bridging would be required to link the chain of islands together.

However, the engineer was dispatched southwards with a corps of surveyors to investigate the practicability of the scheme on the spot. They lived for months in the inhospitable bog beyond Miami, and steamed to and fro among the islets with their transit and level, plotting out the most economical and easiest route, sounding the water depths around the coral reefs to determine the extent and cost of bridging, and the best means of crossing these breaches in the reef.

Then the surveyor returned to New York and sought the railway magnate. The engineer had a complete roll of drawings and a mass of calculations and figures. He related the fruits of his labours, pointed out the route that he suggested should be followed, and hinted that, although the railway could be built, the cost would be tremendous – would involve the expenditure of millions.

The financier, however, was not perturbed in the least by the cost. The project received his sanction, and a few days later the engineer departed to commence operations. Little time was lost upon the essential preparations, and soon the grade was forcing its way out of Miami towards the most southerly point of the United States.

News concerning the enterprise, which up to this point had been nursed in secrecy, now leaked out. The activity around Miami pointed to something unusual being under contemplation. When the object of the extension became known, the financial magnate became the butt of widespread ridicule. His ambitious project was christened 'Flagler's Folly', under which name the railway has since been known colloquially.

'Well, there is one thing for which travellers will bless me when they travel by rail over the Keys,' the moving spirit humorously replied to his detractors: 'they will never be troubled with dust.'

From Miami southwards so far as the eye can reach stretches a dismal tract of swamp where miasma reigns supreme. The Everglades lie below the level of the Atlantic Ocean, and the latter is only prevented from grasping the enormous waterlogged expanse within its ravenous maw by a slender wall of rock which runs right along the coast. But though this barrier resists the incursion of the ocean, at the same time it prevents the imprisoned water on the other side from effecting an escape. The result is that stagnant water, varying from a few inches to several feet in depth, according to the season, spreads over the whole of the depression. It is a huge bog and nothing more, with dank, dense vegetation growing riotously in all directions, forming an ideal home for the alligator, which here is found in large numbers. Some 30 miles of this uninviting marsh confronted the engineers, and until scientific effort discovers some means of reclaiming the country fringing the railway from eternal water, it must remain unproductive.

The engineers found this bog difficult to penetrate. Drainage was impossible, and the raising of an embankment, with the ordinary type of implements at command, was out of the question, because it was impossible to secure a solid foundation for their manipulation. For a few miles south of Miami, a rocky ridge thrust its hump above the level of the marsh, and as its situation was convenient, it was followed to the uttermost limit.

When the builders were compelled to plunge boldly into the marsh, they were beset with difficulties innumerable. Mr Flagler had realised from the outset, after meditating upon the plans and reports of the surveyors, that the only practicable means of seeing his scheme carried to fruition was by means of direct labour under his own engineers, instead of by contract. Consequently, he secured the services of the most capable engineers available, while labour was recruited from all sides. Fortunately, no difficulty was experienced in this direction, because the offer of good wages, with everything found, was considered by the workmen to be an equitable compensation for the risk of malaria.

The engineer-in-chief, the late J. O. Meredith, who died in harness amid the scene of his labours, resorted to highly ingenious methods to overcome the fever-ridden swamp. Not only did the conditions demand that a heavy, solid earthen embankment should be built, with its level well above the highest watermark, but that the ridge of earth should be prevented from spreading at the base under the superimposed weight of a heavy train, and from the insidious attacks of soaking water.

Owing to the absence of rock and gravel in the immediate vicinity, it appeared as if the engineer would have to haul trainloads of material for this purpose from long distances, and at great expense, to be dumped into the unstable mass. But he decided otherwise. He conceived a far more rapid, simple and inexpensive means of building the embankment. Two large, square, shallow-draught dredgers were built, with large grabs rising and falling from the upper end of a projecting diagonal wooden girder or jib. These were towed to a point known as Land's End. Here, on either side of the strip of land forming the right of way for the iron horse, and whereon the embankment was to be raised, an excavation was made. Each cut was 30 inches deep and just wide enough to float the vessel comfortably.

The grabs were then brought into play, and with each swing they withdrew a huge mouthful of the waterlogged soil, swung it round, and ejected it upon the grade. The grabs were heavy and powerful; their teeth crunched through roots and decayed vegetable matter relentlessly. It will be seen that, as a result, each dredger dug a canal for itself as it advanced on either side of the grade, forming two parallel paths, with a belt of dry land between. Now and again their advance was disputed. Just below the water lurked a large rock which defied removal by the terrible teeth, and yet projected too near the surface to enable the dredger to float over.

Then the engineer gave another demonstration of his ingenuity. Instead of wasting time in blasting away the rock, he threw a temporary dam across the ditch behind the dredger, forming a kind of lock. Water was pumped from the fellow ditch to raise the level of the water a sufficient degree to enable the dredger to float over the obstruction.

The only difficulty experienced in this manner of handling the marsh was that the marl torn out by the grabs and deposited upon the right of way was so saturated after its immersion for centuries that it dried very slowly, and delays were frequent and heavy in consequence. One layer of the dump had to be left exposed for a considerable time before the next could be added. But the method of building the embankment proved so eminently successful and efficient, that a new move was made to meet the necessity for allowing the excavated soil time to dry. Four additional dredgers were built, two for each canal, and these were set to work at intervals one behind the other. The foremost dredger laid the foundations of the embankment, the second raised it a further height some days later, and after another interval of time, the third dredger contributed its quota to the constructional work. In this way the task was expedited very materially. In some places, the bog was found to be covered with mangrove trees, the roots of which spread like a thick net through the soil. The consequence was that the grabs tore up a large proportion of roots associated with the soil, and the former had to be used for embanking purposes, as it could not be separated from the inorganic matter. But this fibrous substance dried very quickly, and was so highly combustible that it had to be covered with a thick layer of broken stone to protect it from fire, and also to ensure solidity by packing tightly.

The completed track has a somewhat novel appearance. There is the ridge of earth, flanked on either side by a broad ditch, cut by the dredgers and running as equidistantly from one another as if drawn with a parallel ruler. These side canals, however, serve to drain the permanent way to a certain extent.

When the railway builders made their way through this inhospitable region, they did not meet a vestige of civilisation for over 30 miles. Then they came across pathetic evidences of attempts at reclamation here and there in the form of tumbling homes and isolated parties of half-starved negroes, vainly endeavouring to extract some sort of subsistence from the bog.

But it is when the railway emerges from the Everglades that the most wonderful part of the undertaking is seen. A chain of some thirty verdant islands, composed of coral limestone, stretches out in a graceful curve for about 109 miles, to disappear finally into the depths of the Gulf of Mexico at Key West. These reefs are separated by channels of open sea, of varying widths. These interruptions to the continuity of dry land are spanned by massive arched viaducts wrought in masonry. Where the line traverses the islands themselves, the permanent way either is carried on embankments or through deep cuts. The expensive bridging has been reduced to the minimum, however, for in some cases where the water is shallow the islands are linked together by a massive solid earthen embankment.

This section of the railway may be said to be amphibious in the full sense of the word. In fact, at one point the passenger in the train is carried beyond

the sight of land. The engineer had to build his structure sufficiently strong
and solid as to combat the forces of wind and wave, and at a level beyond
the reach of the spray. When it is remembered that the railway runs through
a territory where tropical storms of terrific fury prevail, and where cyclones
are continually wreaking widespread damage, some idea of the character of
the work requisite to withstand the buffetings of these abnormal visitations
may be gathered.

These climatic disadvantages were brought forcibly before the moving
spirit in the enterprise at the time of its conception, and accordingly he
demanded that the bridge work should be built as strongly as engineering
science could make it. No expense was to be spared, for the financier was
determined that no apprehensions as to safety should be permitted to lurk in
the mind of the timid traveller.

The engineer took him at his word. The depth of water in which the
viaducts are built ranges from 10 to 15 feet and more, while the rails are laid
31 feet above low water. At some places the channel is wide enough to float a
large steamship. The viaducts have been carried out in ferroconcrete, wherein
the masonry is strengthened by means of iron rods, freely intersecting, which
serve to bind the whole mass into a solid, homogeneous whole, so that the
viaduct from end to end becomes practically a single, monolithic structure.

To enable the subaqueous portions of the piers to be built, coffer-dams
were erected around the sites, the space within being emptied and kept clear
of water by means of powerful pumps. By this means the workmen were
enabled to carry out their task of securing the fabric to the solid rock on
the dry coral sea-bed. Where the water ran up to a depth of 30 feet, and the
situation was exposed to the full fury of gales and of the Atlantic, caissons
were sunk for the purpose of constructing the piers to above water level, the
men working in compressed air. The material for constructional purposes was
prepared on large, well-equipped floating plants anchored nearby. The timber
moulds to form the shape of the arches were fashioned and bolted together
on dry land, and towed out to sea by tugs to the point of erection and there
set in position.

Some of these series of arches on the amphibious section of the railway are
only a few hundred feet in length; others measure as many thousands of feet
from end to end. For instance, between Long and Grassy Keys – the islands
are known as 'keys' – the over-sea viaduct is 2 miles from end to end.

The viaduct work was confined to the deepest parts of each channel, being
approached from either end over a substantial earthen embankment. Some
idea of how this expedient saved the costly task of bridge-building may be

obtained from the fact that whereas the distance by the line between Grassy
and Long Keys is 29,544 feet – 5.6 miles – the approach embankments
aggregate 19,100 feet of this total, the long, symmetrical line of arches
totalling 10,444 feet. In the case of the gap between two other keys, the
water is closed by an embankment 21,800 feet in length. In another instance,
the earthen structure stretches for 11,950 feet to connect Upper and Lower
Matecumbe, but inasmuch as this channel is used by vessels, the navigable
channel is spanned by a drawbridge 120 feet in length to permit vessels to
pass between the Atlantic and the Gulf of Mexico. In the first 78 miles of
track running out to sea from the mainland, no less than 14 miles represent
bridge-work, the remaining 64 miles being carried out on embankments
across the islands and shallow straits, or by timber trestling.

On the islands, grading was not accompanied by any great difficulties. The
Keys are for the most part somewhat low-lying, and a certain amount of
excavation and filling was required. The latter work was expedited by building
a crude trestle down the centre of the right of way, on which was laid a large
pipe communicating with dredgers, and through this conduit was pumped sand,
mud and gravel in a continuous stream to form the grade to the required height,
the slopes on either side afterwards being flanked with a thick layer of large
stones. Direct labour was employed on this section of the undertaking also, and
for the most part the ordinary wheelbarrow, pick and shovel supplemented the
efforts of the dredger and pipe line. As the Keys are of coralline limestone, an
excellent material for ballasting the line was readily available.

When a point known as Bahia Honda was gained, the engineer-in-chief
resorted to more expeditious practice. Ten huge mechanical excavators, each
capable of doing every day the work of from 50 to 100 men, were brought
into action. They devoured the spoil to throw up the embankment at such a
speed that one could see the grade's daily growth. It was a tedious operation
to get these excavators to the scene of action, because they had to dig their
own way through the soil to the right of way, a task which occupied from one
to four months, according to the situation of their respective stations.

One of the gravest difficulties in connection with the whole undertaking
was that experienced in provisioning the 3,000 or 4,000 men scattered at
various points, feverishly toiling to fulfil the realisation of the financier's
dream, together with the requisite material. Every drop of water, either for
human requirements or machinery, had to be transported in huge tanks from
a distance of 100 miles. The engineer-in-chief pluckily attempted to cut down
this haulage distance one-half by establishing a water station at a creek 50
miles nearer the front. But he reckoned without Nature.

They had just got the plant going when a wind sprang up and prevented the boats, specially acquired to transport the water from the station to the nearest point on the railway, from approaching within a mile or so of the shore. Hurried arrangements had to be made to draw temporary supplies from Miami once more. A week or two later, the wind veered round and blew just as furiously in the opposite direction, with the same result. This experience sufficed to prove that no reliance could be placed upon the new water station, so it was abandoned.

Similarly, all the broken rock for the concrete had to be brought from the quarries at Miami, and with the cement was stacked in huge heaps at Knight's Key, which constituted the supply depot. The scattered situations of some of the constructional gangs taxed the efforts of the commissariat to a straining point. In many cases the supply boats, in order to get to their destination, only perhaps a mile distant as the bird flies, had to follow a circuitous route of 8 or 10 miles to get there.

When it was seen that Mr Flagler was serious in his intentions, and that the first stretch of viaduct was completed successfully, it was maintained that 'Flagler's Folly', though a wonder of engineering, never could hope to pay its way. Time alone can prove or disprove this contention, but it is worthwhile to observe that, as each section of the line has been completed, strenuous efforts to develop the country penetrated thereby have been made. The Florida East Coast Railway serves an essentially pleasure country – the Riviera of America. Yet, as the line plunged southwards, hotels sprang up at various sylvan spots, and they rapidly assumed positions of importance. The only barren stretch is the Everglades. The commercial conquest of this useless expanse must come later inevitably, and indeed energetic measures to this end are in active progress.

CHAPTER 20

The Land of
Remarkable Railway Bridges

In order to describe fully the complete conquest which the iron horse has accomplished in British India, volumes would be required. In that country, the steel highway has been driven forward in the face of prodigious difficulties of every description; the story is an exciting romance.

But the features which impress the traveller most strongly are the bridges. Some compel more than passing interest because of their great length, such as the Sone Bridge, on the East Indian railway, which consists of ninety-three spans, giving the structure a total length of 10,952 feet, making it one of the longest bridges in the world; or the Godavari over the river of the same name on the Madras North-East line, 9,066 feet in length; others because of their height, as, for instance, the Gokteik Viaduct in Burma, 325 feet high; or the Dhorabhave Viaduct, 178 feet above the stream; while here and there attention is challenged because of the massive proportions of the structure or its unusual design, as, for instance, the Jubilee Bridge across the river Hooghly at Naihati, or the Lansdowne Bridge across the Indus at Sukkur, the main span of which is 790 feet clear.

It may be safe to assert that no country has offered the bridge builder such striking opportunities to display his ability or enterprise as the Indian Empire. The Americans point to the great width of their waterways, and the huge structures which leap across the Mississippi, Missouri or Columbia rivers, but, compared beside the erections which carry the railway across the Indian waterways, they appear puny.

The Indian rivers are famous for their great width, and the extent to which they break up the country through which they make their tortuous ways to the sea. The result is that when the engineer is called upon to cross from bank to bank, especially in connection with the more important waterways, he is faced with some teasing and complex problems, to solve which demands often considerable ingenuity and the expenditure of much racking cogitation. These rivers are bad friends to the engineer at the best of times, but when lashed into fury and swelled to flood they almost defy mastery.

The flood is the bugbear of the bridge builder. One never knows what the enraged water is going to do next. Sir Bradford Leslie, K.C.I.E., M.INST.C.E., who probably has been associated with more great engineering achievements of this character in India than any other living engineer, can recall thrilling moments innumerable. For instance, when he was carrying the Jubilee Bridge across the river Hooghly, the water carried away one of the caissons which he was about to launch for one of the piers. He thought it had been lashed safely into position by means of chains, preparatory to sinking, but the Hooghly 'bore' quickly undeceived him. The Hooghly bore is an ugly customer, for at times it attains a height of 7 feet, and travels upstream for 70 miles in 4 hours. This rapidly moving bank of liquid struck the unlucky caisson, although the latter was of respectable dimensions and weight, snapped the mooring chains as if they were pack-thread, and carried the cylinder away as if it were a small butter-tub. The engineer had a lively chase upstream after his work, and finally secured it stranded in an awkward position about ½ mile above its site.

Immediately arrangements were hurried forward to salvage the caisson. After a day and a half's continuous hard toil, it was recovered and anchored alongside the bank until the next propitious moment arrived for it to be towed out into the stream and sunk into position.

In the early days, the engineers in their bridge-building operations suffered the maximum width of a river to dictate what the length of such a structure should be. Seeing that the normal channels of many of these waterways are narrow in comparison with what they attain under flood, this rendered bridge work exceedingly expensive and intricate. It is no uncommon circumstance for a waterway, when swollen by the rains of the wet season, to spread out for a width of 3 miles or more. It becomes practically insatiable, the soft earth forming the banks falling a ready victim to the powerful eroding action of the scurrying water. The result is worse than that brought about by the scouring of the River Mississippi, which devours huge masses of land continually on either bank. When the Indian river falls, unsightly stretches of undulating sandbanks are revealed, riven by little back channels and small lagoons, which present a general aspect of desolation. Under such circumstances, bridging from bank to bank is a somewhat vague undertaking, for the simple reason that it is difficult to decide what are the limits of the waterway, because erosion continues until the water reaches material which defies this action.

The engineer has met this situation now in an ingenious manner. He determines the channel of the river and keeps it within bounds by means of an artificial wall or training bund, which is carried parallel to the navigable channel, the flow of water through the space between the inner side of the wall and the shore being obstructed by a solid embankment which carries the track. This system was employed first by Mr J. B. Bell to carry the North-Western state railway across the Chenab River at Sher Shah, and proved so eminently successful that it has come into general favour.

One of the latest and most interesting, as well as largest undertakings of this class, is that in connection with the Curzon railway bridge over the Ganges at Allahabad, for the Allahabad-Fyzerbad railway. At this point the river flows between high banks of hard clay about 3 miles apart, and so resistant is this earth to scouring action that erosion has been brought to cessation practically. The width of the waterway, however, is about 1¼ miles, arid when it was decided to span the river, a great length of steel appeared inevitable.

The engineer-in-chief for the work, Mr. Robert R. Gales, M.INST.C.E., however, decided to cut down the length of the bridge work to 3,000 feet. The project was examined at great length, owing to the fact that the difference in the level of the river during the dry and flood seasons is not less than 31 feet, as the Ganges receives the waters of the Jumna about 7 miles above the site selected for the crossing. Careful investigations, however, pointed to the fact that the accumulated waters could be directed safely through a channel some 3,000 feet wide, and accordingly the erection of the training-bund was taken in hand on the left bank. It measures some 4,000 feet in length from end to end, and the top is 5 feet above the flood level of the river. The upstream arm measures 3,300 feet in length, and the extremity ends in a sharp curve to mitigate the effects of scouring. Viewed from the bank, the work resembles a huge letter 'L', with the bottom arm pointing upstream, and the tail overhanging for about 700 feet, while the upright member forms the embankment connecting the training-wall to the shore, and leads the railway track to the bridge.

The training-wall is built up of sandy soil, with stone pitched on the face exposed to the action of the river. At the top it is about 20 feet in width, and carries a wide-gauge railway track from end to end, so that should the floods tear a gap in the embankment, the injury can be repaired immediately by dumping spoil into the breach from railway wagons.

Erection had to be hurried forward, as the season available for operations was so short. In view of the fact that the erection of the wall entailed the handling of some 50,000,000 cubic yards of earth, some idea of the magnitude of the task may be gathered. It was split up into a number of contracts, and when the operations were in full swing no less than 7,000 coolies found employment.

While this work was in progress, the bridge itself was pushed forward. The length of metal is 3,000 feet, divided into fifteen spans, each of 200 feet, carried upon masonry piers. The bridge was called upon to meet requirements not only for railway traffic but for pedestrians and vehicles as well. A single line of 5 feet 6 inches gauge suffices for the former, which is carried upon the bottom deck, while the upper deck meets the second requisition, being 23 feet wide and about 60 feet above the level of the waterway when in flood.

The undertaking was pushed forward with such energy that it was completed in three seasons. The saving in outlay resulting from constricting the river channel, and thereby reducing the length of steelwork, represented no less than £100,000, or $500,000. This offers a convincing illustration as to the ingenious manner in which the bridge engineer in India has succeeded in reducing the costs of spanning the noble waterways of the country.

In a far-away corner of the same country, Upper Burma, may be seen another interesting example of the bridge-builder's craft, carried out under particularly exacting conditions in a forbidding country. This is the Gokteik Viaduct, which carries the metre-gauge single track of the Burma Railway Company across the gorge of the same name. This structure was completed by the Pennsylvania Steel Company, of Steelton, Pennsylvania, and the award of the contract was criticised severely in Great Britain. But the government wanted the valley spanned in the shortest possible space of time and at a moderate price. When the tenders invited from all parts of the world were opened, it was found that the British firms had been outclassed by their American rivals in both these essential factors.

The location of the railway across this gorge was beset with peculiar difficulties. The question of the approach was trying to decide to the best advantage, and in fact so many surveys were made that one of the American engineers remarked 'that he could not see the side of the cliff for survey pegs'.

The gorge itself is also somewhat strange; in fact, it is a curious wonder of Nature. The Chungzoune River flows through the rift, but out of sight, its course being through a natural tunnel, into which it disappears suddenly at a depth of 500 feet. When the line was first surveyed it was in accordance with a low viaduct, the approach thereto being over a suggested section of rack railway working on the Abt system, with grades of 1 in 12½. This was subsequently abandoned, and the surveyor was called upon to find a fresh

location so as to eliminate the rack railway, and to give grades not exceeding
1 in 25, so as to permit the line to be worked by adhesion. This decision
raised the height of the towers by 70 feet and increased its length to 1,350
feet. Even this did not meet with approval, for after prolonged deliberation a
third location was demanded, to give an easier line yet. In this last survey, the
gradients were flattened to 1 in 40, with an attendant increase in the height
of the structure as well as of its length. It was found impossible to improve
upon the viaduct itself, so further surveys were carried out to improve the
approaches, reducing their length and introducing curves at either end of the
viaduct.

At last finality was reached, and the contract was secured by the American
bridge builders on 28 April 1899. They lost no time in hurrying forward the
preparation of the steel. Three months later a special train of forty-five cars,
laden with 977 tons, left Steelton on the 201-mile run to New York, where
a specially chartered steamer was in waiting to receive this steel cargo. The
vessel left the American port on a journey of over 10,000 miles to Rangoon,
where the freight was transferred to the small trucks of the railway and sent
on the up-country journey of 460 miles to the Gokteik gorge. No less than
three steamers were required to transport the 4,308 tons of steel, together
with some 200 tons of requisite tackle for erection, and thirty-five American
bridge erectors.

When the Americans arrived on the scene they were treated to their
first experience of Indian weather. The rain fell in torrents; the roads were
converted into rushing streams, and the low-lying stretches of land into
lakes. This was something new to the Americans, and they chafed at being
compelled to sit down to wait until the weather moderated. To make
matters worse, the line was knocked about severely by the rain, no less than
thirteen washouts occurring between the coast and the gorge. In one place
a locomotive got caught. It could not advance and could not retreat, owing
to breaches in the railway on either side, so quietly settled down to rest in
the waterlogged embankment, and finally slipped into a field of rice, to the
intense disgust of the owner.

The result was that the port became congested with the steel and tackle
awaiting dispatch up-country. The railway company repaired the washouts
with all possible speed, and directly the line was opened the material poured
towards Gokteik in a ceaseless stream. In fact, the American engineers were
somewhat perplexed by the speed with which the material was sent up, and
they had a spirited task in sorting out the pieces of steel as they arrived.
The work proceeded so feverishly that the empty trains could not be backed

out of the shunting yard with sufficient alacrity to admit incoming loads. The bridge builders extended assistance in a novel manner. Shunting was abandoned. The large steam derricks picked up the empty cars bodily off the one track, whipped them round, and deposited them upon a siding, from which the engines pulled them out as best they could.

The railway company provided the builders with a special railway down the side of the cliff, as the approach was not completed. This was a huge switch-back, where the trains ran from side to side, first forwards and then backwards. The descent of the precipice in this manner treated the bridge builders to an exciting ride, which somewhat unnerved them at first, as it was far and away too thrilling to be pleasant. A cableway was also stretched across the gulch, and this was used for transporting material from point to point. In fact, two locomotives were dismantled and sent across this rope in pieces to be re-erected on the opposite side.

When the bridge builders arrived, they found that Mr G. Deuchars, the engineer-in-chief to the railway, had completed the whole of the preparations. The concrete pedestals for the steel towers stretched across the floor of the ridge in two unbroken lines over the top of the natural bridge through which the Chungzoune River makes its subterranean way. All that the bridge builders had to do was to set the steel.

The viaduct was built upon the overhanging principle, in accordance with the American practice, by means of a traveller. This was a cumbersome piece of apparatus weighing 100 tons, with a long arm which reached out over the gorge from tower to tower. To the native, this appliance was a source of infinite wonder. When it was pushed out to its fullest extent, and the long arm appeared certain to lose its balance and to topple into the ravine, they looked on with awe; and when the Americans flew in the face of Providence, as they thought, by venturing to the outermost point to carry out their work, they shuddered. In fact, they never became accustomed to that traveller. Why it did not capsize exceeded their comprehension.

The American workmen were assisted in their operations by 350 natives brought from other parts of the country, and who were accustomed somewhat to bridge building. Once work was brought into swing, it went forward with a rush, the steel towers springing up from their pedestals to a height of 200 feet or so within two or three days. The men toiled 9¾ hours every day, and there was not a halt except when the monsoon blew and it was well-nigh impossible to secure a foothold in exposed positions, or when the torrential rainfall prevailed.

The white men found the heat particularly trying and exhausting. Those perched 200 or 300 feet in the air, and fully exposed to the sun and a temperature of 120 degrees, secured a little welcome shade under an awning that was stretched over the apparatus. They wore the lightest of clothing, while white pith helmets served to offer some protection from sunstroke.

The total length of the work is 2,260 feet, and it is built up to ten spans, each measuring 120 feet, and seven spans of 60 feet apiece. The girders forming the deck are supported on steel towers spaced 40 feet apart. The height of the rails at the highest pier is 325 feet above the floor of the gorge, and 825 feet above the Chungzoune stream. No less than 232,868 separate pieces of steel had to be handled on the site, and the natives had to drive 200,000 rivets to secure the fabric together.

Owing to the remote point at which work was being carried out – 10,000 miles by sea from home – an elaborate cable code was drawn up, each integral part of the viaduct, as well as details of the erecting plant, having a distinctive word. In addition, there were special words for the purpose of reporting the progress of the erection to headquarters. Every week, the chief engineer cabled home a full progress report at a cost of 5s, or $1.25, per word. The men were provided with a well-equipped medicine chest, and a complete photographic outfit constituted an important part of the organisation, photographs being dispatched to Steelton regularly to supplement the cabled and written report on the progress of the undertaking. Only one man was lost in the enterprise, and this was attributable to fever produced from indulgence in alcoholic liquor. No other fatality was recorded either among the natives or Americans, and no serious accident marred the work, which, bearing in mind its magnitude and character, was highly satisfactory.

The actual erection occupied nine months, work being continued uninterruptedly through the wet season, when, fortunately, the greater part of the annual 150 to 200 inches of rain fell during the night. Although the viaduct is 24½ feet wide across the top, which is sufficient to carry a double track, only one road is laid at present. The bridge also enables pedestrians to cross from one side of the chasm to the other, refuge platforms being provided at frequent intervals to enable those afoot to escape being run down by passing trains. Upon completion, the structure was subjected to severe tests spread over a period of two months, and these proving satisfactory, the structure was accepted by the railway authorities. The mammoth steel traveller weighing 100 tons, and which had played such an important part in the rapid erection of the viaduct, was demolished and sold for scrap.

By the provision of this viaduct at the selected height, the track is led to a natural ledge on the opposite cliff-face. While the viaduct was under construction the railhead was pushed forward, the material for the grade being transported across the valley by the overhead cable. By the time trains were able to cross the structure, the end of steel had reached a point some 35 miles beyond.

Although the viaduct is not so lofty as other structures of its class in other parts of the world, yet it occupies a position of distinct importance. Moreover, it constitutes one of the finest expressions of this class of American work that has ever been fulfilled.

CHAPTER 21

Where the Snowplough
Works in Summer

The Scandinavian Peninsula has been the battleground of many titanic struggles on behalf of the railway. In this country, the iron horse has forced its way to the most northerly point in the world where the shriek of a locomotive whistle may be heard. This is Ofoten, a port on the Atlantic seaboard of Norway, beyond the sixty-eighth parallel, and well into the Arctic circle, where the famous iron mines of Gellivare in Sweden find a western point for shipping the ore.

It was in Sweden that steel was pressed into service for the first time in connection with the erection of bridges by the late Major C. Adelskold, R. E., and Member of the Academy of Sciences. This was so far back as 1866, and the daring engineer designed, superintended the preparation of the metal, and also the erection of the bridge. The claim of being the first steel bridge has been advanced on behalf of other structures in different parts of the world, but the records are against all such statements, for they were anticipated by a decade at least in a convincing, practical manner.

Major Adelskold's bridge is highly interesting, not only from the historical point of view, but because of its unusual design, and the methods adopted in its erection. Through the courtesy of Madam Gustafva Adelskold, I am enabled to give the following particulars of its evolution and construction.

The bridge was designed to carry the Uddevalla–Weners–borg–Herljunga railway across the Huvudnas Falls, just above the Tröllhätten Falls. At this point the Göta River forces its way through a gorge 137½ feet wide, just above a fall over a lofty ledge of rock. The depth and velocity of the water prevented any intermediate pier being erected in the waterway, so in order to span the gap it was necessary to lift the girders bodily to set them into position. To enable this end to be achieved, it was imperative that the main girders should be as light as possible. An iron girder, which was the metal in exclusive vogue at that time for this work, 153 feet in length by 12 inches wide, of the requisite strength, would have weighed over 700 tons, and to have handled such a weight would have demanded expensive and elaborate erecting tackle.

Major Adelskold consequently rejected iron as the structural material in favour of light steel girders. Once these were set, he anticipated no further hindrance to completing the structure as a 'suspension bridge'. Up to this time steel girders never had been employed in such work, and the engineer, when he revealed his intentions, was urged by experts and fellow craftsmen not to use 'such a brittle and untrustworthy material' for so long a span.

Major Adelskold, however, was convinced of the soundness of his proposal, and consequently continued his efforts in the face of spirited opposition. The bridge was built at Bergsund, and the dimensions were calculated for a strain of 8 tons per square inch, though the metal was tested to twice that stress before being set in position. The total weight was only 50 tons.

From the engineering point of view, the design is considered somewhat novel, for it bears no resemblance to the general conception of a suspension bridge. It is an inverted structure of this class. The upper members act merely as struts to keep apart the ends of the chains below, which really carry the load through the medium of the triangular members.

The method by which the structure was erected was quite as interesting as the design of the bridge itself. The girders were brought to the western bank of the river. To swing them into position, a derrick was rigged up on either bank so as to overhang the water. The outer ends of these masts, which measured 60 feet in length, were fitted with heavy pulleys, over which ropes were passed and carried from capstans installed for hauling purposes. The pulley ropes on the eastern bank were pulled across the waterway and secured to one end of the girder, while the western bank pulley ropes were secured to the other end of the steel member, which measured 153 feet in length. In this way the girder was lifted, swung over the water, and lowered into position. The event was regarded as so unusual that crowds of people from Gothenburg and Trollhatten assembled on the banks to witness the setting of the steel on 8 February 1866.

Owing to the roar of the waters, the engineer could not make his voice heard, so orders were communicated across the river in Morse code by hand-signalling. The first girder was lifted and set in position in 30 minutes, while the second was handled in half that time. Once the girders were set, it was an easy matter to complete the remainder of the structure.

It may be interesting to relate that the total cost of setting the main girders, together with the hire of the tackle borrowed from a Gothenburg shipbuilding yard, and including the wages of the men assisting in the task, was only £25, or $125. At that time, Major Adelskold's feat was regarded as an audacious stroke of engineering, but today steel is the exclusive material employed in the erection of bridges.

Railway building in these twin countries has been attended always with grave difficulties, owing to the rugged nature of the country and the extreme hardness of the rock. When the sea is left, and the interior plateau is gained, the full brunt of the Arctic weather is experienced, and it is of a character to deter the most intrepid engineer.

One of the most momentous enterprises that has been carried to fulfilment in this northern country is the Trans-Norwegian railway, whereby Christiania is brought into direct communication with the Atlantic seaboard at Bergen. Owing to the prodigious difficulties involved, however, it occupied some thirty years to carry the scheme through, although the line is only 306 miles in length.

In 1870, commercial interests petitioned for the establishment of a shorter route between the east coast and the Norwegian capital. Surveyors, therefore, were deputed to investigate the interior and to ascertain the practicability of building such a railway. After infinite labour, the engineers reported favourably upon the project, but pointed out that the work would be unprecedentedly arduous, and would be highly expensive.

For five years the scheme lay dormant, but in 1875 the government decided to commence the enterprise, with a section of line 67½ miles long, connecting the seaboard at Bergen with Vossevangen. In deference to views prevailing at the time, however, the narrow- or metre-gauge was adopted, and in 1883 it was opened for traffic.

Although no further headway was made with the continuation of the main scheme, it was not abandoned by any means. A mountain barrier, the Dovrejelf range, barred the way to the interior. Its penetration was recognised as one demanding great skill, for the peaks are precipitous, with sides dropping into valleys so narrow as to be mere defiles on the sea side of the chain. Apart from these physical handicaps, however, the rain and snow-falls upon the highest levels were found to be tremendous, and it was essential that elaborate examination should be made concerning these adverse influences before the location was decided definitely.

A cautious policy was practised. No attempt to proceed beyond Vossevangen was made until the mountain wall had been searched through and through. No less than twelve alternative routes were prepared and submitted to the government. These demonstrated the conclusive fact that no route could offer avoidance of the snow and rain. The question was to follow a location, if possible, where these drawbacks were emphasised to the least degree. For this purpose, several meteorological stations were established among the mountains and on the plateau to gather exhaustive data by daily observations.

The outcome was the production of some decidedly startling facts, even to those who were convinced of the extremely inclement conditions prevailing inland. The observers had been instructed to record particularly the maximum fall of snow during 24 hours, the depth of the snow among the mountains during the winter, and the effect of the winds which swept the plateau mercilessly during the latter season. It was found that snow fell every month during the year at Fjeldberg, even June, July and August not being free from such visitations, while at another point the snowfall in winter aggregated no less than 11 feet. At no point along the projected location of the line was a depth of less than 8 feet recorded, while the general average was from 10 feet to 14 feet.

The winds were found to drive the dry, fleecy flakes before them like dust, to pile up huge drifts in sheltered places, running up to 16½ feet deep. Some of these drifts remained throughout the summer, and were found to be of respectable proportions. The sum of these reports presaged the fact that, when the line was completed, the question of maintaining it free from snow-blocks would demand superhuman effort.

At last the government decided to proceed with the undertaking. The advantages and disadvantages of the various locations had been weighed diligently, and promoted the decision to adopt the Gravehals route. The authorities regarded this location with misgiving in the first instance, because it involved the piercing of a tunnel 17,420 feet in length, at an elevation of 2,818 feet. Funds were voted to build the next section from Vossevangen to Taugevand, a distance of 47 miles. In this distance, the line was to be lifted a matter of 4,000 feet to the highest point to be attained between the Atlantic seaboard and Christiania.

The route selected comprised the boring of no less than 12 tunnels, making in the aggregate not less than 11¼ miles, of which the Gravehals tunnel represented over 3 miles. While this difficult section was being prosecuted, the government resolved to come to a definite conclusion as to the route the railway should follow after attaining the summit at Taugevand, so as to enable operations to be continued without delay when the latter point was reached.

The exposed position of the Gravehals tunnel rendered the work exhausting to the men. As the timber line is about 2,000 feet below, the mountainsides are quite bare, and there is no protection against the elements whatever. The work is the longest of its kind in Northern Europe, and has proved probably one of the most exacting to construct. It extends through granite which was found to be exceedingly tough, so that boring was unavoidably slow, especially at times when everything appeared to be pitted against the contractors.

The firm who accepted the contract undertook to complete the work for £158,400, or $792,000, which was considered to be a very low price. It was attacked from both ends, and mechanical boring was adopted. Convenient water power was harnessed to drive the Brandt rock drills, which worked under a pressure of some 1,200 pounds per square inch. Boring proceeded somewhat slowly, more so, in fact, than the contractors had anticipated, but this was due to the extreme hardness of the rock encountered, while the work was handicapped by delays which the contractors could not have controlled. In the first place labour proved scarce and expensive. The men working on the coast, although experienced in drilling and blasting rock, could not be persuaded to proceed up-country to practise their skill. The situation was too remote, and the elements were too bitter, and seeing that extensive railway construction was proceeding at the same time in other and more congenial parts of the country, there was no cogent reason why the men should hie to an inhospitable locality for work.

The tunnel-borers, however, were spared the tribulations which have assailed their colleagues in other parts of Europe. Faults in the rock strata were very few and far between, while subterranean streams and pockets of viscous mud did not overwhelm them. The temperature within the boring, moreover, never rose to an intolerable point, the maximum recorded being 52 degrees Fahrenheit. This was in striking contrast to the conditions on the Gotthard, Cenis, Simplon, and other central European tunnels, where the mercury rose at times to the vicinity of 90 degrees.

Yet the workers in the Gravehals tunnel experienced their own peculiar dangers and exasperating misadventures. The climatic conditions were the most trying, and many men abandoned their tasks after a short experience in this bleak situation, for work at a lower level. This monotony was varied one day by an avalanche, which crashed down the mountainside, smashed into the power-house and carried away some of the machinery. Work had to be suspended for some six weeks while the damage thus caused was repaired. At another time, work could not be carried forward because no water was available, and about two months of enforced idleness had to be endured until the turbines could be set going once more.

On the same section is another heavy piece of work of this character, the Reinunga tunnel, extending for 5,217 feet through a massive mountain shoulder. Here the country is extremely wild, and the location of the line taxed the plotters supremely. The track crawls along a narrow ledge for some distance, poised nearly 500 feet above the high road. The situation is precarious, for landslides and avalanches are of frequent occurrence, while detached boulders rattle down the slopes at times and threaten the railway with extinction. Fortunately, as the metals are laid on a gallery of solid rock hewn in the mountainside, the extent of the damage inflicted by these visitations is limited to the permanent way, though the presence of these untoward obstacles, and the result of their impact with the metals, may interrupt communication for a short time.

Seeing that a difference in level of over 4,100 feet has to be overcome in the 47 miles between Vossevangen and Taugevand, it is a teasing uphill pull all the way. The grades are very abrupt at places, and impose a severe tax upon the locomotives. The passenger, however, has one compensation for slowness in travel. Some of the grandest scenery to be seen on the European continent is unfolded to the train as it glides in and out among the mountain rifts, and consequently, from the tourist point of view, the route possesses illimitable attractions, inasmuch as it offers facilities to gain some of the most beautiful parts of the country, which hitherto have been unapproachable, except in the face of an arduous and tedious journey by primitive means of conveyance.

After crossing the summit level the railway commences an easy descent, for the inland plateau is gently undulating, and the valleys being wider, the surveyors were assisted appreciably in their task of discovering an easy location. The downward run continues until Bromma, 205 miles west of Bergen, is gained at an altitude of some 450 feet. Then comes another rise to overcome a low range, which is accomplished through a tunnel 7,644 feet in length.

This tunnel proved a more exacting and troublesome undertaking than either the Gravehals or Reinunga works. The boring was attempted at first on the time system, but the advance was so slow and unsatisfactory that this principle was abandoned. The whole tunnel was then handed over to a contractor, but he found the rock so hard that a piece-work system was instituted. In this arrangement, the workmen were stimulated to supreme effort by the offer of tempting premiums. Issuing from this tunnel, there is another descent for some miles, when another ridge intervenes, necessitating a sharp climb of 700 feet, followed by a smart downward run to Roa, where a junction is effected with the Norwegian eastern railway system.

Contemporaneously with the building of this line between Vossevangen and Roa, the original section between Bergen and Vossevangen had to be overhauled. The metre-gauge was in vogue upon this division, whereas the rest of the line was being built on the standard gauge to secure uniformity with the other lines. Accordingly, the narrow-gauge was replaced by standard-gauge track striking pieces of railway engineering in Europe, and testifies to the remarkable skill and dogged perseverance of the Scandinavians in breaking down tremendous obstacles as they arose, with complete success. It is no light undertaking to attempt such an enterprise as this in such a latitude across a terribly exposed, storm-swept plateau, among the most sparsely populated regions of Europe, and where the winter lasts for eight or nine months. The rainfall is tropical in its severity, while the storms are of terrific fury, as the workmen found to their cost.

Some idea of the magnitude of the work consummated by the engineers may be gathered from a few general details. The line passes through no less than 184 tunnels, which represent an aggregate length of nearly 24 miles. To carry the line across depressions which could not be filled, fourteen bridges, ranging from a single-span stone structure of 60 feet to a metal bridge 566 feet from end to end, had to be built. Between the two terminal points, fifty-five stations and stopping places have been provided. In order to fashion the permanent way, the engineers had to excavate about 35,000,000 cubic feet of earth, and nearly 30,000,000 cubic feet of rock on the highest parts of the mountain section, this latter task being assisted by the expenditure of over 1,800,000 pounds of dynamite.

The anticipated task of maintaining communication, especially on the higher and more exposed sections of the railway, has been appreciated to the full. To deal with the snow three powerful rotary ploughs have been acquired, and one is kept in constant readiness. It is no unusual circumstance for this equipment to be called out in the middle of summer to cope with a block in one of the deep cuttings. The drift is a danger against which especial attention has to be devoted, for the wind catches up the fine, dry flakes and whirls them in clouds across the country. To prevent this being deposited upon the line, and thus obstructing traffic, timber screens have been erected beside the line, this defence continuing in an almost unbroken line for 60 miles between Mjolfjeld and Gjeilo.

The provision of the line, however, is of far-reaching importance to the commercial interests of Norway. Formerly, 54 hours were required to travel between Christiania and Bergen, but now, by cutting almost straight across the peninsula, the journey can be covered in 14 hours. To forge the link of 215 miles between Vossevangen and Roa, to complete this undertaking, occupied ten years, and the £3,333,000, or $16,665,000, expended upon the enterprise is considered an excellent investment for the country.

CHAPTER 22

From Buenos Aires to Valparaiso Overland

Though Meiggs was denied the glory of having built the first South American trans-continental railway, yet the idea has been carried to fruition, but at a point much farther south than he contemplated. Again, whereas the audacious Philadelphian engineer proposed only to establish his Atlantic terminus on the upper reaches of the Amazon, the completed line runs down to the water's edge on either coast, the two opposite ports connected in this manner being Buenos Aires on the Atlantic, and Valparaiso on the Pacific, coasts.

The Transandine Railway itself, which completes this connection, however, only extends from Mendoza at the foot of the mountain chain on the Argentine side, to Los Andes on the Chilian slopes of the range. These two points are 156 miles apart, but the metals had to be lifted 11,500 feet into the air to bring them together.

When it was decided to connect Mendoza and Los Andes together in this manner, the first-named town was in direct touch with the Atlantic Ocean, the Buenos Aires and Pacific railway having thrown its meshes inland to the foot of the mountains. This was not a difficult matter, owing to the flatness of the country, pampas plains for the most part prevailing. The result is that in the climb from Buenos Aires to Mendoza only 2,470 feet has to be overcome in 650 miles. Consequently, the gradients are so slight as to be practically imperceptible. Indeed, so simple was construction that it was found possible to lay the metals in an absolutely straight line for no less than 210 miles – the longest stretch of 'straight' line in the world.

It was in 1886 that the first preliminaries in the actual construction of this final link in the coast-to-coast railway were made. The surveys showed the feasibility of the scheme, though it was pointed out that to climb over the Andes would entail work of a peculiar character, and that the cost would be tremendous. The critical point was the negotiation of the summit itself, for the mountain pass is at an altitude of 12,796 feet. Though commenced in 1886, the scheme experienced many changes of fortune which hindered construction time after time. Financial and labour troubles were the two most retarding factors. By 1891 only 57½ miles were open to traffic; four years later only witnessed the passing of the ninetieth milestone. Such slow progress was deplorable in comparison with the building of the Oroya and Mollendo railways.

Then came a delay of four years, but in 1899 work was resumed and was pushed forward to completion. On the Chilean side, owing to similar troubles, construction was possible only in spurts, and even when the financial details were adjusted satisfactorily, the scarcity of labour remained a thorny problem.

The surveys showed that the most practical route westwards from Mendoza was by following the course of the river of that name right into the mountain range. In this manner, extensive blasting and heavy cutting could be avoided, except where the mountainsides dropped abruptly into the river, and then these would have to be tunnelled.

The constructional engineers followed this location, but only to run full-tilt into another difficulty which had not been foreseen. The Mendoza is a South American replica of China's ill-fated Hoang-ho. In the low season its placid waters roll leisurely to the ocean, but when it is swollen by the melting snows, it tears along with fiendish velocity. As its banks are composed only of the soft alluvium brought down from the mountains, the foaming waters do not find this a very difficult obstacle, and accordingly carry it away in tremendous quantities. As a result, the river is for ever changing its channel.

To the railway engineers, such eccentricities proved serious factors. They realised speedily that here was a situation peculiarly exasperating, for long lengths of track were swept away bodily time after time. It never could be anticipated where the turbulent water would break its bounds next. A stretch of permanent way, left safe and sound in the morning, sometimes was wiped out of existence before nightfall. All that could be seen of the work possibly was the rails dipping into the water on one bank and reappearing on the other, the intervening section describing a graceful festoon in the depths of the muddy torrent. At times the waters were more freakish. They would burst upon the track with such violence as to wrench the metals apart; then only the jagged, twisted ends jutting mournfully into the air on either side of the new river channel were the sole remnants of the track.

The engineers tried innumerable expedients to preserve the line from these erratic attacks, but without any material success for some time. At last they decided to provide the river with an artificial embankment, and to lay the track well back from the waterway. Trainloads of huge masses of stone were brought to the vulnerable points and pitched at the foot of the embankment, which was raised to a height well above flood level. Thousands of tons of stone were dumped in this manner, and it was found that it afforded complete protection, because the water could not dislodge the masonry pitching to eat its way into the soft earth beneath. The artificial dyke solved the problem of how to keep the rushing, boisterous Mendoza within bounds.

Avalanches and snowslides were another constant menace. Their accustomed paths had to be noted carefully and then studiously given a wide berth. These convulsions are of impressive severity in the Andes, and the impetus the slides gain, owing to the steepness and length of the declivities down which they tumble, imparts terrific force to them. When a slender railway stands in their path, it is caught up like straw and scattered in all directions. Possibly the landslides are more to be dreaded than the movements of the snow. In the Andes, the denuding forces of Nature are exceptionally heavy. Many a mountain slope which, from a cursory inspection, looks substantial and solid, upon closer investigation proves to be merely a thick layer, perhaps many feet in thickness, of soft detritus. The slightest vibration is sufficient to set the mass in motion, and it slides slowly and irresistibly downwards. At some places it was found impossible to avoid such unstable ground, so the engineers ingeniously cut a passage through the soft rubble, taking care to reach the solid mountain flank beneath upon which to build the track, while the detritus was held back by means of massive concrete masonry walls.

Under such circumstances it is imperative that the track should be of the most solid character, if it is designed to fulfil the conditions of a trunk highway. The roadbed is well built, laid with metals to a metre-gauge, and ballasted heavily. All earthworks are carried out on liberal lines, and the bridges are built throughout of steel.

When the main range is gained the line becomes more devious, the banks are sharper and more numerous, the short tunnels and the bridges across the rivers more frequent, for the location caused the line to swing from bank to bank as being more economical construction than to blast and carve a way for the line through the solid rock of the cliffs. At places the rises became so abrupt as to defy operation by adhesion. Then short lengths of rack where cog-wheels on the locomotive mesh with a toothed rail laid between the ordinary rails, and working similar to a rack and pinion, had to be inserted to enable the train to climb upwards.

A striking evidence of the distance saved by the railway is afforded between Mendoza and Upsallata station. As the crow flies, the distance is 40 miles due east; by rail it is 17 miles farther, but by the old mountain road which converges upon the line at Upsallata it is no less than 100 miles! The latter makes a wide, sweeping detour after leaving Mendoza in order to avoid the foothills, and to ensure an easy gradient for animal traffic.

The wildest part of the range is encountered when the Mendoza River is left and the railway enters the Amarillo, or Yellow Gorge. Incidentally, the line through this rift was one of the most costly and difficult sections to build. Las Cuevas, at an altitude of 10,388 feet, was the objective, and so great is the difference in level within a few miles that some daring development work had to be carried out. The first sign of this steep climb is a Meiggs V-switch. The rack was adopted more extensively, this being introduced between short stretches of easier grade or sections of level, so that the railway really ascends in the form of a series of gigantic steps. The rack is of the three-toothed type similar to that so familiar on the Swiss mountain railways.

In winding through the gorge, some of the most impressive vistas of Andine majesty are unfolded. There is the snow-capped crest of Aconcagua, beetling 23,500 feet to the sky, Tupungato 21,451 feet, Tolosa 19,000 feet, and many another white-hooded mountain giant. The Transandine ranks as one of the greatest scenic railways in the world, for it unlocked the door to what previously was regarded as one of the most inaccessible sight-seeing centres on this globe. Already its station at Inca has developed into a popular mountaineering rendezvous, whence the ambitious essay to scale the caps of the Cordilleras. Some idea of the stupendous character of the railway's ascent in this region may be gathered from the fact that in the last 8 miles to Las Cuevas it rises no less than 1,414 feet, and at this latter station the track lies nearly 2 miles above the Atlantic.

Las Cuevas is at the foot of the summit ridge which is pierced by the tunnel carrying the railway into Chile. This part of the work proved the most trying, for it involved wrestling with innumerable difficulties of great magnitude and peculiar character, such as are experienced very seldom in tunnelling operations. Though the range is not pierced at such an altitude as by the famous Galera tunnel in the country next door, yet it is three times as long.

The engineers had to drill, blast and excavate their way through the rock of the ridge for 10,000 feet – nearly 2 miles – and at times the obstacles that loomed up suddenly proved extremely perplexing. The completion of this work delayed the opening of the railway considerably, for calculations and anticipations were upset rudely when excavation commenced.

Some time passed before the precise design of the tunnel could be settled. At first, it was decided to describe a spiral in the peak so as to accommodate the level of the Argentine division with that of the Chile section of the line. The tunnel was to be driven from either end by the engineers of the respective railways, which were two distinct undertakings. The two armies were to meet at mid-tunnel immediately beneath the famous statue of Christo Redentor, commemorating the treaty of peace between Argentina and Chile, which stands upon the boundary line of the two countries in the pass above.

On the Argentine side, the camps for the tunnel works were established at Las Cuevas, about 1½ miles below the portal. When boring was commenced, the engineers' advance was threatened. The depth of the loose, friable earth eroded from the peaks above, which had accumulated during the flight of centuries, proved much greater than was supposed. This entailed most elaborate timbering to prevent the roof caving in and burying the excavators. As all lumber had to be brought up from Mendoza, for this desolate region is far above the timber line, heavy delays arose pending the arrival of the wood. Then they had to move forward warily foot by foot, as the detritus proved treacherous to handle. The engineers ploughed their way through this material for 300 feet, and felt relieved when at last they struck solid rock, which they rightly thought was the main body of the mountain. Elaborate arrangements were made to drive ahead more rapidly, but when the mass had been penetrated for nearly 200 feet, the engineers received another rude shock. The rock was false. What they had fondly thought to be the mountain itself was merely a huge crag which had become detached and had slipped down bodily.

Here was a critical dilemma. The work was far too risky for aught but expert tunnel builders – engineers who had made a speciality of such undertakings, and who were possessed of competent ability and facilities to cope successfully with any contingency likely to develop. As a result of careful deliberations it was decided to hand the whole tunnel – lock, stock and barrel, from end to end – to one firm. Selection fell upon the British engineers, Messrs C. H. Walker & Company, who rescued the famous Severn tunnel from flood, and successfully completed it in the face of unheard-of difficulties.

These engineers at once attacked the problem boldly. It was found that the false rock on the Argentine side extended for no less than 1,670 feet, so that it must have been a most violent shiver of Nature, indeed, which let loose that mountain spur. The situation, however, was grasped so completely that within two years the range was pierced.

Yet it was not so much the engineering difficulties that this firm feared when they essayed the task, but the altitude at which it had to be accomplished. Again, there were difficulties incidental to transport, and the situations of the workings so far from any base. These were very great. It must be remembered that during the winter months – that is, from April to October – the tunnel workings and camps were cut off practically from the outside world. To plan one's arrangements during the short summer so that when isolated there was no lack of material, food for the workmen, housing accommodation, as well as provision made for a thousand-and-one other details which were bound to arise, demanded considerable foresight, for work had to be maintained as steadily during the winter snows as under the summer sun.

It is not every workman who will volunteer, or is physically capable, to brave the dangers attending the wielding of pick, shovel, wheelbarrow and explosives in the rarefied atmosphere and the adverse climatic conditions prevailing in winter among the highest altitudes of the Andes. The cold is intense, the snowfall is tremendous, and the winds rage with terrific fury. The frozen snow and ice are driven like sand in all directions, and with such force that they cut like a knife, and penetrate every crevice.

Labour, indeed, proved a wearisome difficulty. Chileans figured most prominently among the workmen, and they proved to be very good labourers. There were a few Italians among them, with Englishmen occupying the controlling positions. At each end of the tunnel, elaborate hospitals were erected replete with competent medical attention, for in addition to accidents there were the innumerable maladies provoked by the reduced atmospheric pressure which, unless skilfully tended in the incipient stages, are apt to develop very serious symptoms. Pneumonia was the chief cause of illness, attributable to insufficient clothing and care on the part of the Chileans. But after all is said and done, work at such an altitude is terribly exhausting under the most favourable conditions.

On the Chilean side, the constructional work was more imposing in character. It is only 46 miles from the Pacific portal of the tunnel to Los Andes, where junction is effected with the state railway systems. In this short distance there is a difference of some 8,000 feet in levels, and the drop in the first 7 miles from the tunnel mouth is no less than 3,150 feet. The engineers were hard pushed to devise ways and means to lay the track so that it could be operated by the usual railway methods. Heavy grades, ranging from 6 to 8 per cent, could not be avoided to communicate each successive gallery carrying the metals along the mountain sides. The rack had to be resorted to freely, and the result is that the line describes a remarkable zigzag course, strikingly recalling the wonderful Stelvio road in the Tyrol.

At one point there is a very impressive piece of engineering. The line winds along the hillside high up on the bank of the rushing Aconcagua River, disappears into a tunnel through a spur, and then emerges at the other side on the brink of a narrow chasm – the Soldier's Leap. This is a mere wedge-shaped fissure in the rock, but a few feet in width, and through which the river tumbles over 200 feet below. A narrow bridge carries the line across the rift to a narrow ledge blasted out of the opposite cliff-face where the mountains overhang the water.

The resources of the engineers will be taxed to a supreme degree in order to keep the line clear from snow during the winter. In fact, it was asserted freely that for about six months in the year the upper levels of the line would be well-nigh impassable. The engineers on the spot, however, have risen to the occasion. They have studied the massive hills of snow which, lashed into furious whirl storms by the hurricane winds, sweep rapidly and irresistibly forward, often burying the railway to a depth of 30 feet or more. A powerful rotary plough was placed in service to tackle this obstacle, and although found highly successful in the places where the line was open, it could not be utilised in the deep cuttings. Special situations demand special methods. So the engineers set to work to devise their own means of combating Boreas in his wildest fury. They evolved a push-plough of a special wedge-shape pattern, which can attack a 16-foot drift and cut a channel clean through it with ease. The trouble is not so much the snow, but the large masses of rock which are rolled down the mountain sides, and lurk in the white mass. When a rotary strikes one of these formidable boulders when running at full speed, the auger-like rotating mechanism is smashed to pieces, and the whole apparatus is thrown out of action. With the special push-plough, however, no such disaster is to be feared. The nose of the apparatus glides over the concealed obstruction without suffering any damage whatever, and the boulder can be removed by manual labour, as a skilled gang of snow clearers are attached to every snowplough train.

A new line is approaching completion among the Andes which compels attention, even in South America, the land of railway wonders. This is the new main line which is to connect La Paz, the capital of Bolivia, with the coast. Hitherto, in order to gain the metropolis of the interior land-locked state, one has had to embark upon a circuitous journey either via the Antofagasta railway and its connections, or by means of the Peruvian Southern railway from Mollendo, by way of Lake Titicaca and Puno.

The new line starts from the coast at Arica and follows as straight a line to La Paz as the configuration of the country permits. The outstanding feature of this enterprise is the extreme altitude at which it lies for the greater part of its length, this ranging between 12,000 and 14,000 feet above the Pacific. Another fact is that the summit is not overcome by a tunnel, but the line passes right over the crests. The line measures 292 miles in length, and the sudden rise from the coast into the mountain country is effected by means of the toothed rail or rack system, the aggregate length of which is no less than 40 miles.

Some idea of the conditions that confronted the railway builders was afforded in the course of the surveys. In many places the engineers had to blast a trail out of the hard, solid rock with dynamite in order to advance. There are about 70 tunnels, though none are very long, for the most part piercing shoulders and spurs of the main range which could not be compassed or removed. At places very heavy bridging is essential, the spanning of one gorge in particular having presented a pretty problem. This ravine is 150 feet in width, and is crossed in a single span 150 feet above the raging river.

Here, again, the extreme rarefaction of the atmosphere is a serious disadvantage against which the engineers have had to contend, while the fluctuations in temperature are extremely great. A difference of 113 degrees in the course of a day is by no means uncommon. At noon the thermometer will stand at 100, by nightfall it has dropped to 0.13 degrees. Such a rise and fall are tremendous, for at Greenwich, it may be pointed out, the same daily fluctuation averages about 17 degrees.

Again, in the highest altitudes through which the line threads its way, water boils at 180 degrees, as compared with 212 degrees on the coast. In order to enable the workmen to prepare their food in such exposed, lofty situations, special vessels have had to be devised to prevent the water boiling over, for this result ensues long before the food is cooked properly, and the loss of water, even of only a pint, in such parched regions is a serious matter. In some places the country is as arid as the Sahara, and the water has had to be transported over great distances in barrels slung on the backs of mules. Large packs of these animals have been pressed into service for this work only. Similarly, the building material has had to be carried from the coast to the constructional camps strung out along the proposed route, by means of this ship of the Andes.

The work was carried out from both ends simultaneously, one tentacle being thrown out from the junction with the Bolivian State railways westwards, and the other eastwards from the coast. The cost of providing the capital of Bolivia with this direct outlet to the Pacific approximates £3,000,000, or $15,000,000. Bearing in mind the high cost of the other Andean railways, this last conquest of the South American mountain backbone may be considered low.

CHAPTER 23

A Little-Known Central African Railway

Buried in the heart of Central Africa, with one border skirting the most southern of the chain of Great African Lakes which nestle in the huge depressions of the continent, is a small, little-known British colony. This corner of the empire is Nyasaland, a tongue of promising territory which thrusts itself southward into Portuguese East Africa.

Though the wealth of this little territory, measuring 550 miles in length, and varying from 80 to 90 miles in width, is incalculable, exploitation of the resources has been handicapped by the complete absence of transportation facilities. The early pioneers and civilising influences visiting the country were impressed with the outlook, and sought to attract settlers. The more hardened and adventurous accepted the invitation, and, finding the country in every way as described, devoted their energies to the cultivation of coffee, which held out most promising inducements. The physical configuration of the country, providing a diversity of hill and dale and ample watering facilities, served to bring about a certain movement towards settlement. Roads were driven in all directions, and, indeed, the internal communication today leaves little to be desired.

But the country suffered severely from being cut off from the world at large. There is only one channel by which the country can be entered, and that is from Chinde on the coast, via the Zambesi River until the mouth of the Shiré River is gained, this latter waterway being followed so far as Port Herald. The distance is about 210 miles, and the stern-wheel, shallow-draught steamboats occupy from four to six days on the journey according to the state of the rivers.

For about three months in the year the Shiré River can be navigated for a further 40 miles to Chinde, and occasionally Chikwawa, 310 miles from the coast, can be reached by water. In the early days a hope was entertained that it would be possible to travel by water from the coast to Lake Nyasa, but this is impossible, as the Murchison Falls, which connect the Upper and Lower Shiré rivers, are an insurmountable obstacle. Had this navigation been possible, the country would have been provided with an excellent artery of communication, and would have brought Blantyre, the capital, into direct touch with the coast. As a matter of fact, however, the normal head of navigation on the Shiré River is Villa Bocage, in Portuguese territory, just above the point where the waterway joins the Zambesi.

In order to remedy this grave disability, which was hindering the expansion of the country to an acute degree, the British Central Africa Company decided to provide a main line of railway between Blantyre and Port Herald. The opportunities were unique, as transport was difficult and costly, while it was pointed out, also, that by means of the iron road the slave-trade around Lake Nyasa could be broken up effectively. Sir Bradford Leslie, K.C.I.E., M.INST.C.E., the eminent engineer whose bridge building and other works are scattered throughout the Indian Empire, was approached to extend his valuable assistance and skill in the prosecution of the undertaking. The scheme was not ambitious so far as railways are concerned, but there were many peculiar difficulties which had to be overcome. The line promoted was only 114 miles in length, but in that distance a difference of 3,700 feet in levels had to be overcome. The broken character of the country proved that some heavy work would be necessary, for the deep, wide rifts in the mountainsides, though dry in summer, are raging torrents when the wet season breaks.

Sir Bradford Leslie, being interested in the extinction of the slave-trade, gladly cooperated in the scheme, and although he did not visit the country to inspect the outlook on the spot, he prepared estimates from data of the physical conditions extended, upon the basis of his Indian work.

It was intended, in the first instance, that Chiromo should be the base for constructional operations, the primary idea being to connect Blantyre with the river at this point. This represented the building of about 84 miles of line, and promised to remove the isolation and inaccessibility of the capital. At this time a cart road was the sole means of communication, and when this could not be used, everything had to be carried on the heads of native porters, while passengers had to travel to and fro by 'machilla', a kind of hammock slung from a pole.

But access to Chiromo was found to be so unreliable, owing to the shallow depth of water in the river and the numerous sandbanks upon which the vessels became stranded, that it had to be abandoned as a base. A further 30 miles of line had to be added to the project, to enable it to be carried northwards from Port Herald. The contractors found themselves hampered at every turn, and it is probable that no railway was ever constructed under such peculiar and exasperating difficulties. Railways, as a rule, have been carried from a base on the coast, where supplies could be landed without very great difficulty, but in this instance this was quite impossible. Then, again, the work was being carried out at an extreme distance from home, and an elaborate organisation was requisite to keep the forces in the field supplied with every little necessity.

When the line was commenced, the country was in a very primeval condition. Skilled labour was quite non-existent, and unskilled labour was very scarce. This problem was accentuated by the fact that Nyasaland was being drained of its resources in this respect by agents from the Transvaal, who had received permission to recruit Negro labour in this country. The railway authorities endeavoured to meet this situation by importing coolies from India for the purpose of construction, but this action was sternly forbidden by the government authorities.

The effort to provide the country with the very communication it needed so sorely to bring about its settlement, furthermore, was hampered in another direction. The government authorities in London insisted that the railway should be built according to the standard of the Rhodesian railways, notwithstanding the fact that Rhodesia was in a very much more advanced position economically, whereas Nyasaland had not reached the moulding stage. This was a somewhat inexplicable attitude to assume, and was of a nature that might have jeopardised private enterprise in this field of endeavour. However, the engineers and builders accepted the terms and the work proceeded.

Under this arrangement the 3 feet 6 inches gauge was adopted as on the Rhodesian railways, so that in the dim future, when the two systems are connected, through running will be possible. The rails weigh 41½ pounds per yard, and as timber is devoured by white ants and boring beetles, it could not be used in any form. Consequently, steel sleepers, or ties, had to be adopted.

Everything required in connection with the undertaking had to be shipped from England; the country did not assist the builders one little bit. Not an ounce of coal could be obtained locally, there was no lime, and bricks could not be made to assist in the erection of the piers. The country is even deficient in a good quality of stone suited to building purposes, so masonry work was equally out of the question. The only alternative was the utilisation of concrete. The Portland cement for this purpose, by the time it gained Port Herald, cost between five and six times the price for which it could be bought in England – in other words, the expense of carriage was from four to five times the value of the article. This applied to other material beyond cement. In fact, the transportation to such a remote district was a heavy item. The articles were dispatched to Beira, where they were transhipped into coasting steamers, and 5 hours later were landed at Chinde, where they were loaded upon the shallow-draught river boats and conveyed to Port Herald.

The line follows a northerly course after leaving the southern terminus, and roughly clings to the bank of the river so far as Chiromo. Here it swings across the waterway over a bridge about 420 feet in length, to gain the valley of the Ruo River. This bridge is the outstanding feature of the railway, on account of its interesting lifting span, which is of novel and unusual design. When the railway was plotted, the government stipulated that there should be no interference with navigation on the river, although the waterway, as a highway of traffic, has fallen practically into desuetude since the railway was constructed. However, official requirements had to be met, and these demanded an opening 100 feet wide, and giving a clearance of 30 feet in height at high water. The ordinary type of draw or swing-bridge, to satisfy this requisition, was quite out of the question, because the need to open the bridge is very rarely experienced, and when the demand does arise, the time occupied in the operation is of minor importance. Heavy expenditure under this heading, therefore, was not justifiable.

Moreover, as native labour was to superintend the work of opening and closing the bridge, the simplest arrangement possible was essential, and, furthermore, had to be capable of hand manipulation. The designing engineers, Sir Douglas Fox & Partners, and Sir Charles Metcalfe, Bart., evolved an ingenious solution. On the top of two adjacent piers carrying the span in its normal position, a tower was erected on either side of the opening, with two simple, single, vertical racks on either tower. At the top of each tower, a platform extending the width of the bridge was provided, together with a large sprocket wheel at either end. A chain passed over each sprocket wheel, one end being attached to a corner of the bridge, and the other to a heavy counterweight.

To open the bridge, all that the natives have to do is to wind a winch which rotates the sprocket wheel, and as the counterweight descends, the whole span rises vertically and horizontally, being guided in its movement by the rack on each tower. The counterweight is the full width of the bridge, and when the span has been lifted to its fullest extent, the counterbalance weight lies across the track, to form a high barrier to anyone attempting to cross the bridge when the span is open.

It will be seen that the bridge acts on the principle of a sash window, where the sash weight counterbalances the weight of the moving portion, and in lifting only the friction of the moving parts has to be overcome. To guard against disaster from tampering or misuse, the bridge, when either raised or lowered, is locked. To lower the bridge, it is only necessary to reverse the winding direction of the winch. The span of steel moved in this manner weighs 55 tons, and the whole operation of opening and closing occupies about ½ hour, eight men under a native superintendent sufficing for the movement of the winches. It is an unusual type of lifting bridge, but it is doubtful whether a simpler and cheaper means of meeting the situation could have been devised, while the maintenance expenses – a vital consideration in such a remote country – are reduced to insignificance.

About 12 miles out of Chiromo the railway commences a heavy climb, as it has to gain a summit level of 4,000 feet to reach the plateau. The ascent is through very tumbled country. The ruling grade is 1 in 44, and the minimum curve is of 363 feet radius. As the valley winds amazingly, the line is a continuation of curves winding round crags and bluffs. Here and there the mountainsides are torn by wide clefts that have had to be spanned by bridges, which are supported on steel towers, carried on pedestals or plinths built of concrete. One of the largest bridges of this class is that across the M'Swadzi River, which is 290 feet long.

The Ruo valley is left after the 64th mile is passed, and the line makes a difficult and tortuous ascent along the Tuchili River for nearly 10 miles, when it swings over to the Luchenza River, which is followed until the summit level is gained, 109 miles out of Port Herald. In the next 5 miles, a descent of 500 feet has to be made to gain Blantyre. This is the present terminus of the railway, though an extension has been projected northwards to Fort Johnston at the head of Lake Nyasa, and another limb southwards from Port Herald for 60 miles to the Portuguese town, Villa Bocage, the head of navigation on the Shiré River.

In the course of the 114 miles there is at present only one intermediate station with an existing township, at Chiromo. Three other stations have been provided, however, in the anticipation that settlements will spring up and blossom into towns as the country opens up.

Construction was sadly delayed by the difficulties in regard to labour. The native proved an indifferent workman, the maxim being to accomplish as little work in a day as possible. Then, when the rainy season – lasting about three months – set in, the whole of the working force migrated from the grade in a body to cultivate patches of land, and were not seen again until the weather changed. The climate played sad havoc with the Europeans who ventured to the scene of operations to superintend native effort, and the mortality from tropical diseases among the whites was very heavy. In order to protect what European labour is required in the repair shops and the administration offices, the headquarters have been established at Limbi, 5 miles from Blantyre, where the full benefit of the elevation is gained, this point being at an altitude of 4,000 feet above the sea, and one of the most healthy parts of the country.

An amusing story is related by Sir Bradford Leslie in connection with the construction of the railway. Prior to the commencement of this undertaking, labour in the country was rewarded in cloth – there was no money currency, and in fact the natives knew nothing about coinage or its value. However, when the line was commenced, the government insisted that the natives should not be remunerated in kind, but in cash. Wages were paid once a month, and the natives immediately were urged by Hindoo traders to transfer the money for cloth. The latter played upon the native's ignorance of money to distinct personal advantage, but the natives had to pay dearly for their goods. Moreover, they came to the conclusion that the textiles they received in exchange for their cash were inferior in quality to that given to them in direct settlement of work done. Consequently, they assailed the engineer and complained that his money was bad, in support of which contention they displayed the small quantity of indifferent material they received in exchange for their wages. They certainly did not evince a very marked appreciation for the railway company's system of paying for labour in sterling.

Although the undertaking cost more than had been estimated, the results justified fully the expenditure, for the railway, in point of construction, compares very favourably with other lines of a similar character on the continent. The engineer in charge of the work, Mr A. G. Pears, overcame his unique difficulties in a highly satisfactory manner, and its completion in about seven years is a striking tribute to his organisation and methods, while the unceasing expansion of the country supports the initiative of those who fathered the enterprise.

CHAPTER 24

The Invasion of the Far East I – Early Days in China

There has been much discussion during recent years concerning the remarkable awakening of China in every ramification of progress and industry, but without a doubt the most wonderful manifestation of this movement has been in regard to railways. In 1870, when the United Kingdom was criss-crossed with no less than 15,537 miles of the iron road, and the United States was threaded with 52,922 miles of railway, the huge tract of Asiatic territory known as the Chinese Empire, of sufficient area to absorb easily both the United States and the British Isles, and outnumbering the combined population of the two latter nations by more than 6 to 1, did not possess 100 yards of the steel highway.

This remarkable state of affairs was not due to lack of enterprise or initiative on the part of far-seeing financiers and engineers. It was attributable directly to one influence – Fung Shui, an unfathomable and insurmountable difficulty – which thwarted every attempt to bring the great nation on the eastern borders of the Pacific Ocean into line with other countries. The Flowery Land is ridden with mystery, superstition, and a religious fanaticism. These offered an insurmountable barrier to development in any form. The balance between the 'White Tiger' and the 'Azure Dragon', two inscrutable forces, had to be maintained at all costs, and unless every member of the Celestial community strove to maintain this equipoise, the fates in store for him were beyond comprehension.

An effort to break through the influence of Fung Shui was made in 1875 by a group of Englishmen. The firm of Messrs Jardine, Matheson & Company, who have large interests in China, desired to connect Shanghai to Woosung with 12 miles of railway, and they secured the services of the late Mr. G. J. Morrison, an accomplished engineer, to carry the project to fulfilment. Great difficulty was experienced in securing the requisite permission to proceed, because the Chinese entertained a deep-rooted objection to the invasion of their country by the foreigner. However, the application proved successful and the line was built.

The opening of this short road was received with acclamation by the lower classes in close proximity to the line. They experienced a peculiar delight in travelling in the carriages drawn by the steam horse, and all was proceeding merrily. The opposition of the Chinese to the newfangled idea had been overcome, argued the promoters of the enterprise, and they looked forward to further railway expansion. But they did not reckon with the offended opposition and ignorant vested interests, as represented by influential landowners and high personages. The wrath of the gods was anticipated in no uncertain manner, but as this did not appear to have vent spontaneously, the opponents resorted to ingenious methods to achieve their desires. They induced a soldier to throw himself before an approaching train, under the promise of a payment of $100 to his family. The latter, possibly entertaining the belief that the presence of his body stretched across the metals might arrest the progress of the train, or at least throw it off the track, without inflicting injury upon himself, submitted to the ordeal, with the inevitable result. He was killed. Instantly the intriguers published this circumstance as an instance of the intense displeasure of the gods, and the countryside rose up with one voice, calling for the destruction of the innovation.

The agitation startled the government. An inquiry was held upon the suicide, and the unanimous verdict was that the line was unsafe. It was condemned forthwith. The government even went farther under public pressure. It purchased the railway, lock, stock and barrel, at cost price, and turned it over to the enraged populace to do with it according to their inclinations. The frenzied fanatics tore the track up piecemeal, threw the rolling stock out of the country, and, to propitiate the gods, erected a temple to the Queen of Heaven upon the site selected as the terminus in Shanghai. The promoters of the ill-starred enterprise retrieved as much of the discarded remains of the line as possible, and transported them to the island of Formosa for another undertaking. Such was the inglorious end that befell the first attempt to introduce Stephenson's invention into the land of the Celestial.

Curiously enough, among those most prominent in the opposition to this movement was Li-Hung-Chang, subsequently China's foremost and most enlightened statesman. He had spared no effort to prevent the construction of the first railway, and when it was completed he left no stone unturned to bring about its demolition. Shortly afterwards, however, he became converted to the new method of locomotion. Among those few enterprising and enlightened Chinese gentlemen who realised the widespread advantages accruing from the adoption of railways in other parts of the world, and who foresaw its possibilities in his native land, was General Tong-King-Sing. He had followed the Shanghai-Woosung experiment with deep interest. Undeterred by the fate which had overwhelmed the effort of Messrs Jardine, Matheson & Company, he decided to build another line, but he took care first to win the most powerful opponent to such a movement to his side. The general was identified with a steamship company which required cheap coal. Li-Hung-Chang, then Viceroy of Chichli, was interested in some collieries at Tongshan, some 30 miles inland from the nearest port at Pehtang.

The general approached the viceroy, and the two, with the aid of some other influential friends, decided to exploit the deposits. But the question arose as to how the coal could be carried cheaply to the coast. General Tong-King-Sing maintained that there was no means of transportation which could compete with the railway, and he skilfully won the viceroy round to his side. In this manner the viceroy was converted from an implacable enemy to a strenuous advocate of railways. They approached the government for the requisite permission, and the latter, impressed possibly by the great men associated with the enterprise, sanctioned the project. The preliminary arrangements were hurried forward, an Englishman, Mr C. W. Kinder, who might be described as the Father of the Railway in China, being enlisted as engineer-in-chief.

Before actual constructional work was commenced, however, the government – no doubt owing to pressure – repented of its action and withdrew its approbation. As a result, the company were forced to build a canal, which was completed for some miles, but the head of this waterway was some 7 miles from the coal-pits. From the end of the canal to the port, the government authorised the construction of a tram road, but it stipulated that mules should be employed exclusively for the haulage of the trucks. The company was forced to make the most of this indifferent bargain, and so the coal was transported from the collieries to the port under very adverse circumstances.

These slow methods, however, did not appeal to the engineer, and secretly he decided to effect an improvement. He fashioned a locomotive from the best materials he could command, a portable engine which was used at the mines being mounted on a truck in such a way as to secure self-propulsion. This was used for haulage between the collieries and the head, of the canal. As no ill results attended its use, the government finally approved of its utilisation. Shortly afterwards the line as a railway was extended to Tientsin, and opened for traffic in October, 1888. Subsequently the railhead was pushed onwards to Shan-Hai-Kuan. From the small 7-mile road upon which the enterprising engineer surreptitiously placed a fearsome-looking locomotive the railway has spread its tentacles throughout the Chinese Empire, the original road has been extended, and has effected connection with other systems, giving communication in the north with Mukden, Harbin and the Trans-Siberian railway.

The original road is intensely British, both in its character and operation. It was built on the English model, and differed greatly from the usual class of pioneer railway. The gradients are easy and the curves are of wide radius. At one point the location of the line ran through two private cemeteries, but as the graves of the ancestors could not be disturbed under any considerations whatever, the line had to make a wide swerve to avoid this obstruction.

All the materials for the railway were obtained from Great Britain, and the solidity of the construction is an outstanding feature. Every bridge is carried out either in steel, concrete, brick or stone, whichever was found to be the most economical. This feature somewhat surprised American engineers, who are accustomed to less durable work in the initial stages, especially as it did not appear justifiable in such a fickle country as China. The latter were also astonished at the low price at which the requisite materials were landed in the country, and the fact that mechanical appliances could not compete with coolie labour in point of cheapness. As a matter of fact, the country traversed at that time was exceedingly poor, the inhabitants experiencing a terrible struggle to eke out a pitiable existence. Indeed, around Tongshan, at the time the railway made its appearance, it was estimated that over 50,000 natives died of starvation in two months. When the iron horse invaded this territory a change for the better set in, inasmuch as it offered a ready and inexpensive means of conveying the produce from the land to market.

One piece of engineering skill has always ranked as a distinct wonder in the neighbourhood. This is the bridge over the Lan-ho, 2,170 feet in length, in which there are five spans, each of 200 feet. It was designed by the late Sir Benjamin Baker, and aroused interest because of its unusual design, which was condemned severely by American engineers. This famous bridge builder, however, was by no means content to abide by hide-bound rules and regulations, and though in this structure he departed from the orthodox very decidedly, he forced his detractors to admit that the bridge was absolutely safe, and was able to meet any traffic that it was likely to be called upon to bear.

Another feature compels attention. Just before reaching Shan-Hai-Kuan, the line strikes across a valley about a mile in width. Here there is a bridge having an opening of some 1,000 feet, through which a narrow stream makes its way. Originally the track was carried about 10 feet above the floor of the valley, but the very next wet season caused the small stream to swell into a wide, foaming torrent, rising to 16 feet above high watermark, and it swept over the embankment like a mill-race. When the waters subsided, the engineers, instead of overhauling their earthworks, lowered the track to the bottom of the valley, so that no obstruction should be offered to future floods, while the roadbed was protected by a paving extending for 50 feet on either side, with bushes planted on the superimposed earth. This expedient was found to meet the situation completely and to protect the track from destruction by the flood waters, which fall quickly after attaining their highest level.

In the early days, the trains constituted a source of infinite amusement. They were what are known as 'mixed' trains; i.e. they carried both passengers and freight. The passenger coaches were of varying classes, the Chinese travelling in long, open trucks, with tarpaulins to protect them from inclement weather. The natives appeared to enjoy this experience highly, especially when the train attained its maximum speed of about 25 miles an hour, which they admitted was quicker travelling than by an animal-drawn cart. The whole 100 miles was covered in about 5½ hours, including stops, some of which, at intermediate points, were of long duration. At these points, however, the time was whiled away by watching the antics of the Chinese travellers, who were sorely perturbed lest the steam horse might start before its scheduled time. This initial trunk line played an important educational part in the railway expansion of China, and the cost of travelling was cut down to the lowest figure. The first-class fare for the whole distance was 5s 5d, or $1.30 for 100 miles, which, in comparison with the scale prevailing in other parts of the world for similar accommodation, was absurdly cheap. The Chinese at first regarded the railway with childish delight, those who could afford the expense travelling to and fro for the mere pleasure of travelling.

Consequently, it is not surprising that the railway soon established itself in popular favour. Indeed, resentment from the earliest days had proceeded only from the upper classes; the peasants hailed it with unfeigned pleasure. Accordingly, as railway expansion set in, any opposition that was encountered was fostered by ignorant, affected, wealthy interests. After Li-Hung-Chang became a staunch friend of the new means of travel, he established his own ways of dealing with opposition, which were peculiarly Chinese. On one railway which he supported, traffic was interrupted frequently by displaced rails and sleepers. When he, in his official capacity, sought to ascertain the reason for such disturbance, he was informed that it was due to the spirits, who resented its intrusion. He made no reply to this ingenuous reply, but hinted that if he caught the spirits interfering with the line, it would go hard with them. Needless to say, no further trouble was experienced on that line in regard to breaks in the track.

Within the past few years, several momentous railway undertakings have been carried to successful conclusion, and today there is feverish activity in covering the empire with the iron thread on every hand. Foremost among these enterprises are the Shanghai–Nanking, the Pekin–Kalgan, and the Canton–Kowloon lines. Railways, indeed, are being driven through the country by various interests and nations, including British, United States, Belgian, French, Portuguese and German. In fact, there is spirited competition among the various powers to bring about the complete conquest of the Celestial Kingdom by the iron road.

Although the initial venture in regard to introducing the railway into China had been so disastrous, Messrs Jardine, Matheson & Company were by no means deterred. They waited a favourable opportunity before repeating their experiment. It came twenty-three years after their first ill-starred adventure, for in 1898 they received permission to connect Pekin with Nanking by rail, a distance of some 200 miles, together with other enterprises of a similar character. This railway was undertaken by a group of financiers known as the British & Chinese Corporation, and they carried the first part of the scheme through to success. The arrangement was drawn up that this line should coincide in every particular with a typical first-class European railway, and this has been secured to the strict letter of the agreement. Indeed, it stands as the finest-built line in China. It proved an expensive undertaking, due in a great measure to the solidity of the constructional work, but the policy has been well repaid. The railway serves a wealthy district, where the possibilities of expansion are extensive, for the territory is rich in all resources.

Curiously enough, this line includes the stretch of 12 miles between Shanghai and Woosung, which it was attempted to connect by the iron road in 1875, and which the natives tore up and destroyed in an unceremonious manner. The promoters of that enterprise may be said to have achieved a sweet revenge, especially as 'Fung Shui' does not appear to have been perturbed by the second attempt to set the Tiger and Dragon at variance.

This line is what is known as a 'fast road'; that is, owing to its comparatively easy alignment, there being several stretches of straight road, while the track is well ballasted, it is favourable to high speeds. Indeed, on the opening day, the special train which travelled over the line with privileged guests covered the 193 miles in 5½ hours, notwithstanding that on the last 25 miles the speed had to be dropped to a maximum of 25 miles per hour, as the road had not been ballasted thoroughly. On some portions of the line, the train notched a speed of 57 miles an hour, and apparently was appreciated greatly by the Chinese guests.

CHAPTER 25

The Invasion of the Far East II – Modern Developments in China and Japan

The Chinese, once they were awakened to the possibilities of the railway, were not content to permit their country to be covered with foreign-built lines. They decided to become active participators in the movement – in other words, they acquired all the knowledge they could, and then undertook constructional engineering. Their aptitude for this work finds an excellent expression in the Pekin–Kalgan railway, 125 miles in length. This road was built throughout by Chinese effort, the engineer-in-chief being His Excellency Chang-Tien-Yow, who is today the foremost Chinese engineer in this field in China. He was educated in the United States, where he acquired valuable knowledge concerning this branch of engineering, and completed his training under Mr Kinder, the builder of the oldest railway in the Celestial Kingdom.

The road is excellently built, and the engineer displayed his ingenuity in coping with the problem of carrying the line through the Nankow Pass. This pass guards the entrance of the main road through the Great Wall, and to overcome the obstruction a gradient of 1 in 30 had to be introduced for a distance of 13 miles. At the foot of the pass three Mallet locomotives of British construction are maintained, and they crawl to the summit of the pass, at an altitude of about 1,500 feet, in 2 hours – a speed of about 6½ miles an hour.

The alignment of the railway up this pass is noteworthy. The road clings for the most part to the side of the mountains, crossing deep rifts and wide clefts, as well as cutting through spurs and humps and compassing massive crags.

Four tunnels were found to be unavoidable, one, 3,580 feet in length, burrowing 200 feet beneath the Great Wall. When the summit is gained, the railway enters a flat plateau, the only difficulty here, as on the flats around Pekin, being the preservation of the road from the attacks of floods. That this is no slight factor is proved from the fact that in the vicinity of Pekin a washout which overwhelmed the line cost no less than £32,000, or $160,000, to repair. The completion of the work, however, offers convincing testimony that the Chinese, under competent supervision, are perfectly capable of building railways without the aid of foreigners, and that no fault can be found with their work so far as solidity and durability are concerned.

For centuries, the Chinese have been famed for their prowess in matters pertaining to civil engineering. At times this skill pursues a quaint course, but probably the most extraordinary illustration was in connection with the Shanghai–Nangchow–Ningpo railway. By an imperial edict a Chinese official was appointed as engineer-in-chief.

At one point it was necessary to throw a bridge across a river. How it was to be accomplished passed the comprehension of the engineer. But he evolved a solution which, to say the least, would be difficult to equal in originality. He built the bridge on dry land, on one bank of the river. When this was completed satisfactorily, he diverted the waterway, so that the river ran beneath the bridge through a new, specially built channel, and the old one was filled up! In another instance, where a similar situation presented itself, a pier in the centre of the waterway became necessary. The river ran swiftly and the water was deep. The engineer knew nothing about coffer-dams, caissons, or other methods which the foreign engineer would have adopted. As the men could not work on dry land to build the bridge, he proceeded to provide them with this requisition. Hundreds of tons of spoil were dumped into the river at the point where the pier was to be erected until an island was formed, and on this the necessary constructional work was carried out.

Possibly the greatest and one of the most important lines, however, is the Pekin–Hankow railway, which is 760 miles in length, and which eventually will be an important link in the great road that is under construction, whereby through communication will be provided from Kowloon via Canton, Hankow, Pekin, Mukden and Harbin to the Trans-Siberian railway. This line was carried out with Belgian and French money for the most part, and £5,000,000, or $25,000,000, was sunk in the enterprise. The undertaking was commenced in 1900, but the Boxer Rebellion interfered seriously with its progress. The insurrectionists expended their full fury upon the railway, and inflicted damage to the value of nearly £1,000,000, or $5,000,000, which, however, was paid over by the government as compensation. It has been built cheaply, and does not compare, in point of solidity, with the English-built lines. At the same time, however, there are some outstanding engineering achievements. The most important is the bridge across the Yellow River, which consists of 102 spans, giving a total length of nearly 2 miles. It proved a particularly trying structure to erect, owing to the treacherous character of the riverbed, while the scouring action of the water, which is particularly severe, demanded elaborate protective works around the bottom of the piers. After various schemes were tried and had proved futile, large mattresses of brushwood interwoven with rushes were fashioned, and laid around the feet of the piers, hundreds of tons of heavy pieces of stone being dumped on these to keep them in position. This has been found more or less successful to prevent the soft silt from being washed away, and to protect the supports to the bridge from being undermined. The structure, however, is scarcely strong enough for heavy traffic, and consequently trains upon arrival at the ends of the bridge have the large locomotives uncoupled, and are drawn across the river by special light engines retained for the purpose.

One of the most important lines from the commercial point of view, however, is the Canton–Kowloon railway stretching from Kowloon, in British territory, to the busy centre of Canton, and thence continued northward to Hankow to provide connection with the other great systems of the country, and also with Europe by means of the Trans-Siberian railway. This project has passed through many vicissitudes. The British & Chinese Corporation received official sanction to build a road between Canton and Kowloon as far back as 1898, but the project became shelved. An American syndicate, which had secured the concession to connect Canton with Hankow, asserted that they had secured rights to carry the line from the former point to the coast. Such action would have dealt a serious blow to British commercial supremacy, and the money was subscribed to buy out the American concession, which in the meantime had been sold to a Belgian syndicate, and regained.

The section between Kowloon and Canton, 100 miles in length, was divided. The Hong-Kong government was held responsible for the 23 miles through British territory, while the balance of the line through Chinese territory was carried out by the Chinese government.

The English section proved tremendously difficult. The country traversed was exceedingly rough and mountainous. The difficulties encountered proved so abnormal that the cost of the undertaking has exceeded the original estimates by nearly 150 per cent. Some idea of the arduous character of the work may be gathered from the fact that nearly 2½ out of the 23 miles in British territory are represented by tunnels. The most arduous enterprise of this class was the Beacon Hill tunnel, 7,000 feet in length, driven through the heart of the mountain ridge that rises up 3 miles from the coast. The tunnel is perfectly straight, and ranks as the largest work of its type in the Chinese Empire.

It is driven through a depth of disintegrated granite on either approach, where heavy timbering became necessary until the solid rock was gained. Water was encountered and gave considerable trouble. At first labour was a serious problem, as the natives could not be induced to toil underground, and coolies had to be imported from India. After the work was well started, Chinese labourers, who had been working on the South African gold fields and had returned home, were available, and proved highly useful workmen, especially when the wrestle commenced with the hard, solid rock.

The tunnelling task, however, was equalled by the work in the cuts and on the fills. Some of the cuttings are of enormous depth, and the engineers have had to guard against the danger of heavy landslides, which, with washouts, are two of the greatest menaces to the railway in China. Heavy earthworks were required, because the line follows roughly the coastline, which is serrated, and to preserve alignment it was necessary to strike straight across these indentations where the water in many places proved to be very deep. The treacherous character of the seabed, which for the most part is a silt, demanded the provision of massive foundations upon which to raise the grade, and months were expended while a huge fleet of junks dumped hundreds of tons of rock into the water. Occasionally the work as completed was washed out by heavy rains, while now and again the typhoon left evidences of its wrath. A noticeable feature in the grading was the amount of work performed by women, who had recourse to their native basket slung on a pole for the conveyance of excavated earth to the fills.

The railway, however, has been built upon the most solid lines, and although its cost has proved so high, the money appears to have been expended to advantage. The traffic, although not so extensive as it will be, is increasing promisingly, and there is no doubt that when Hankow is reached a heavy volume of business will flow over this highway. The Chinese are proceeding with their section, and it is anticipated that not many years will elapse before the two points are connected.

The French engineers are erecting monuments to their railway engineering skill in the Flowery Land, the province of Yun-nan being the centre of their activity. The Yun-nan railway experienced a very chequered career through its early stages, for in endeavouring to connect the French possession of Lao-Chay with Yun-nan-Sen, the capital of the province, they had to break down enormous obstacles. The country is exceedingly mountainous, the height of the ridges being paralleled by the depth and precipitous nature of the gorges. Still the heavy and extensive bridging necessary proved no deterrent to the French bridge- builders, who are masters in this art, as the many remarkable structures in France testify conclusively.

The one factor to be feared seriously was the climate. This corner of China is one of the most insalubrious in the whole empire. Even the natives cannot withstand it, and their ranks are decimated heavily by tropical diseases. The labour question was one of everlasting perplexity, and the promoters of the enterprise found that skilled workmen, even of north China, evinced no desire to contribute to a distinguishing feat amid such miasmatic surroundings. The absence of transport facilities hit the undertaking sorely, and the engineers were compelled to make the best avail they could of the existing vehicles of conveyance – mules and the heads of natives.

The most difficult section of the line was in the valley of the Namiti. Here it was a stern fight for supremacy with physical obstacles for mile after mile. The weight and dimensions of every article had to be restricted within severe limits to facilitate handling and carriage by the primitive systems extant, and when the question comprised the component parts of steel bridges, the problem demanded searching deliberation. It was found, however, that the mules could handle weights up to about 600 pounds, and that the natives could struggle along with loads varying between 200 and 300 pounds, but neither man nor beast could cope with anything exceeding 7 feet in length.

Such handicaps would appear to militate against the achievement of any startling engineering performances. Yet, as a matter of fact, the French engineers displayed a striking instance of their remarkable ingenuity and capacity to meet awkward situations. The Namiti gorge disputed the progress of the line. It is a deep, wide, V-shaped fissure, one side dropping down perpendicularly for several hundred feet. The line pierced its way through one bluff, and had to jump across the rift to enter the opposite wall of rock. It was a matter of 200 feet across, and the rail level had to be carried 300 feet above the river below.

The situation demanded a novel solution. Erection by false-work was out of the question, as also was a cantilever bridge; again, the question of transporting the material to the site had to be borne in mind. Monsieur Georges Bodin, the presiding engineer of the Parisian Société de Construction des Batignolles, however, rose to the occasion, and evolved an unusual type of bridge, and at the same time elaborated a novel method of carrying out its erection.

The bridge consists of two essential parts forming leaves, or bascules. When set in position they have the appearance of a widely opened, inverted V. To carry out the task of erection, first a shelf was excavated in each cliff-face at the requisite height to carry the anchorages below the tunnel-mouths overlooking the gap. The top members of each bascule were riveted up, laid vertically flat against, and fixed firmly to, the cliff-faces. From this foundation each bascule was completed.

While the mantling of the steelwork was progressing, other gangs were busy at work cutting out large niches in the cliff-face, some height above the tunnel portals, and on these platforms powerful winches were erected. Each of these carried heavy chains measuring 900 feet in length. The transport of this essential piece of tackle was interesting. Large gangs of coolies were disposed in Indian file 7 feet apart, and the chains were trailed over their shoulders like a gigantic serpent. In this way they wound around crags, climbed steep bluffs and threaded narrow defiles for some 13 miles. These chains were passed around the winches and the outer ends were attached to the upper points of the bascules.

When each bascule was completed it was pinned firmly to its anchorage, the lashings securing each leaf of steel to the rock face were knocked away, and the two arms were held merely by the chains. Gangs of coolies were stationed at each winch under the supervision of a French engineer, and at the word of command the chains were slowly paid out, causing the bascules to heel over towards one another. Care had to be exercised that the lowering proceeded evenly from either side until the two arms met at a point. Workmen then swarmed up the arm on either side and rapidly drove in the pins and rivets which secured the two leaves firmly in position. The whole task of lowering and securing took only 4 hours, which was a noteworthy achievement.

Two short steel towers were now erected on the haunches, or central part of each bascule, to support the steel deck of the bridge, the members of which were brought up to the mouth of the tunnel and launched by being pulled out over rollers. With the spanning of the Namiti gorge, the most difficult part of the railway line was completed. When the enterprise was undertaken, it was computed that the railway could be completed for £3,840,000, or $19,200,000, but by the time this gorge was spanned a revision in the estimates showed that the cost would approach £6,620,000, or $33,100,000.

In Japan, the strides in railway development within a comparatively few years have been quite as notable as in China. In the former country, however, the conversion from primitive means of communication to steam locomotion commenced at an earlier date, and was attended with greater success. As in China, the railway invasion of Japan was fathered by an Englishman, Mr. H. N. Lay, who visited Tokio as a guest of the then British Minister, the late Sir Harry Parkes, in 1869. He approached the government and stated that he was prepared to furnish the funds necessary to commence the railway conquest of the country.

He made his offer at a peculiarly appropriate moment. The military regency which had ruled the country for so many centuries had drawn to a close, and the new government welcomed the proposal. Foremost among the supporters of the project were the present Count Okuma and the late Prince Ito. Mr Lay undertook to raise a loan of £1,000,000, or $5,000,000, and this was accepted, while Mr Lay was entrusted with the carrying out of the scheme. The promoter of the enterprise secured the services of Mr E. Morell as engineer-in-chief, and in 1870 the work commenced. But friction arose between the English capitalist and the government, who did not approve of the financier's methods. The agreement was nullified, and the Oriental Bank was established to carry out the undertaking, Mr Morell being retained in his engineering capacity.

He set to work in grim earnest. The question of gauge had to be settled first. This vital detail was threshed out in all its bearings, a gauge of 3½ feet was selected, and the building of the first line between Tokio and Yokohama – a distance of 18 miles – commenced. Once the fashioning of the grade began, other schemes were put forward. Among them was a line from Kobe to Osaka, a distance of 20 miles, which was put in hand, while an extension of the latter line to Otsu was surveyed. The first railway in the country was opened on 14 October 1872, amid elaborate festivities, in the presence of the Emperor. Within six years of Mr Morell's arrival, no less than 70 miles of line had been laid and opened. This was a highly satisfactory and energetic start for a young country, and the success of the experiment spurred the government to more ambitious schemes. These, however, were doomed to temporary derangement owing to internal troubles, and the rebellion in South Japan in 1877, which drained the imperial exchequer to such a degree that no funds were available for railway building operations.

Among these early enterprises was a trans-insular railway to connect the Pacific coast of the island with the shores of the Sea of Japan, with ferry steamers on Lake Biwa to connect the inland break in the railways due to that sheet of water. By this time, the Japanese engineers considered themselves competent to build railways, for they had proved apt pupils under Mr Morell's training. Native talent found its first opportunity on the Kioto–Otsu undertaking. This was a peculiarly difficult enterprise, but the Japanese engineers rose to the occasion, though English engineers were retained to advise them and to design the bridges. On this line, tunnelling had to be carried out, and this was the first occasion on which the Japanese engineers were faced with this work in their own country. Still they succeeded in complying with the original plans to perfect satisfaction, and had the pleasure of learning, when the road was opened in 1880, that the cost of construction was less than the estimates.

The completion of this undertaking marked the decadence of the foreign engineer in railway building in Japan. Native engineers were found to be capable of fulfilling the difficult position of assistants, and consequently only a few British engineers were retained in the capacity of advisers or consultants.

Private enterprise also entered the field, and numerous schemes were sanctioned. The first of these was the Nippon Railway Company, organised through the instrumentality of the late Prince Iwakura, a strong advocate of railway expansion, mainly for the purpose of assisting the peers to secure a profitable investment. It took several years of ardent campaigning to enlist the sympathy of the latter in such a project, but at last they fell victims to the Prince's persuasion, and the Nippon Railway Company was born.

This company projected the building of no less than 510 miles of railway. The two greatest contributions to this scheme were the Tokio–Takasaki railway, on which the government guaranteed a profit of 8 per cent, for ten years, and the Tokio–Sendai section, guaranteed similarly for fifteen years. Numerous other private companies followed, many of which received liberal government subsidies. But while private initiative was displaying considerable energy, the government railway enterprise slackened, and threatened to collapse, until Prince Yamagata proposed that trunk lines should be laid along all the main routes of the country, when the movement received a fresh impetus. Thus in 1883 there was renewed national activity in construction, and although many of these undertakings were beset with difficulties of a physical character, they were pushed through to completion.

One of the most notable of these early achievements was the Takasaki–Naoyetsu line, which was commenced originally to facilitate the transportation of constructional material for another road. The engineers were baulked by the Usui Pass, and this gap was left open, the two sections on either side of the range being opened for traffic in 1887. The intervening division was undertaken subsequently, being deferred from time to time in the hope that an easier location than had been plotted would be found. Though the engineers searched the mountains diligently, they failed to secure any improvement free from heavy work, and at last the mountain division was taken in hand. The grades were so steep, however, that the rack had to be introduced, the Abt system being selected. The engineers found this section particularly trying, as they had to drive no less than twenty-six tunnels through mountain spurs in a distance of 7 miles, while the deep clefts in the mountain's flanks called for massive masonry bridges. This work, however, was completed in 1893, and it served to provide through communication between Tokio and Naoyetsu.

It is doubtful whether the iron road ever has made such a phenomenal growth in other parts of the world within a short time as has characterised its development in the East. In China there was not a mile of line in 1877. Today, over 10,000 miles of railways have been built, are under construction, or are projected. In Japan, the network has grown from 18 miles in 1872, to 5,141 miles at the end of the 1910 fiscal year, of which total 4,634 miles belong to the State, and 597 to private companies, while the former at that date had 2,790 miles in hand, and private enterprise about 160 miles.

CHAPTER 26

The Conquest of the Cascade Mountains

Although the first trans-continental railway across the North American continent tapped San Francisco, this was not the route that was advocated in the first instance. Public fancy was inclined rather to the suggestion that the Pacific should be gained more to the north, at the estuary of the Columbia River. This feeling was fostered, no doubt, because that country loomed more prominently in the popular eye, as a result of the famous expedition of Lewis and Clark during the years 1804–06, wherein they trailed across the unknown corner of the continent and gained the Pacific via the Columbia River. The operations of the Hudson Bay Trading Company and its numerous rivals also had served to familiarise the public with this great territory.

It is strange to observe how, directly Stephenson had demonstrated the possibilities of the steam locomotive, imaginative minds drew pictures of stupendous railway building achievements across great continents, broken up by unsealed mountains and unfathomed broad rivers, as if the building of a track for the iron horse was the same as a child building toy houses with wooden bricks. As a result, the North American continent became crisscrossed in all directions by railways – on paper – and it was a good thing for the country at the time that these schemes never got any farther than that stage.

Since Huntington succeeded in his first great effort, the country has been spanned by a round dozen lines. Four systems, however, stand out pre-eminently. These are the Northern Pacific and the Great Northern, two lines which, in the first instance, were built after the pioneer manner, and the Western Pacific, and the Milwaukee, St Paul, and Puget Sound roads respectively, which were constructed upon experience gained in connection with the earlier lines, and therefore in accordance with modern ideas.

The Northern Pacific undertaking suffered strange vicissitudes. It was suggested, discussed and anticipated for years before it was ever taken in hand. It was a born engineer and practical railway builder who drove the scheme finally to a definite conclusion. This was Edwin F. Johnson, and his words carried weight because of his great engineering reputation and the soundness of his views. He waged the agitation so relentlessly that the government at last embarked upon a unique enterprise. A series of expeditions were inaugurated, known as the Pacific Railway Surveys, and the men for this task were drawn from every department of the public service. Their task was to report upon the practicability of threading the great mountain barriers to reach the western sea. The results of their efforts were set out in some thirteen large volumes, and they constitute possibly the most exhaustive work ever carried out in regard to the plotting of railways through a country. But, like the majority of such government outbursts, they represent so much wasted money: they were so valuable that they became forgotten. The surveyors and railway builders of today prefer to work out their own destinies.

Then came the Civil War, and that ruled any railway building enterprise under the aegis of the government completely out of court. But Johnson was not to be dissuaded from his enterprise. He laid his scheme before many prominent railway men in the country, and they decided to carry out the work. Johnson was deputed to act as chief engineer, and was urged to locate the line.

In 1870, the task of laying some 2,500 miles of track was commenced. The mouth of the Columbia River was selected as the outlet on the Pacific Ocean. Work was commenced simultaneously from both ends, the eastern terminal being near Lake Superior. By 1873 the line had reached the Missouri River on the east, and here a pause had to be called to erect a massive steel bridge, 1,400 feet long, 50 feet above the river, which absorbed £200,000, or $1,000,000.

When the first stretch of prairie line was completed, it was used only in the summer months. There was not enough traffic to pay for the coal burned in the locomotives during the winter, in the estimation of the administration, while they feared the expense and losses that would be inflicted by the terrible blizzards and snowstorms which rage in this country. Consequently, after the crops had been garnered and conveyed to market, all the engines, trucks and cars were withdrawn from service upon a great length of line, which was abandoned practically until spring came round.

This state of affairs continued until the Indians rose up against American law and order, wiped out several men, and precipitated a general reign of terror. The government, in order to pour troops into the disaffected territory, requested the working of the railway during the winter of 1876/7, which proved to be one of the most severe in history. Yet the line suffered less from snow than the systems in the eastern states, and, moreover, possibilities of traffic were discovered which hitherto had been considered non-existent. Needless to say, the railway never has been closed during the winter since.

Before the railway had proceeded halfway across the continent, the need for overhauling and relaying the first part of the track was felt. A higher standard of construction was therefore laid down for all the new work. Moreover, in order that the line should be completed within the shortest time possible, it was split into large sections, and the grade was driven east and west from several points simultaneously.

The mountains proved a severe stumbling-block and precipitated great delay. The country was so broken that lofty timber trestles had to be erected to be filled in with earth at a later date. Then two large tunnels had to be bored to carry the track through the Rockies, one, the Bozeman tunnel, being 3,610 feet long, and the other, the Mullan tunnel, 3,857 feet from end to end. Yet construction proceeded so successfully that the links were joined up on 3 September 1883, the last spike being driven in Hellgate Canyon, Montana. The spike used for this auspicious event was the very first that had been driven in connection with the line when it was commenced years before.

The railway has passed through many financial tribulations. On two occasions the intermediary of a receiver has been found necessary. It was hit by a panic in its very earliest days, and it failed ten years after completion, the second breakdown precipitating one of the worst financial scares in the history of the states. From the ashes, however, a new company was reconstructed, a bolder and more enterprising body of men gripped the reins, the system was pulled to pieces from end to end and rebuilt. Today, it is not only one of the finest railways in America, but one of the most popular and successful as well.

Running parallel to the Northern Pacific across the continent, but some miles nearer the international boundary, is another great artery of steel which has become a great transportation force in the United States. This is the Great Northern, likewise built through the energy of one man, Mr James J. Hill, the empire builder of the Great American west. Mr Hill is a born railway magnate, and when he shook the dust of his native land – Canada – from his feet, it was merely because the Dominion at that time offered him no scope for his energies and initiative.

His life is one romance; a prolonged conquest with the unknown country, with the railway as his weapon, and with which he has overcome tremendous obstacles. The Great Northern was driven slowly across the country from the Great Lakes. Advance was risky, as the country traversed failed to promise an ounce of produce; but whenever the organiser saw that development in the country ahead was likely to take place, he drove the line forward. His motto was that 'The railway must be a pioneer, leaving the settler to be brought in afterwards.' He lost no opportunity to gain revenue. For instance, when the mineral wealth of Montana attracted widespread attention, he made a journey to Butte. He found that it was costing the mines £3 8s – $17 – per ton to ship their copper to Omaha. He pondered on the subject, and suddenly announced his intention to carry his railway into Butte. He did so, and the first stroke he consummated was to transport the metal to the same eastern point at £1 13s, or $8, per ton – about 50 per cent, below the previous rate.

The desolate character of the plains of Montana, and the towering heights of the Rocky Mountains which stood right in the way of the line, were far from being attractive from the financial point of view. Yet he was convinced that traffic could be created, and was fortunate in infusing his colleagues with his enthusiasm. But if the railway's future was precarious, that of the settler was much more so. For some miles the line ran through territory inhabited by the Indian, and which the Red Man stubbornly persisted in maintaining was his property. The result was that the white man could only live on sufferance. If he stopped too long while passing through the country he was told to move on. Mr Hill relates an amusing instance of Red determination to seize the main chance at the settler's expense. 'When the settlers drove their cattle across Indian country in order to gain the railway, the Indians exacted a toll of 50 cents, or 2s for the privilege of driving the cattle across 3 miles of their territory! They even wanted an additional amount per head – I don't remember what it was – for the water they drank while crossing the Missouri River!'

Among the Rockies the engineer met with a spirited resistance, and the result is that the railway describes a tortuous course as it climbs up the one, and drops down the other, side. At places one may stand on the edge of a cliff where the track has been cut, and watch it following the spur for miles, steadily falling meanwhile to the head of the valley, where it describes a sweeping curve to wind back along the face of the cliff on the opposite side of the depression. Straight across it is, perhaps, not more than a mile or so, but the long detour of several miles was necessary to avoid a heavier climb. The fight for the grade is emphasised in watching an approaching train coming up the hill. It rounds the bluff on the opposite side of the valley, two ponderous 170-ton locomotives pulling and straining amid clouds of smoke and steam. Their joint labour produces a speed of about 15 miles an hour, and the roar created by the steam in harness is heard distinctly across the ravine. One follows the train on its winding course, for it is fully in sight the whole time as it swings round the curve at the end of the valley, and presently rushes by one with a terrible roar. Some 12 minutes have passed since the train first came into sight.

Among the Cascades, the spectacle is more impressive. Travelling westwards, the train pauses at the mountain's summit, and an electric locomotive is attached to haul the cars through the Cascade tunnel, a bore as straight as an arrow through the mass of rock for three miles. In ten minutes the train regains daylight, and the electric locomotive makes way for a ponderous 170-ton vibrating mass of steel and steam for the downward descent. When the railway was first opened, the crest of the range was overcome by a big switch-back, but it did not meet with official satisfaction, so it was abandoned in favour of the tunnel driven through the crest.

Directly the engine driver releases the air-brake the train commences to move. The descent is at the rate of 116 feet to the mile, and, as may be conceived, no steaming is required to give the train momentum down the banks – it travels by gravity alone, held in check by the powerful airbrake. The train plunges into a line of snow sheds, and when it emerges, two tracks at different levels may be seen, and in the far distance, on the opposite side of the valley, is the black band of steel writhing among the crags to pass from sight round a distant shoulder. The train swings down the uppermost gallery, crosses a lofty trestle set over a rift on a curve, dives into a tunnel wherein a horseshoe loop is completed, so that when it issues from the other portal the train speeds along the second track in the opposite direction. Then it makes another twist to swing to the opposite mountain slope. Looking back from the lowest level, the line can be seen cutting three ugly gashes among the trees clothing the mountain flanks.

The construction of this series of loops was exciting, and dangerous to the navvies, as one of their number related to me. Excavation was carried out on the two levels simultaneously, but those on the lower terrace had to maintain a vigilant eye and a keen ear. Huge ballast cars were hauled on to the upper gallery loaded with debris, and they shot this over the side to build up the grade. The result was that the men below were subjected to a heavy, intermittent bombardment, for massive pieces of rock were among the spoil. These, given a start downhill, bounced from point to point with terrific force, until they crashed into the depths of the canyon. The men had to dodge these missiles as best they could. Sometimes they were lucky; at others they were not, and many a man received a nasty wound, a jarring blow, or a broken limb from a piece of rock in flight. Accidents from this cause were numerous, and fatalities were not infrequent.

When the Western Pacific was projected, it was decided to profit from the mistakes made on the early lines in the first instance. Grades in particular were to be kept down, especially among the mountains, where a maximum rise of 1 in 100 was only to be allowed. This line completes the original idea in connection with the Denver and Rio Grande line by giving the latter an outlet from Salt Lake City to the Pacific at San Francisco.

The railway is 725 miles in length, and it was split into three sections for constructional purposes. The first extended from Salt Lake City to Oroville at the Pacific foot of the Sierras main range, the second from the latter point to Oakland on the coast, while the third was a trying short section right down to the water's edge at San Francisco from Oakland. Building was carried out on the three divisions simultaneously. Remarkable enterprise was displayed by the liberal resort to any new time- and labour-saving methods and implements. In the San Diablo Range, the path of the track was interrupted by a depression 123 feet deep and 1,120 feet wide. That hollow had to be filled to preserve the grade. To expedite the task, an ingenious tool was devised. This was an electric scraper, and the idea was to pull this down the side of the mountain, thereby removing several tons of earth at a time, and to shoot it into the gulch. But the scraper did not come up to expectations. Breakdowns were so frequent that at last it was dismantled in disgust and thrown on one side to rust. Then another ingenious idea was tested. This was called a 'merry-go-round', something very similar to a roundabout. It comprised a revolving table overhanging the edge of the dump or embankment. A track was laid on the circumference of this turntable forming a loop. The laden trucks were run round this curve and their contents were shot overboard at the point desired, the empties continuing round the loop to the track to return to be refilled. The advantage of this arrangement was that the spoil could be discharged just where it was wanted much more quickly and easily than by the ordinary method, where the cars are pushed to the edge of the temporary track, emptied and then pulled back. As the bank grew outwards across the valley, the merry-go-round was pushed forwards, so that it always stood on the brink of the earthwork.

Among the mountains, some magnificent work was accomplished. As the directing engineer remarked to the writer, it was a stiff problem to descend the western flanks of the Sierras with a 1 per cent, grade. The line crosses the mountains 2,000 feet lower than the Central Pacific, and one advantage is that there are no snow sheds anywhere.

When one sees how rigorously the maximum grade has been guarded one marvels. The mountains are negotiated through Feather River Canyon, which is a duplicate of the Kicking Horse Pass that carries the Canadian Pacific main line down to the coast. The canyon is entered at Oroville, and for almost 100 miles the line rises steadily at 52 feet per mile, following the river until it at last gains an altitude of 4,817 feet. But hugging the river causes the line to meander very tortuously, for the waterway zigzags like the teeth of a saw.

Moreover, Feather River is a fearsome waterway. In its calmest moods it rushes along swiftly, but when swollen by the melting snows and countless mountain brooks it thunders and boils like a whirlpool. To escape the fury of the waters the track had to be laid well up the mountainside, and where a fork of the river is crossed, a massive metal bridge had to be built for the reason advanced by the engineer that 'Nothing but steel could be used with safety when the river is in full flood.'

Curiously enough, although Feather River Canyon had never before been selected as a passage-way through the mountains for the iron road, it was favoured by the Indian as being the easiest passage through the Sierras. Theodore Judah had noticed its advantages for the first trans-continental. But the Red Man's trail was along the opposite bank to that preferred by the railway. At first sight it would appear as though the surveyors might have profited advantageously from the sagacity of the aborigines, but they declined to do so for a striking reason. The locaters had to pay due respect to the snowfall and the paths of avalanches. In such a gorge, the former may be only a few inches on one, and as many feet on the other side, and the dangers from slides are proportionate. Such conditions prevail in this canyon. The bank selected by the engineers is exposed to the sun throughout the day, and the snowfall is very slight, whereas on the other and shaded bank it is very severe.

In ascending the canyon, very heavy development work had to be carried out. At one point, a huge loop had to be described on the mountainside, and the summit negotiated by a long tunnel beneath the Beckwourth Pass. The latter acts as a funnel or shaft for the warm 'Chinook' winds, which, entering the pass, melt the snow almost as soon as it falls. Consequently, on this section snow is an insignificant enemy, and does not strike such terror into the hearts of the railway authorities as, say, on the Canadian Pacific, or the overland route. The records at Beckwourth give the maximum depth of snow as 24 inches, so that Boreas will be kept within bounds very easily by an ordinary snowplough. By placing the track well below the snow line, and with the assistance of the kindly Japanese warm wind, the heavy expense of snow sheds has been avoided.

This is no mean saving either, for in many cases the cost of building these protective sheds has been more per mile than the railway itself sheltered within. On one line, the average cost of this protection is £15,000 per mile, and it is necessary for 40 miles!

On the eastern sides of the mountains, the railway runs into the ill-famed Humboldt River territory, which has proved a thorn in the sides of many railway builders. This fine waterway at times bursts its bonds, floods the country, and finally follows a new course. In order to avoid any troubles from this cause, the line was kept well clear of the district, though it involved many artificial works such as bridges, embankments and tunnels, while the river is crossed twenty-four times in 185 miles.

Between the foothills of the Sierras and Salt Lake City, two other mountain ranges had to be overcome – the Pe'quop and Torano chains respectively. A tunnel solves the first, and a striking piece of development work compasses the second. This is a horseshoe curve 5 miles in length, which rises gently eastwards at the prescribed maximum grade. Had the engineers cut straight across as the crow flies, miles would have been saved, but the banks would have been three times as heavy. The eastern point of this horseshoe brings the railway to the fringe of the Salt Lake desert, a rolling waste of salt and borax in which lies the inland sea of the same name, and whose waters in the distant past lapped the foothills of the Torano range. The rail strikes across the desert in a beeline for 43 miles, the permanent way being as level as a billiard table, with the rails resting on a solid mass of salt, 8 feet or more in thickness. This marked the first attempt to cross this dismal expanse by railway. Many a traveller essaying the perilous journey as a shorter cut to the country beyond has been overwhelmed by thirst or the intolerable heat, to lie down to his last rest, his bones afterwards being found bleaching in the glare of Old Sol, beating down from a cloudless sky.

One notable feature of this road is the tunnels. There are forty-two in all, aggregating over 45,000 feet in length, while there are forty steel bridges totalling a length of 9,261 feet. In one division among the Sierras, extending for a distance of 75 miles up the Feather River Canyon, grading ran into £20,000, or $100,000, per mile. Altogether some 40,000,000 cubic yards of earth were handled to form the grade. The contractors had to spend £20,000, or $100,000, alone to cut a wagon-road in order to transport supplies to their camps along the grade.

Contemporaneously with the construction of the Western Pacific railway, a third line – the Chicago, Milwaukee and Puget Sound – was being pressed across the continent for the purpose of bringing Chicago and the Atlantic seaboard into direct touch with the Pacific ports of Seattle and Tacoma on Puget Sound.

This great artery sprang from very humble beginnings. In 1865 there was a short stretch of line in the State of Minnesota which, under energetic and wise expansion, threw its tentacles in all directions, until by 1908 it had grown into a huge system known as the Chicago, Milwaukee and St Paul railway, possessing 7,451 miles of track. How it came to launch out upon this long reach to the Pacific is an interesting story, typical of railway development in the North American continent.

The eastern division of the parent system served an absolutely treeless country, though the land was among the finest imaginable for agriculture. The railway required plentiful supplies of timber, not only for its own needs, but also for those of the settlers scattered along its roads. Every foot of wood had to be cut in the far northwest lumber territory, and had to be hauled for hundreds of miles over a rival railway before it entered the territory served by the Chicago, Milwaukee and St Paul railway. Considering the enormous consumption of this commodity, the money paid over every year to the rival railway in freight charges represented a respectable figure.

Thereupon it was decided to tap the forests and to secure an outlet on the Pacific Coast at the same time. Although it was estimated that the 1,400 miles of track necessary for the purpose would cost about £20,000,000, or $100,000,000, it was calculated that the saving in freight charges for hauling timber would defray the greater part of the interest on this capital.

Work was commenced in 1906: on 1 April 1909, the last rail was laid, and the golden spike was driven home into its sleeper, with no more ceremony than if a mere siding had been completed, instead of a new trans-continental line, conforming with all up-to-date requirements as to grade, curvature and general standard of work.

The completion of such a project within three years was truly an epoch-making achievement, and, as might be supposed, a long string of record-breaking feats accompanied its realisation. In thirty-six months £17,000,000, or $85,000,000, were expended in the boring of tunnels, the erection of 20 miles of bridges, cuts and fills to fashion a new steel highway, and to pave it with 200,000 tons of rails. Some days the mechanical track-layer, with its load of sleepers and rails, advanced so rapidly that 5 miles of track were laid between sunrise and sunset.

Curiously enough, this new line was commenced from the banks of the same river as signalled the commencement of the first railway to the Pacific – the Missouri River – but at Mowbridge, a point some miles to the north. At the very commencement, heavy expense was incurred in the building of a huge bridge across the waterway, which alone absorbed, £400,000, or $2,000,000. It crosses North Dakota and Montana, where it was no uncommon circumstance to encounter isolated homesteads, the owners of which had to travel 150 miles to post a letter – a duty which, under the circumstances, was performed about once in 6 or 12 months.

In Montana, the line drops into the valley of the Yellowstone River to cling to its banks. While the river winds in and out in an amazing manner, the railway follows practically a straight line through the valley, and for 117 miles it is one of the fastest stretches of track in the whole continent, there being an imperceptible rise. On paper it seems but a simple task to build such a piece of straight, level track, but in this instance it proved very expensive, for the river is crossed about once in every mile, there being 115 bridges in the 117 miles.

After leaving the Yellowstone River the work became more difficult, for three ranges of mountains had to be overcome. The battle with Nature, which had been fought by the Southern, Western, Northern Pacific and Great Northern Railways respectively, had to be waged again.

At times the preservation of an easy grade proved a very knotty problem. The end was achieved only by prodigious earthworks, frequent tunnelling, as well as lofty trestling across the ravines. The curves were kept very easy, galleries being cut in the projecting humps to enable the line to follow the contour of the mountain sides, while the summits were conquered by driving tunnels through their crests at as low an altitude as practicable.

The most noteworthy tunnel is the St Paul Pass, and here a striking record was set up, the mountain being pierced at a greater speed than has been achieved in any previous undertakings of this character. It was bored from both ends simultaneously, and although it was solid, hard rock for practically the whole of its length, an average advance of some 540 feet per month was maintained, the highest rate of progress being reached with a monthly progress of 732 feet.

Among the Cascades, the tremendous ravines separating one peak from another taxed the ingenuity of the engineers sorely. It was practically what in railway parlance is described as 'cut-and-fill' all the way; that is, the digging of deep cuttings here, and the raising of lofty embankments there. The cuts through the shoulders of some of these monarchs became quite respectable defiles in themselves by the time the steam shovels had retired from the scene. And the cuts were equalled in their magnitude by the 'fills.' One, 'Topographers' Gulch', is exceptionally notable. The track creeps through a deep cutting on either side to the edge of the mountain, the sides of which drop away in a steep slope to a depth of 282 feet. At track level the gulch was 800 feet across. A viaduct was at first suggested to span the gap, but it was found that the approaches were unsuitable to such a solution of the problem.

The engineer resolved to make a daring effort. He would not bridge the gulf; he would not go round it, but he would fill it up! There was plenty of material on the spot for the purpose. The question was the quickest way of accomplishing this end. When it is remembered that a twenty-storey building could have been dropped into that ravine, and that its roof then would have been only level with the proposed permanent way, it will be seen that it was a big fill indeed. How was it done? Why, by means of water jets – hydraulic sluicing – being directed against the mountainside, dislodging the earth and speeding it down conduits into the depression. Little did the western railway foreman anticipate, when he first suggested washing down a hill to fill a rift by means of a hose as already described, that his much ridiculed proposition ever would be called upon to fill up a chasm like this.

A powerful pumping plant was set up, hundreds of feet of hose were laid down, and fitted with huge, powerful nozzles. Gigantic and powerful streams of water were thrown against the mountain face, and the debris thus dislodged was diverted into flumes, or wooden troughs, which emptied themselves into the valley. Before a yard of debris was tossed into that abyss; £12,000, or $60,000, had been spent. When the full blast of water was brought to bear on the face of the hill, the gravel rushed down into the depression like lava pouring from a volcano in eruption. The water jets literally moved a hill into the ravine. In the course of a few weeks a neck of solid earth stretched across the abyss, affording a path for the railway.

The crossing of the Columbia River was another heavy undertaking, exceeding in character the bridge across the Missouri. At this point the river is wide, with the navigable channel in the centre, but there is a heavy rise and fall of the water according to the season, the feet of the mountains on either side being lapped when the river is in flood. The peculiar conditions necessitated a high structure, with massive stone piers supporting the steelwork. Sixteen wide spans were required. The task was carried out by the railway companies' own bridge-engineering staff, in which class of work they are specialists and peculiarly fitted to such huge enterprises.

Such is the story of the Railway Rush across the United States to the Pacific. Yet the public clamours for further lines. The facilities extended already to travel from the Atlantic to the Pacific seaboards in less than four days have served only to cause the public to emulate 'Oliver Twist' and to ask for more.